Femicide and the Law

This book discusses the legal and criminological aspects of femicide. It scrutinizes the three key US criminal doctrines usually applied in femicide cases: provocation; the felony-murder rule; and self-defense. The work also explores the influence of the American Model Penal Code as it relates to the various relevant criminal doctrines applicable to femicide. It advances a detailed and innovative proposal to amend the Code, providing a socio-legal framework and response to issues inadequately addressed by legislative proposals in this context to date. While the focus is primarily on femicide in America, the issues discussed are of global relevance due to the tragically widespread nature of this crime. The book thus makes a significant contribution to the legal discourse of many other countries with similar legal structures.

Hava Dayan is Head of the MA Program in Crime, Law and Society, School of Criminology, University of Haifa, Israel.

Femicide and the Law
American Criminal Doctrines

Hava Dayan

Routledge
Taylor & Francis Group
LONDON AND NEW YORK

First published 2018 by Routledge

2 Park Square, Milton Park, Abingdon, Oxfordshire OX14 4RN
52 Vanderbilt Avenue, New York, NY 10017

Routledge is an imprint of the Taylor & Francis Group, an informa business

First issued in paperback 2020

British Library Cataloguing-in-Publication Data
A catalogue record for this book is available from the British Library

Library of Congress Cataloging-in-Publication Data
Names: Dayan, Hava, author.
Title: Femicide and the law : American criminal doctrines / by Hava Dayan.
Description: Abingdon, Oxon : New York, NY : Routledge, 2018. | Includes bibliographical references and index.
Identifiers: LCCN 2018006433| ISBN 9781138572690 (hbk) | ISBN 9781351331784 (web pdf) | ISBN 9781351331777 (epub) | ISBN 9781351331760 (mobipocket)
Subjects: LCSH: Homicide–Law and legislation–United States. | Women–Crimes against–United States.
Classification: LCC KF9305 .D39 2018 | DDC 345.73/0252082–dc23
LC record available at https://lccn.loc.gov/2018006433

ISBN: 978-1-138-57269-0 (hbk)
ISBN: 978-0-367-58998-1 (pbk)

Typeset in Galliard
by Wearset Ltd, Boldon, Tyne and Wear

To those who stood up to their grim-fated destiny and heroically rose from ashes
And to those murdered before they got a chance

Contents

Preface

December 21 was the shortest day of the 2004 calendar year, as it is every calendar year. But it was also the longest day of Andy's life. At midday, she was forcefully evacuated by the police, taken with her four young children to a secretly located women's shelter. The police officers were sure that she was about to be killed by her husband, in a matter of a few hours at most. She knew her life was in danger because he had been violent towards her and the children before, to the point of choking her on one occasion, and had explicitly and continuously expressed his adamant fury and indignation at her resolute wish to end the marital relationship. Andy thought she still had a few days to safely leave home, but the police officers thought differently about the danger her husband posed. As she would learn, their appraisal of the situation was accurate and correct. She was indeed lucky to have been forcefully and immediately evacuated. Had they waited for her to decide to leave, it would probably have been too late to save her. Perhaps the tragic deaths of so many women who came before was what heightened police alertness and sensitivity to the phenomenon of femicide, guiding their steadfast decision to evacuate her.

At the time of her evacuation she was not fully aware of the many emotional, economic, physical, social and legal hardships and obstacles she would have to overcome before she could build a peaceful and quiet life, apart from her dangerously violent ex-partner. Had she known at that point in time the agonizing difficulties she would face in the future, most likely she would not have cooperated with her own evacuation to a safe and remote shelter. Emotionally crushed and devastated by her continuously abusive marital relationship, perhaps she would have chosen to stay at home and peacefully face death.

More than ten years have gone by since the day Andy was evacuated. She is fine and her kids are doing very well. She survived the tangible and definite threat to her life and was lucky enough to have been rescued in time. But many other women have not been so fortunate, and the lives of many are still in peril. Andy's tragic experience exposed me to a whole range of women fleeing from dangerous homes, and aroused my personal and academic curiosity about the disturbing and grievous social phenomenon of femicide. In the years to come I found myself recurrently drawn to exploring this perplexing issue academically. In this respect, my socio-legal academic background was extremely useful in achieving a well-rounded understanding of the phenomenon of femicide. Moreover, it enabled me to formulate an alternative and necessary socio-legal structure to serve as the foundation for a just and impartial policy on the matter. I feel privileged to have been able to undertake a critical exploration of the socio-legal structure relevant to the phenomenon of femicide, to contest its criminal and victimological adequacy, and to offer alternative legal structures that may assist in preventing and eradicating this fatally tragic phenomenon.

This book therefore owes a moral and social debt to all the women whose death created a clear legacy, to pursue every possible avenue by all necessary means to prevent additional femicide. May they rest in peace, and may this socio-legal treatise help save other women facing the threat of death.

Acknowledgments

I would like to thank Prof. Emanuel Gross for his invaluable mentorship and support. This book could not have been written without his guidance, trust and encouragement.

An earlier version of Chapter 2 was published as 'Uxoricide Under the Auspices of the Model Penal Code: A Legislative Proposal to Amend Section 210.3(b) of the Model Penal Code', in the *Georgetown Journal of Gender and the Law*, Volume 15.2, 2014 (with Emanuel Gross); an earlier version of Chapter 3 was published as 'Assaultive-Femicide and the American Felony-Murder Rule', in the *Berkeley Journal of Criminal Law*, Volume 21:2, 2016 [© 2016 by the Regents of the University of California Citation: 21 Berkeley J. Crim. L. 1 (2016) By permission of the Regents of the University of California]; and an earlier version of Chapter 4 was published as 'In Between the Hammer and the Anvil: Battered Women Claiming Self Defence and A Legislative Proposal to Amend Section 3.04(2)(b) to Circumstances of Domestic Violence', in the *Harvard Journal on Legislation*, Volume 52, 2015 (with Emanuel Gross).

achieving a well-rounded understanding of the phenomenon of femicide. Moreover, it enabled me to formulate an alternative and necessary socio-legal structure to serve as the foundation for a just and impartial policy on the matter. I feel privileged to have been able to undertake a critical exploration of the socio-legal structure relevant to the phenomenon of femicide, to contest its criminal and victimological adequacy, and to offer alternative legal structures that may assist in preventing and eradicating this fatally tragic phenomenon.

This book therefore owes a moral and social debt to all the women whose death created a clear legacy, to pursue every possible avenue by all necessary means to prevent additional femicide. May they rest in peace, and may this socio-legal treatise help save other women facing the threat of death.

Acknowledgments

I would like to thank Prof. Emanuel Gross for his invaluable mentorship and support. This book could not have been written without his guidance, trust and encouragement.

An earlier version of Chapter 2 was published as 'Uxoricide Under the Auspices of the Model Penal Code: A Legislative Proposal to Amend Section 210.3(b) of the Model Penal Code', in the *Georgetown Journal of Gender and the Law*, Volume 15.2, 2014 (with Emanuel Gross); an earlier version of Chapter 3 was published as 'Assaultive-Femicide and the American Felony-Murder Rule', in the *Berkeley Journal of Criminal Law*, Volume 21:2, 2016 [© 2016 by the Regents of the University of California Citation: 21 Berkeley J. Crim. L. 1 (2016) By permission of the Regents of the University of California]; and an earlier version of Chapter 4 was published as 'In Between the Hammer and the Anvil: Battered Women Claiming Self Defence and A Legislative Proposal to Amend Section 3.04(2)(b) to Circumstances of Domestic Violence', in the *Harvard Journal on Legislation*, Volume 52, 2015 (with Emanuel Gross).

Introduction

This book explores the grievous phenomenon of femicide. Despite the critical legal discourse taking place in the United States concerning violence against women, and the legislative reforms introduced in various U.S. jurisdictions, comprehensive legislative reform on femicide has yet to be proposed. Consequently, the American criminal doctrine relating to femicide remains incomplete. The prevailing legal structure precludes the provision of adequate and uniform legal justice for victims, leading to tragic legal consequences for women throughout the United States. The book examines and discusses the legal and criminological aspects of femicide, a phenomenon that is prevalent worldwide and is therefore relevant to countries other than the United States.

As the American criminal legal structure is deeply rooted in English common law, its substantive criminal doctrines are widely shared by many countries. In this respect the book's exploration of legal criminal doctrines in the United States may provide a significant contribution to legal discourse in many other countries with legal structures similarly steeped in English common law. The book treats femicide within the legal framework of the American Model Penal Code because of the Code's enormous influence and leading role in shaping state criminal codes. Since its publication it has had a notable impact on legislative reforms made to subsequent state criminal codes, and in fact its wording provides the current prototype for the doctrine of self-defense in all U.S. jurisdictions. Moreover, it has significantly influenced the development of principles of criminal law as a whole through extensive case law based on the Model Penal Code as a normative source used to interpret state criminal law. In these two respects the Model Penal Code is the closest thing, both *de jure* and de facto, to what can be viewed as the "American Criminal Code."

The book examines three key substantive criminal doctrines usually applied in femicide cases: provocation, the felony-murder rule and self-defense. These doctrines will be analyzed with respect to their application to femicide perpetrators and battered women facing legal procedures for using deadly protective force while being assaulted by their intimate partners.

For the sake of legal clarity, and to prevent arbitrary interpretations of the law by fact finders, a clear and explicit statutory legal arrangement must be promoted in the context of femicide. The book therefore articulates a focused and detailed legislative proposal to amend the Model Penal Code as it relates to the various relevant criminal doctrines applicable to femicide. The book's legislative proposal contains unique and innovative elements and provides a socio-legal framework and response to issues not adequately addressed by legislative proposals in this context to date. The proposed statutory amendments to the U.S. Model Penal Code are applicable, *mutatis mutandis*, to many other countries. It is my fervent hope that these recommended amendments will serve as a prototype for legislative reforms in other parts of the world as well, contributing to the legal response to the egregious social phenomenon of femicide.

1 Femicide and related American criminal doctrines

A preliminary overview

Femicide

The book explores the grievous phenomenon of femicide. This phenomenon is conceptually situated within the broader perspective of violence against women. Such violence is a form of gendered violence, targeted at women or girls.[1] The phenomenon of violence against women is perceived to be part of a larger social phenomenon of male patriarchal dominance achieved and maintained through coercive control.[2] Such violence may take various forms (physical, visual, verbal, emotional, economic, political or mental), and may occur at various stages of a female's life (as a fetus, an infant, an adolescent, an adult and as an elderly woman). It may take place in different spheres of life (at home, at work and in the social arena) and may be embedded within and performed through various social spheres (political, legal, racial, religious, ethnic and cultural). The nature of the violence itself may be of varying degrees, forming a continuum with harassment at one end and fatal assault at the other.[3] The violence may be explicit, formal and organized but also discrete, sporadic and covert.

While recognizing that violence against women is a multi-faceted and complex issue, this book will limit the scope of its discussion to a particular subtype of gender violence: femicide. Femicide (or feminicide) is a homicidal form of violence targeted at women and expressed through their actual killing.

Femicide is the major cause of the unnatural death of women[4] and the seventh leading cause of the premature death of women worldwide.[5] In many cases family members, frequently the victim's children or mother, are witnesses to the act of femicide.[6] Furthermore, femicide, particularly the intimate partner type, often involves the murder of family members or bystanders such as relatives,

1 Radford and Russell 1992: 10.
2 Ibid.: 4.
3 Ibid.: 3–4, for a description of the notion of a continuum of violence against women.
4 Weil 2015.
5 Weil 2016.
6 Dobash and Dobash 2012: 662–667.

the couple's children or the victim's new partner.[7] Patterns relating to the murder of women display empirical proximity to the family arena: the women are primarily murdered within the framework of "their family," i.e., by their partners, usually "after lengthy periods of prolonged physical violence accompanied by other forms of abuse and coercion."[8] Indeed, empirical studies on intimate partner femicide in the United States report 79–90 percent rates with regard to history of violence in the relationship. Smith et al.'s study of femicide in North Carolina found a history of violence in about 96 percent of the cases,[9] and Websdale found similarly high rates (86 percent) in femicide cases in Florida.[10] It is important to distinguish intimate partner femicide from domestic violence, although in some cases the murder of the female partner is the culmination of an existing pattern of violence against her. While violence directed at a female partner aims to achieve control and obedience, killing her is intended to bring about her ruin – more specifically her death.[11]

Femicide has certainly gained global notice in recent years along with efforts towards its eradication.[12] Alarmed by the fact that femicide was increasing throughout the world, the Academic Council of the United Nations conducted a series of symposiums in 2012, urging member states to undertake steps to prevent femicide.[13] The United Nations Vienna Declaration on Femicide, in conjunction with the Commission on Crime Prevention and Criminal Justice (2012), refers to various modes of female killings that may be carried out in different social, political, cultural and religious circumstances. According to the Declaration, these can take the form of, inter alia: (1) murder of women as a result of intimate partner violence; (2) torture and misogynist slaying of women; (3) killing of women and girls in the name of "honor"; (4) targeted killing of women and girls in the context of armed conflict; (5) dowry-related killings of women; (6) killing of women and girls because of their sexual orientation and gender identity; (7) killing of aboriginal and indigenous women and girls because of their gender; (8) female infanticide and gender-based sex selection feticide; (9) genital mutilation-related deaths; (10) accusations of witchcraft; and (11) other types of femicide connected with gangs, organized crime, drug dealing, human trafficking and the proliferation of small arms.[14] Different types of femicide relate to the different stages of female life. These may include female feticide (the killing of female fetuses), female infanticide (the killing of female

7 Ferrara et al. 2015.
8 Dobash et al. 1992: 81.
9 Smith et al. 1998.
10 Websdale 1999.
11 Ben Ze'ev and Goussinsky 2008: 118.
12 Corradi et al. 2016.
13 Ibid.: 983.
14 Laurent et al. 2013: 4.

infants), uxoricide (the killing of spouses), sororicide (the killing of sisters) and matricide (the killing of the female parent).

The term femicide was coined by Russell and introduced in the book written with Radford and published in 1992. In their seminal book, femicide is defined as the misogynous killing of women by men,[15] which takes many different forms shaped and changed by culture and context.[16] Russell and Radford argue that these diverse forms may refer to racist femicide, homophobic femicide, lesbicide, marital femicide, femicide perpetrated by strangers, serial femicide, mass femicide and the deliberate transmission of AIDS that results in death. Radford prefers an expansive definition of femicide, one that does not refer exclusively to intentional killing of women, but rather "situations in which women are permitted to die as a result of misogynous attitudes or social practices."[17] Among such social practices she mentions a broad spectrum of practices embedded in patriarchal gender-based violence: the death of women and girls resulting from botched abortions, unnecessary surgery of females and misogynous neglect or starvation of female infants and women.[18] According to Russell, femicide is the end result of various forms of terror against females that result in death:

> Femicide is on the extreme end of a continuum of antifemale terror that includes a wide variety of verbal and physical abuse, such as rape, torture, sexual slavery (particularly in prostitution), incestuous and extrafamilial child sexual abuse, physical and emotional battery, sexual harassment (on the phone, in the streets, at the office, and in the classroom), genital mutilation (clitoridectomies, excision, infibulations), unnecessary gynecological operations (gratuitous hysterectomies), forced heterosexuality, forced sterilization, forced motherhood (by criminalizing contraception and abortion), psychosurgery, denial of food to women in some cultures, cosmetic surgery, and other mutilations in the name of beautification. Whenever these forms of terrorism result in death, they become femicides.[19]

Femicide as a concept and a term was promoted as an alternative to the gender-neutral term "homicide" in order to highlight the killing of women because they are women. According to Radford and Russell, the term "femicide" had a political purpose, intended to alter the prevailing understanding of the violent death of women. They claimed that naming the phenomenon "gives women's

15 Radford and Russell 1992. Russell emphasizes the idea that males commit femicide with sexist motives, and chooses to replace the word woman with female to show that girls and infants can also be victims of femicide. See generally, Russell and Harmes 2001: 13–14; Russell 1990: 104–108.

16 Radford and Russell 1992: 7.

17 Op. cit.

18 Op. cit.

19 Russell 2011.

experiences and understandings priority over men's intentions and as such is consistent with one of the basic tenets of feminism – women's right to name their experience."[20] Thus the coining of the phenomenon was part of feminist action and theory to find, create and redefine words that reflect and record women's experiences in general and violence against them in particular. It was the feminist notion that "Names provide social definitions; make visible what is invisible; define as unacceptable what was accepted; make sayable what was unspeakable"[21] that spurred the intentional coining of the term and naming of the phenomenon. The naming did not create the phenomenon of women killing. Women were killed long before the phenomenon was named and delineated. However, the gender-neutral term "homicide" lacked the gender-sensitive terminology crucially needed for the real and fact-based description of particular gender-based fatally violent events. The new term for the old phenomenon of women-killing aimed to re-conceptualize the homicide phenomenon and reconstruct women's social experience by voicing what was until then unvoiced: the recognition that the violent death of women is a crime in and of itself, not to be confused with the gender-neutral terms "homicide," "killing," "murder" or "manslaughter."[22]

The term was not only coined for the sake of describing reality as such. Reframing the term as a social and political problem had a constructivist purpose.[23] It aimed to re-construct social reality through a gender-sensitive perspective. The practice of "naming" and "renaming" this gendered-based violent social phenomenon was part of a larger feminist goal and practice from the 1970s onwards, aimed at mobilizing society and producing social change by raising awareness and making visible something that up to then had been invisible. According to Radford and Russell, it was vital to begin by coining the term, because "Naming an injustice, and thereby providing a means of thinking about it, usually precedes the creation of a movement against it."[24] Thus the term "femicide" also had a political purpose, to produce changes in the social order that legitimized or tolerated gender-based killings. In Radford and Russell's words, "by going beyond an academic discussion of the evidence, by making the fight against femicide a major theme of this anthology, we hope it will play a strategic role in consolidating feminist resistance to femicide."[25] According to Corradi et al., "the groundbreaking contribution of Radford and Russell in coining the term was to emphasize that homicide deletes from the sociological eye that special, gender-based evidence of woman-killing, which is

20 Radford and Russell 1992: 3.
21 Kelly and Radford 1996: 19–20.
22 Corradi et al. 2016: 977.
23 Ibid.: 978.
24 Radford and Russell 1992: xiv.
25 Ibid.: 7.

different from the murder of men", and to reframe it as a unique social and political problem.[26]

The book will focus on a particular sub-type of femicide: intimate partner femicide (killing by spousal as well as non-spousal female intimate partners). Scholars agree that this is the most typical form of femicide in Western countries,[27] and that it seems to intersect with the larger phenomenon of domestic violence[28] where victims of assault and murder are almost all women. As elaborated in Chapters 2 and 3, the criminological characteristics of this particular lethal and fatal form of gender violence relate to the typical identity of both the victim and the killer, and to the typical murder scene. In this type of femicide, the victim is female and the killer is almost always male,[29] most often the victim's intimate partner. Consequently, the murder scene itself is usually none other than the home.[30] This particular form of femicide in which a woman is murdered by her intimate male partner is estimated to account for the vast majority of female homicides[31] and is distributed evenly throughout various racial and social strata.[32] Socio-demographic data about such killers suggest that they are almost always "ordinary guys,"[33] and that the phenomenon is common throughout the world.

Across the United States, intimate partner homicide accounts for approximately 40 to 50 percent of all femicide cases, while only 5.9 percent of the victims of this type of homicide are male.[34] These patterns were also reflected in the World Health Organization report on violence, which found differences in male versus female violence against partners, with women in the United States more likely to experience physical and sexual violence at the hands of a male intimate partner.[35] This victim gender asymmetry was also noted also by the National Violence Against Women Survey, which also showed that women in the United States are more likely to experience physical and sexual violence at the hands of a male intimate partner.[36] According to U.S. Bureau of Justice

26 Corradi et al. 2016: 978.

27 Campbell et al. 2007; Dobash and Dobash 2012.

28 Gender-based violence has broader criminological aspects than just domestic violence, as violence against females is also a characteristic of crimes committed outside the home environment, for example sex crimes.

29 Radford and Russell 1992: 10. In some other forms of femicide (e.g. honor killing, feticide and infanticide) females may collaborate or may be forced to collaborate with the killers.

30 Indeed, gender-wise, the home is considered to be the most dangerous place for women. See ibid. at 7: "the home is the most lethal place for women living in nuclear families."

31 Of femicide cases, 90 percent are carried out by family members, and of these 70 percent are spouses. See Campbell et al. 2007: 254; Serran and Firestone 2004: 12; Smith and Zahn 1998: 156–157; Coss 2006: 53, 57–58.

32 See Mackinnon 2001: 717.

33 See generally, Dobash et al. 2004.

34 Campbell et al. 2003: 1089.

35 Heise and Moreno-Garcia 2002: 89.

36 Tjaden and Thoennes 2000.

Statistics figures, about one-fourth of all murders committed annually in the United States are perpetrated against women, and of these killings about one-third of the women are murdered by an intimate partner.[37] American women are killed more often by an intimate partner (husband, lover, ex-husband or ex-lover) than by any other type of perpetrator.[38] Stout reported that married women comprised the majority of women killed by intimate partners in the United States, with wives of offenders making up 57.7 percent of intimate femicide victims. The next largest category of intimate femicide victims is that of girlfriends (24.9 percent), followed by common-law wives (7.9 percent), ex-wives (4.9 percent) and female friends (4.7 percent).[39]

While data observations for 1976–1996 indicate declining intimate partner homicide rates across the United States,[40] this is not the case regarding intimate partner femicide rates. The overall decreased rate of intimate partner homicide in the United States is the result of fewer murders of male intimate partners by female perpetrators. At the same time, across the United States the percentage of female victims killed by their intimate partners is on the rise.[41] Thus, the percentage of intimate partner homicides involving male victims decreased in the years 1976–1996, whereas the percentage of female victims in such homicides increased from 54 percent to 72 percent.[42]

Most women killed in the United States are white women.[43] The victims range in age from 16 to 91, with a modal age group of 25–29 for the victims and 30–34 for male offenders.[44] Geographic distribution of femicide in the United States indicates increased percentages across the southern states[45] and in cities with higher poverty rates.[46] Black women are over-represented in the distribution of femicide victims by race.[47] In fact, Campbell et al. argue that femicide is the leading cause of death in the United States among young African-American women between the ages of 15 and 45.[48] Stout argued that intimate partner femicide tends to be intra-racial and intra-ethnic.[49] However, since femicide among other racial minority groups such as Latinos, Asian Americans and Native Americans has not been studied yet,[50] the racial characteristics

37 Fox and Zawitz 2007.
38 Campbell et al. 2003: 1089. See also Warner 2010: 183.
39 Stout 1992: 34.
40 Dugan et al. 1999; Gauthier and Bankston 2004: 117; Wells and DeLeon-Granados 2004: 229.
41 Fox and Zawitz 2007.
42 Campbell et al. 2003: 1089.
43 Stout 1992: 34–35.
44 Ibid.: 35.
45 Gauthier and Bankston 2004: 118; Pridemore and Freilich 2005: 219.
46 Della Giustina 2010: 125–126.
47 Gauthier and Bankston 2004: 106; Campbell et al. 2003: 1089; Della Giustina 2010: 121.
48 Campbell et al. 2003: 1089.
49 Stout 1992: 35.
50 Della Giustina 2010: 148.

of the phenomenon in the United States are not fully known. The over-representation of black female victims of femicide, and perhaps also of females from other minority groups, may be linked to socio-cultural factors.[51] This needs to be further explored using socio-criminological methodologies before any conclusive legal recommendations can be made.

A legal analysis framework of femicide

Femicide in the form of the killing of an intimate female partner is a multi-faceted and complex social phenomenon with myriad aspects worthy of academic research, among them political, cultural, legal, economic, geographic, racial and religious. Scholars agree that since femicide is distinct from other forms of homicide it requires a specific framework of analysis.[52] Moreover, when analyzing intimate partner homicide with the aim of understanding and addressing the phenomenon, victim gender disparity highlights the vital need for a gendered criminological approach that takes into consideration the overwhelming majority of female victims. Indeed, a woman's disproportionate risk of lethal victimization at the hands of an intimate partner has generated much discussion among scholars, leading to the conclusion that feminist theoretical frameworks are the best prism through which to examine the phenomenon.[53] A gender-sensitive perspective is vital for adequate examination of femicide, exploring the phenomenon while searching for the underlying basic assumptions and socio-cultural structures that enable and perhaps even foster such killings.[54]

The legal field is an important area of inquiry into the social construction of gender-based violence. This book adopts the perspective that views law as a powerful social mechanism, not only because it reflects social reality, but more so because it plays a major role in the construction of reality, in this case gendered social reality.[55] By way of social reality construction, law has the power to refute and disregard alternative discourses and to claim a special place in defining the reality[56] of those affected by the law.[57]. Owing to its social constructive power, law defines crimes and victims and plays a significant role in the formation and treatment of violence. In this respect it also has the power to deny, exclude and trivialize gender-based violence, and more so to implicitly encourage it, even if inadvertently.[58]

A comprehensive examination of femicide must therefore critically demystify law and render its legal constructions more transparent, particularly regarding

51 Wallace 1986: 182.
52 Landau and Hattis-Rolef 1998: 76; Websdale 1999; Taylor and Jasinski 2011: 342.
53 Taylor and Jasinski 2011: 356.
54 Ibid.: 354.
55 Smart 1989.
56 Ibid.: 162–164.
57 Levit and Verchick 2006: 45.
58 Kelly and Radford 1996: 19.

the underlying basic legal assumptions and criminal mechanisms and doctrines by which law can contribute to the perpetuation and toleration of fatal gender-based violence.[59] This goal can be attained by employing methodologies used to uncover and expose gender-based biases hidden within supposedly "neutral" laws, and by identifying the gender-based consequences that such laws create.[60] Such a legal framework of analysis should examine whether seemingly neutral and objective laws contain a gender bias by not considering women's experiences, by implicitly favoring one sex over the other and by promoting illegitimate and offensive gender-based violence.[61]

The book will focus on the legal and criminological aspects of this phenomenon as they are reflected in the particular field of criminal law. While acknowledging that the legal perspective on femicide has global and historical aspects worthy of study and analysis, the scope of this book will be limited to the examination of the socio-legal aspects of femicide in contemporary American criminal law. In this regard the discussion about female homicide as part of the vast legal discourse in the United States on violence against women has not been sufficiently nor comprehensively articulated.[62] The book will offer socio-legal insights and practical legislative proposals regarding what I consider to be the best-suited framework for the criminal analysis of the phenomenon, and for the treatment and prevention of femicide in the form of intimate partner killing. It takes an in-depth look into the underpinnings of American criminal doctrines related to femicide, in order to expose and unravel socio-cultural structures that may give way to the killing of women and may even perpetuate such violence under the supposed aegis of its criminal doctrinal structures and statutory terminology.

The book will focus on three criminal doctrines relevant to the phenomenon of intimate partner femicide: the doctrine of provocation, the felony-murder rule and the doctrine of self-defense. A critical review of the legislation and legal structure of these doctrines will be presented as they are manifested in U.S. criminal law, particularly in the U.S. Model Penal Code. Somewhat similar to the way Levit and Verdick (2006) described legal feminism, the compatibility of the relevant doctrines to gender-based violence in general and to intimate partner femicide in particular are assessed in Chapters 2 through 4. This is achieved by identifying the various gender-based biases in the three main criminal doctrines and their consequences for women's killing. The practical sphere is addressed in Chapter 5, presenting several concrete recommendations for integrating gender-sensitive insights about femicide into mainstream criminal doctrines and into seemingly neutral yet biased existing laws.[63] Specifically,

59 Smart 1995: 2.
60 Levit and Verchick 2006.
61 Scales 2006; Levit and Verchick 2006.
62 Radford and Russell 1992: 4–5.
63 Levit and Verchick 2006: 46.

several statutory amendments are proposed to rectify what I see as issues not adequately addressed in current doctrine and legislation regarding the proper treatment and prevention of femicide.

American law on criminal homicide

Before examining the three specific criminal doctrines – the doctrine of provocation, the felony-murder rule and the doctrine of self-defense – it is important to set the stage by outlining the legal framework of homicide in the United States. The United States was founded by English colonists subject to British rule and to the English legal system. Consequently, American criminal law as a whole is generally based on its forebear, English common law doctrine. However, the historical British roots of the first American colonies did not necessarily mean that English common law was automatically transplanted, since "some of these colonies were settled in the early seventeenth century by religious dissenters eager to legislate for themselves."[64] We would thus expect differences, however slight, between English common law and U.S. law on criminal homicide.

English common law did not initially distinguish murder from manslaughter, and it was only around the sixteenth century that criminal homicides were divided into murder and the lesser offense of manslaughter.[65] The common law courts defined murder in terms of the concept of "malice aforethought" and treated manslaughter as a residual category for all other criminal homicides.[66] The English common law concept of "malice aforethought" converged into four main states of mind:[67] the intent to kill (that included awareness of such an outcome even if the actor did not have particular desire to kill the deceased), the intent to cause grievous bodily harm (whereby the knowledge that the particular conduct could cause such harm was assimilated into the required intent), unintentional killing (killing with extreme recklessness regarding the homicidal risk) and killing while intending to commit a felony. These four main states of mind did not require that the killing be committed with premeditated or

64 See Binder 2004: 107. British colonial authorities did not maintain that English law, whether customary or statutory, had to be automatically extended to conquered territories; "the colonial charters conferred by the Crown did not declare the applicability of the common law as such" (ibid.: 108). British authorities generally authorized local authorities to promulgate laws compatible with English laws. Hence, prior to independence, English law made common law rules authoritative in the colonies only insofar as local lawmakers enacted them. The significance is that English common law was not transplanted as such, and that it was slightly different in each state because in each state it was a creature of local decision during the colonial period (ibid.: 115.)

65 See *Model Penal Code and Commentaries (Official Draft and Revised Comments)* 1980: 44.

66 See ibid. at 44: "thus, in its classic formulation, manslaughter consisted of homicide without malice aforethought on the one hand, and without justification or excuse on the other hand."

67 See generally, LaFave and Wakeman 1972: 528–562. See also *Model Penal Code and Commentaries (Official Draft and Revised Comments)* 1980: 14–15.

subjective intent, as the knowledge or awareness of the plausible death outcome was assimilated into the intent required for a murder conviction. Thus, in English common law, the definition of murder extended to include homicide cases currently treated as manslaughter. If we add the abundance of capital crimes[68] to the extended definition of murder in the English common law, we can most probably argue that it was harsh and punitive with respect to criminal homicide.

During and after American independence, a number of states enacted statutes or constitutional provisions accepting the English common law as default legislation.[69] Thus, English common law greatly influenced American post-independence criminal law, but was not incorporated as such in its entirety. American reformers were particularly skeptical of the criminal common law, as they viewed the abundance of capital crimes as archaic and bloody,[70] rejected the feudal sources of the criminal common law[71] and were suspicious of judicial lawmaking.[72] Accordingly, American legal scholars aimed to innovate criminal law, particularly in the field of homicide,[73] and instituted these innovations through legislation more than through adjudication.[74] American criminal law was thus an intentional, codified and explicit law advanced by the principle of separation of powers between the executive, judicial and legislative branches. Indeed, the legislative authorities of post-independence America were particularly energetic in legislating on the subject of homicide law, and by the end of the nineteenth century almost all U.S. jurisdictions had enacted such legislation.[75]

Apart from legislative efforts to codify American homicide law, legal scholars attest that substantial parts of common law pertaining to homicide law "survived virtually intact."[76] Nonetheless, alongside the general assimilation of the

68 See Binder 2004: 119.

69 Both in general and with respect to particular crimes (see ibid.: 113). However, in so far as U.S. jurisdictions applied common law to resolve cases, they applied their own practiced, local common law since, prior to American independence, English common law was applied only as locally practiced. See ibid.: 114.

70 See ibid.: 115.

71 See ibid.: 116.

72 American reformers believed that punishment could only fulfill its principal purpose of deterrence if based on judicial ex post-facto case law and on statutes that clearly define proscribed conduct in advance. See ibid.: 117, 122.

73 See ibid.: 118, 123.

74 See ibid.: 118.

75 See ibid.: 123, referring to felony-murder rule statutes, and 120 for homicide grading statutes.

76 See *Model Penal Code and Commentaries (Official Draft and Revised Comments)* 1980: 19: "It was the pattern in this country prior to the Model Penal Code to incorporate the common law in some jurisdictions and to build upon it in others." See also Wechsler 1983: 220:

> criminal law began with the reception of the English common law and antecedent legislation, plus a small addendum of colonial enactments. It was an obscure system, if indeed it may be called a system, fraught with technicalities and bloody punishments that it endeavored to

English common law, several innovations were introduced into American law on criminal homicide. These innovations were instituted during the nineteenth century and departed from the English criminal common law in an attempt to rank the relative gravity of the various forms of murder. This took the form of a murder gradation scheme (dividing murder into degrees)[77] as well as the codification of the felony-murder rule.[78] Thus, instead of the common law's all-encompassing conceptualization of murder, American post-independence criminal law on homicide introduced a grading scheme that differentiated between the gravity of various types of murder. Other than killing while committing a felonious act (that did not require subjective *mens rea*), all killings without subjective intent (such as killing while being reckless) were seen as less grievous forms of murder. Willful, deliberate and premeditated murder, as well as murder that occurred in the commission of or in an attempt to commit enumerated felonies, were regarded as the most grievous kind of murder, graded as first degree murder with correlative capital punishment.[79]

By and large, American criminal law was more lenient towards criminal homicide than English common law with its definition of murder and its correlative capital punishment. This leniency led to the extension of the common law doctrine of provocation and of the doctrine of self-defense.[80] As will be elaborated in Chapters 2 and 4, in relation to both these doctrines American criminal law expanded the circumstances whereby defendants could assert legal claims to mitigate their criminal liability for the killing they had committed. Over time the criminal doctrines of self-defense and provocation shifted further away from their English forebears and reinforced the expansive American approach towards the range of applicability of the legal doctrines that mitigated the defendant's criminal liability for murder. The American doctrine of the felony-murder rule also added technical bars for murder convictions in line with the merger doctrine. Thus all three criminal doctrines that will be critically examined with regard to the femicide phenomenon have the power, both *de jure* and de facto, to reduce murder convictions of femicide perpetrators to manslaughter.

---

impose on the unfortunates within its toils … legislation did reduce the number of the capital offenses but generally went no further than to fix the lesser penalties to be imposed. If it undertook a definition of offenses, the text was very likely to be drawn from Blackstone's repetition of judicial formulations. Principles, rules and doctrines measuring the scope of liability and of defenses were dealt with very rarely in the statutes and remitted consequently to the common law.

77 The legislative reform dividing murder into degrees originated in Pennsylvania's 1794 reform statute which restricted capital punishment to first degree murder. This legislative reform was led by reformers who viewed the abundance of capital crimes in English common law as barbaric, and strived to reduce and differentiate between penalties based on a more enlightened approach. See Binder 2004: 119; *Model Penal Code Official Commentaries* 1980: 16.

78 See Binder 2004: 120.

79 See Wechsler 1968: 1446.

80 See *Model Penal Code and Commentaries (Official Draft and Revised Comments)* 1980: 49–50.

Furthermore, these legal constructions have the power to exonerate or inadvertently tolerate the killing of women through the "legal understanding" accorded by these three doctrines to femicide perpetrators. For this reason, instead of focusing on the general criminal doctrine of homicide, the book tackles criminal doctrines that function in practice as partial defenses while according diminished criminal liability to women killers. In light of the vast power of the law to construct and perpetuate social reality, such mitigating legal criminal constructions contribute to the perpetuation of femicide, even if inadvertently.

The U.S. Model Penal Code approach to criminal homicide

Despite the legislative efforts of post-independence America, state criminal codes are not systematic and lack comprehensive codification.[81] This lack of coherent codification was an outcome of the English common law tradition that focused on the development of substantive law through case law,[82] as well as the fact that comprehensive American federal statutory legislation was neither available nor applied. Furthermore, the extent to which the common law on homicide was modified varied considerably from jurisdiction to jurisdiction.[83] Consequently, current American criminal law varies from state to state and is comprised of a codified body of 52 different criminal codes (50 state codes, the code of the District of Columbia and the federal code that is applicable to all states and deals with inter-state offenses).[84] This complex legal construct was not resolved by federal criminal law (that could have constituted a framework for all states), because the latter was not systematic or relevant to the practical functioning of the states.[85] Criminal jurisdiction over crimes relating to the federal structure of the United States (crimes relating to military bases, ambassadors, federal law enforcement agencies or crimes that cross state borders) is in federal hands.[86] Under the Constitution of the United States, the enforcement of criminal law relating to most crimes (murder, rape, robbery, assault, theft) falls within the jurisdiction of the states.[87] Owing to this

81 See Wechsler 1982–1983: 220:

> notwithstanding the importance of the penal law to society and to the individual, we did not have an integrated, reasoned *corpus juris* in (the criminal) field. Such statutes were fragmentary, old, disorganized and even accidental in their coverage, producing a medley of enactments and of common law that only local history explained.

82 See Dubber and Robinson 1999: 6.

83 See generally, *Model Penal Code and Commentaries (Official Draft and Revised Comments)* 1980: 16–18.

84 See Dubber and Robinson 1999: 1–2.

85 For an analysis of the historical reasons for the lack of a uniform federal criminal law see Binder 2004: 116–117.

86 See Dubber and Robinson 1999: 3.

87 See *U.S. Constitution*, Article 3, Section 2(3); See *Bill of Rights* 1791, Section 6.

state-level criminal jurisdiction, it is very difficult to establish a uniform federal criminal law that would be applicable to the entire United States.[88]

It was in the middle of the twentieth century, in view of this inadequate legislative infrastructure, that the American Law Institute turned to the work of criminal codification, which in turn led to the drafting of the U.S. Model Penal Code.[89] Since its formulation, the Code has had a notable impact on legislative reforms made to subsequent state criminal codes,[90] and in fact its wording provides the current prototype for various criminal doctrines in all U.S. jurisdictions.[91] It also had an immense impact on the development of criminal law principles as a whole[92] through extensive case law based on the Model Penal Code (MPC) as a normative source for the interpretation of state criminal law.[93] In this respect, the MPC is the closest thing, both *de jure* and de facto, to what can be viewed as the "American Criminal Code."

In its treatment of homicide, the MPC abandoned the degrees of murder that had been legally constructed by post-independence American states (first, second and third-degree murder) and chose to employ in their place the three basic common law categories of criminal homicide (murder, manslaughter and negligent homicide[94]). According to this approach, only homicide that was committed purposely or knowingly was placed in the murder category.[95] The most important change proposed by the MPC in the realm of criminal homicide was the broad criterion for mitigating the defendant's criminal liability

88 See Dubber and Robinson 1999: 3.

89 Op. cit.

90 See Herberling 1975: 914–915.

91 By means of extensive case law based on the MPC as a normative source for interpreting state criminal law, see op. cit.; Dubber and Robinson 1999: 5. The legislative amendments by the various states of the United States attest to the critical impact of the MPC, which resulted in certain similarities found in the criminal codes of the various states, albeit not all the legal arrangements proposed by the Code drafters were adopted. For example, many states preserved the common law felony-murder rule, even though the Code drafters abolished this murder offense. Similarly, many states still apply different rules to attempted offenses and completed offenses, whereas the Code advocates equivalent punishment for both. In general, considerable variation still exists between the states on various criminal issues, with variation entrenched in the absence of effective federal legislation. See Gillespie 1989: 183–184.

92 Even the MPC Official Commentaries accompanying the proposed draft MPC (the draft Code was published in 1962 and the Official Commentaries relating to the various sections were published shortly thereafter between 1980 and 1985), provide an interpretive source for the development of legal discipline and judicial legislation in the various U.S. jurisdictions. See Dubber and Robinson 1999: 6. For empirical findings of the influence of the MPC on case law, see Wechsler 1982–1983: 222.

93 Even the Official Commentaries accompanying the proposed draft Model Penal Code (the draft Code was published in 1962 and the Official Commentaries relating to the various sections were published shortly thereafter between 1980 and 1985) provide an interpretive source for the development of the legal discipline and judicial legislation in the various jurisdictions of the United States. See Dubber and Robinson 1999: 6.

94 See section 210.1(2) of the *Model Penal Code and Commentaries (Official Draft and Revised Comments)* 1980: "Criminal homicide is murder, manslaughter or negligent homicide."

95 See Wechsler 1968: 1446.

applied in two of the traditional English common law criminal doctrines of homicide: the doctrine of provocation and the doctrine of self-defense.[96]

As elaborated in Chapter 2, the doctrine of provocation has historical roots in English law and views provocation by the victim as a factor instigating intense anger, which thereby diminishes the moral guilt of the person accused of the murder. The doctrine of provocation enables mitigation of a murder conviction upon proof that the defendant had been provoked to kill by the deceased victim. The MPC's approach further extended the mitigation offered by the traditional doctrine of provocation, by introducing the legal concept of "extreme mental or emotional disturbance," as in section 210.3(b) of the Code. Consequently, according to this approach an intentional homicide can be reduced from murder to manslaughter if it is committed "under the influence of extreme mental or emotional disturbance for which there is reasonable explanation or excuse,"[97] thus judging the matter from a subjective rather than an objective point of view.[98] The main departure of American doctrine from its traditional English roots on this matter relates to "the enlargement of the class of cases which would otherwise be murder but which could be reduced to manslaughter under the Model Penal Code definition because the homicidal act occurred in the "heat of passion" upon adequate provocation."[99] The MPC's formulation of the provocation doctrine enables mitigation of a murder conviction if the provocative event aroused in the defendant extreme mental or emotional disturbance. The mitigation that could be granted according to the MPC formulation is thus far more extensive than that accepted by the English common law in that it encompasses emotional and mental circumstances that were not accepted as adequate provocation in English common law. Furthermore, the MPC's articulation of adequate provocation expanded the component of subjectivity in the context of applicable claims for mitigation under the doctrine of provocation.[100] Such an extended formulation may lead to the exoneration of homicide defendants from murder convictions.

The MPC also extended the traditional English common law self-defense. As will be elaborated in Chapter 4, this doctrine constitutes an exception to the rule prohibiting the use of force, and is particularly dramatic in the context of its application to acts of homicide, which are considered to be justified upon implementation of the doctrine. The criminal doctrine of self-defense originally

96 See Wechsler 1982–1983: 230 with regard to the MPC's formulation of the doctrine of provocation.

97 See Section 210.3(1)(b) of the *Model Penal Code and Commentaries (Official Draft and Revised Comments)* 1980: when "a homicide which would otherwise be murder is committed under the influence of extreme mental or emotional disturbance," it would constitute manslaughter (according to section 210.3(1)).

98 See ibid.: "the reasonableness of such explanation or excuse shall be determined from the viewpoint of a person in the actor's situation under the circumstances as he believes them to be."

99 *Model Penal Code and Commentaries (Official Draft and Revised Comments)* 1980: 49.

100 Ibid.: 49–50.

developed in medieval England[101] and functioned as a common law ruling in U.S. jurisdictions up until the twentieth century.[102] As the United States emerged as an independent socio-cultural and political entity, its criminal doctrine departed from its English forebear in so far as it abolished the duty to retreat and softened most of the additional traditional English requirements for its application. The endemic changes to the doctrine of self-defense are related to unique socio-cultural and geographical characteristics of the British colonists in America of the eighteenth and nineteenth centuries, in the context of which, for example, the prerequisite of retreat was regarded as overly "soft" for the American settlers.[103] By the end of the frontier era, the abolition of the duty to retreat as a prerequisite for the application of the claim of self-defense was widely accepted in American society.[104] This already extended approach was statutorily promulgated and even further expanded by the MPC.[105] According

101 The doctrine was developed in circumstances wherein the government was unable to provide security and the crime rate and number of homicides was among the highest in European history. See Gillespie 1989: 35. The British legal principles concerning the application of the claim of self-defense are ancient and attributed to the Norman invasion of England in the eleventh century. For a review of the impact of this invasion and the subsequent changes to the English legal system in general and to the doctrine of self-defense in particular, see Leverick 2006: 1; Gillespie 1989: 32–35. For an historical review of medieval England and a cross comparison with the United States in the nineteenth and twentieth centuries, see Beeghley 2003: 41–77.

102 The American doctrine of self-defense was codified in the twentieth century. This doctrine, which was particularly developed by the Western states of United States, was not codified at the time of America's inception and therefore functioned in the same way as principles of American common law. The same holds true for the Eastern states (in which comprehensive codification of the criminal law had been carried out even before the twentieth century), in which the doctrine of self-defense had not undergone codification and was therefore applied as part of the criminal common law in these states as well. See Gillespie 1989: 48.

103 In the Western states, settlements were sporadic and geographically remote from any center of government that could have enforced law and order; retreat in such circumstances was regarded as improper submission (Gillespie 1989: 42). Abolition of the duty to retreat requirement, as well as the ethos of "standing one's ground", were reflected in the mythological figure of the virtuous cowboy in American culture who represented the "real American man":

> The figure of the lone hero – be he cowboy, sheriff or outlaw – had reached truly mythic proportions in the popular mind in the last decades of the nineteenth century. He was a "man's man," a two-fisted fighter, never a coward or a bully, never entangled by the Victorian society that his idolizers were tied to, beholden to no one but himself.
>
> As Teddy Roosevelt described:
>
> A cowboy will not submit tamely to an insult, and is ever ready to avenge his own wrongs, nor has he an overwrought fear of shedding blood … he does possess, to a very high degree, the stern, manly qualities that are invaluable to the nation.
>
> (Quoted in ibid.: 46)

104 See also Carpenter 2003: 663.

105 The MPC added to the circumstances in which a person could retreat without danger all other circumstances in which the attack takes place in the victim's home or workplace. See Model Penal Code and *Model Penal Code and Commentaries (Official Draft and Revised Comments)* 1980: 54–56.

to the Code's formulation, killing committed while using deadly protective force is judged from the defendant's subjective point of view and could be deemed justified self-defense. Consequently, this formulation enables the mitigation of the criminal liability in cases whereby the defendant of a criminal homicide claims that he used protective deadly force as a defensive response. Such extension may offer defendants in the United States a possible acquittal from the murder conviction they would have otherwise faced under the traditional common law criminal doctrine of self-defense.

The majority of U.S. state criminal codes follow the MPC's approach with respect to the extension of these two criminal doctrines: the separate legal category for the use of protective deadly force in the doctrine of self-defense[106] and the extended conceptualization of the doctrine of provocation.[107] The Code was not as influential with regard to the formulation of the felony-murder rule.[108] According to the felony-murder doctrine, the felon's intent in committing a felony is attached to the killing and transformed into the common law's malice aforethought required for murder.[109] The MPC's formulation with respect to the traditional common law felony-murder rule restricted the rule by requiring an additional *mens rea* for a felony-murder conviction. This proposed restricted version of the felony-murder rule is followed by only three U.S. jurisdictions.[110] Thus, we can argue that in the realm of criminal homicide law, U.S. jurisdictions chose to follow the MPC approach only in so far as it legally extended the leniency towards mitigated criminal liability of defendants facing a murder conviction.

Femicide and related American criminal doctrines

Gender-related legal issues in the United States have progressed significantly over the past 30 years, and in practice form one of the most prominent features of current American criminal law.[111] This is particularly conspicuous against the

106 This version of the self-defense doctrine will be further elaborated in Chapter 4.

107 The conceptualization of the "Emotional or Mental Extreme Disturbance" (EMED) mitigates murder convictions based on the defendant's subjective state of mind. This version of the doctrine of provocation will be further elaborated in Chapter 2.

108 This version of the felony-murder rule will be elaborated in Chapter 3.

109 See Fletcher 1981: 413; *Model Penal Code and Commentaries (Official Draft and Revised Comments)* 1980: 13.

110 Currently followed only by New Hampshire, Delaware and Arkansas. New Hampshire requires "knowledge" for capital felony murder or first-degree felony murder, and "recklessness under circumstances manifesting an extreme indifference to the value of human life" for second degree felony murder (see New Hampshire Revised Statutes Annotated, Section 630: 1). Delaware requires recklessness for first-degree felony murder or criminal negligence for second-degree felony murder (see Delaware Code Annotated Tit. 11 Section 635–636). Arkansas requires the manifestation of extreme indifference to the value of human life during the commission of any felony for first-degree felony-murder conviction (see Arkansas Statute Annotated Section 41–1502).

111 See Sangero 2006: 116; Dubber and Robinson 1999: 7.

backdrop of the MPC, which has remained unchanged since it was drafted in the 1950s, and is greatly lacking in all gender-related aspects of criminal law. As a result, the Code includes a distorted legal arrangement with regard to the application of its various relevant criminal doctrines in situations of violence against women in general, and femicide in particular.

Defendants who claim that they killed their female intimate partners "under the heat of passion" are usually treated by the prosecution and the courts alike according to the doctrine of provocation. However, this doctrine has been significantly extended in U.S. jurisdictions that follow the MPC with its inclusion of "extreme mental or emotional disturbance" (EMED) as a partial mitigating factor. Hence, de facto, the American legal conceptualization of EMED as espoused by the MPC may provide legal immunity from full criminal liability and may exonerate male defendants from a murder conviction for the femicide that they committed. Furthermore, defendants who kill their female intimate partners while lethally battering them to death may be exonerated from a murder conviction in light of the American criminal doctrine of felony murder. As will be elaborated in Chapter 3, the extended American felony-murder sub-doctrine of the "principle of merger," commonly found in U.S. jurisdictions and in the MPC alike, bars such prosecution on the grounds of the battery being a lesser-included offense within the criminal homicide. Thus, the American legal conceptualization of the felony-murder rule and its "principle of merger" correlate offer legal immunity from full criminal liability and exonerate defendants from a murder conviction for the assaultive-femicide they committed.

However, this leniency towards criminal homicide is not gender-symmetric. Specifically, American criminal law is not as lenient when it comes to the prosecution of battered women. The current American doctrine of self-defense is inadequate and cannot be employed by female defendants that use protective deadly force under circumstances of domestic violence. This has dire and unjust legal consequences for women who defend themselves against a grievous and dangerous attack perpetrated by their intimate partner with deadly protective force. Consequently, and lamentably, these battered women will face the tragic and fatal legal result of a murder conviction. Thus, overall, it seems that current American criminal homicide law still lacks gender-equal justice. As will be elaborated in Chapter 4, once prosecuted for the killing caused by their defensive response, battered women should be able to resort to the extended American doctrine espoused by the MPC formulation regarding justified use of deadly protective force within the doctrine of self-defense.

Under the current American criminal doctrines of provocation, felony-murder rule and self-defense, femicide perpetrators are treated leniently while battered women are treated harshly. Male defendants will, at worst, be convicted of manslaughter for killing women, while female defendants will be convicted of murder for killing the men who battered them. Such an anomalous legal structure reflects both gender inequality and criminal injustice.

In order to provide a comprehensive legal analysis of the gender problems found in the American criminal doctrines relevant to femicide, each of the following chapters will focus on the specific characteristics of femicide and on the corresponding criminal doctrine, as generally applied. The analysis will explore three main issues: uxoricide (spouse killing), assaultive-femicide (killing through battering) and the potential legal implications of a preemptive defensive strike on the part of a battered woman. Following this methodological approach, Chapter 2 will deal with intimate partner femicide, presenting a criminological overview of the phenomenon and a critical review of the common law doctrine of provocation as applied in the MPC. Chapter 3 will focus on the criminological characteristics of assaultive-femicide and present a critical review of the common law criminal felony-murder rule found in the MPC. Chapter 4 will offer a critical review of the common law doctrine of self-defense and discuss its legal implications for battered women who engage in a preemptive strike where there is a tangible threat to their life. Chapter 5 will then translate the legal insights of all earlier chapters into a series of proposed detailed statutory legal reforms to the MPC, addressing the above three primary issues applicable to femicide as well as their correlative criminal doctrines within the Code. These proposed legislative reforms will be presented as amendments that offer suitable and tailor-made changes required for the proper adaptation of these current criminal doctrines to the treatment and prevention of femicide. The relevant criminal doctrines as worded in the U.S. Model Penal Code are: the doctrine of provocation as in section 210.3(b), the doctrine of felony-murder rule as in section 210.2(1)(b), and the doctrine of self-defense as in section 3.04(2)(b).

2 "Either mine or dead"

Intimate partner femicide and the American criminal doctrine of provocation

Many scholars argue that the Model Penal Code provision that seeks to mitigate criminal liability in the context of the doctrine of provocation is overly broad, and recent empirical findings about the context of the murder of intimate partners suggest that these killings do not occur in circumstances of emotional turmoil or momentary loss of control, but rather knowingly and deliberately (often against the background of the female partner's wish to end the intimate relationship).

The chapter will demonstrate the harsh consequences of the doctrinal expansion afforded by the Model Penal Code in the context of the murder of intimate partners, and will argue that mitigation of criminal liability in circumstances of such conscious and deliberate action is inconsistent with a proper doctrinal foundation for mitigating criminal liability. Although American writers have already criticized the excessive mitigation of criminal liability in states that have adopted the Model Penal Code doctrine of provocation, this chapter offers a real contribution to the cause of dealing with intimate partner homicides, both because it focuses on this issue specifically and because it is a platform for a concrete proposal for the legislative amendment of the Model Penal Code, as will be further elaborated in the last chapter of the book.

The chapter will elaborate the socio-legal problems stemming from the application of the doctrine of provocation, as it is statutorily entrenched in states that have adopted the text of the Model Penal Code and its legal concept of "heat of passion" in the context of murder of intimate partners. In order to obtain a substantive critical overview of the legal concept of "heat of passion" in the context of intimate partner femicide, I will first outline the historical and socio-legal characteristics of the American doctrine of provocation. In doing so, I will offer a legislative history of the American doctrine of provocation with its original British roots (early common law approach) and its two additional indigenous adaptations: the doctrine of provocation based on the "reasonable person," and the "heat of passion" doctrine of provocation based on the Model Penal Code. Having explored the three main versions of the doctrine of provocation used in America, this chapter will focus on the dire consequences of the application of the most common American version of the doctrine of provocation, the "heat of passion" approach, to instances of femicide. I will analyze the "heat of passion" doctrine of provocation based on the Model Penal Code approach (as codified in Section 210.3 of the Model Penal Code) and provide general recommendations for a proper socio-legal American doctrine of provocation in circumstances of intimate partner femicide.

Love, jealousy and provocation: a socio-legal view of intimate partner femicide

Women are not murdered by women. Most often, they are murdered by men.[1] It is rare, too, for them to be murdered by strange men. They are murdered by their partners.[2] Theoretically, then, even though it is possible to distinguish between two different concepts, femicide (the murder of women) and uxoricide (the murder of spouses), empirically the phenomena share common characteristics. The characteristics common to both phenomena relate to the fact that the women are killed by male family members. The features unique to uxoricide (the murder of spouses) relate to the circumstances and motives typical of these cases of homicide: *the majority of uxoricides typically occur in close proximity to the female partner expressly seeking separation from the man and an end to their intimate relationship*. Therefore, cases of uxoricide (including both married and non-married spouses) are usually post-separation homicides.[3] The link between the woman's desire to separate and the homicide is repeatedly supported by studies conducted in various countries.[4] In practice, the period immediately after separation is the most dangerous: 50 to 70 percent of the acts of murder occur while the couple lives separately,[5] and often they are committed after the female

1 As with the murder of men, women are almost always murdered by men (i.e., most murderers are men). U.S. Department of Justice, Bureau of Justice Statistics 2013: 4.

2 For socio-legal discussions and insights on this issue, see generally Campbell et al. 2007; Ramsey 2010: 83; Serran and Firestone 2004: 12; Browne et al. 1999: 149–150; Coss 2006: 57.

3 Naturally, most separations between partners (including separations initiated by the female partner) do not lead to murder; nonetheless, intimate relationships which terminate at the initiative of the man tend not to end in murder, whereas intimate relationships which terminate at the initiative of the woman expose those women to the risk of death. There is a vast amount of literature as well as supporting studies concerning the causal connection between the murder of the female partner and her desire and initiative to end the intimate relationship. See Campbell et al. 2003: 1095; Dawson and Gartner 1998: 382; Dobash et al. 2004: 582; Farr 2002; Hannawa et al. 2006: 540–541; Johnson and Hotton 2003: 59–60, 68–70, 80–82; Saunders and Browne 2000: 420–421, 443; Serran and Firestone 2004: 3–5, 12; Wilson and Daly 1998: 301; Wilson and Daly 1993: 3–4, 9–12; See generally, Campbell et al. 2007: 254; Coss 2006: 59–60; Browne et al. 1999: 159–161.

4 Such studies have been conducted, for example, in the United States, Australia, Canada and New Zealand. See Ben Ze'ev and Goussinsky 2008: 39, 42, 86; Edelstein 2011: 148, 164, 168, 171, 183 (discussing empirical results from Israeli society and specific findings relating to particular populations, including Ethiopian immigrants, Russian immigrants and the non-Jewish population in Israel).

5 A large proportion of them occur during the first months following separation and after the man has failed, despite his best efforts, to restore the relationship. Researchers argue that the woman's risk of being murdered during the period of separation is two to four times greater than the risk of being murdered while living together with her partner. See Ben Ze'ev and Goussinsky 2008: 105.

partner has implemented her intention to separate.[6] Another unique characteristic of intimate partner femicide is the particular socio-demographic profile of the murderers: the profile of the murderers of female partners is unlike the typical profile of murderers in general.[7] In contrast to murderers in general, murderers of their female intimate partners are heterogeneous in age, often do not have a criminal record, and are much more likely to be middle class than other murderers.[8] It is important to emphasize that, although in some cases the murder of the female partner is the culmination of an existing pattern of violence against her, intimate partner homicide is distinct from domestic violence.[9] While violence directed at a female partner aims to achieve control and obedience, murdering her is intended to bring about her ruin – and more specifically, her death.[10]

Together with the link between the murder of the female partner and her desire to end the intimate relationship, many researchers have also pointed to the connection between sexual/romantic jealousy and intimate partner homicide.[11] Murder out of jealousy[12] seems to undermine the goal of the murderer as, paradoxically, the man acts to destroy the very person whose presence he

6 Coss 2006: 59. In any event, researchers define the initial few months after the woman seeks to separate as a period in which she is at high risk of being murdered by her partner (although it must be recalled that most women who wish to separate are not at risk of being murdered and therefore it is necessary to define the group at risk in a more specific manner). See Dobash et al. 2004: 582 (discussing the high risk following a separation initiated by the woman).

7 Murderers in general tend to have common characteristics: a problematic childhood, under-education, likelihood of unemployment, previous criminal convictions and a tendency for alcohol and drug abuse. See ibid.: 599–601.

8 Ben Ze'ev and Goussinsky 2008: 90.

9 The murder of a woman is undoubtedly one of the most extreme forms of male violence. However, in the opinion of Ben Ze'ev and Goussinsky, it should not be understood as the culmination of a chronology of violence but as a separate phenomenon – different in motives, circumstances leading to the act and emotions surrounding it. Ibid.: xiii.

10 Murder and violence in this specific context must be regarded as separate phenomena because the motivations underlying the two actions are dissimilar. While violence towards women, according to the accepted view, is a strategy of control, directed at obtaining obedience and displaying power and force, the murderer aims to achieve another purpose: the destruction of the woman. Ibid.: 118.

11 See, e.g., Lee 2003: 27, 283 (quoting a study concluding that 60 percent of the men who murdered their partners claimed that they had done so because of the victim's sexual relationship with another man).

12 Ben Ze'ev and Goussinsky argue that romantic love contains the potential for jealousy because romantic love testifies to the existence of an important relationship, and the threat of losing this relationship in favor of another may incite jealousy. Such a loss severely harms a person's self-esteem and the threat is grave because it entails the loss of an important relationship. Usually, jealousy is interpreted as a sign of concern and love for the partner (and indeed there will be no jealousy where the partner feels a complete sense of indifference towards the relationship), but it does not necessarily reflect love (for example, a man who loathes his wife may feel jealous when someone else looks at her with lust, and in such a case the jealousy is connected more to egoism than to love). See Ben Ze'ev and Goussinsky 2008: 83; Ben Ze'ev 2000: 51–60, 94–99 (discussing the emotion of jealousy and the link between jealousy, love and intimate partner relationships).

seeks, and the murderer does so because he wants to continue to be close to the victim: "*With his own hands, a man causes the destruction of someone else, because he does not wish to lose that person.*"[13] Jealousy and the behavioral patterns associated with the term are seen as an expression of true "love,"[14] but concomitantly negate the woman as an autonomous being and allow (not to say encourage) the demonstration of feelings through violent behavioral patterns. This social construct of "romantic jealousy" therefore produces social and personal tolerance towards displays of violence in "romantic" contexts,[15] and the sublimation of violence when it occurs in circumstances of "love."[16] Understanding the patterns of intimate partner homicide is therefore only possible in the light of society's understanding of the social construct of love as noble, lofty, pure, eternal and total.[17] In view of this social ideal, the separation from the beloved partner is perceived as separation from the eternal and total ideal, and therefore as death:[18] Male murderers are threatened therefore not by the existence of the woman in their lives, but just the opposite – by her absence in their lives: thus

13 Ben Ze'ev and Goussinsky 2008: 84. This paradox inspired the researchers of this phenomenon to assume that the murder of intimate partners is not the outcome of love but rather the consequence of extreme, morbid and pathological sexual jealousy. Later in this chapter, I shall discuss the connection between this prima facie paradox and the development of the legal construction of "loss of control" in the doctrine of provocation, in the circumstances of the murder of intimate partners.

14 In this context, it is customary to quote a fifth century comment attributed to St. Augustine: "He that is not jealous is not in love." Saint Augustine, *Source unknown*, 4th/5th century AD. See Ben Ze'ev and Goussinsky 2008: 83.

15 To address this issue, a bill was introduced in the Israeli parliament by MK Ahmad Tibi which proposed prohibiting media publications describing the murder of women in romantic terms, or in terms describing the violent event as one relating to family honor, as "linking a violent event such as murder to positive expressions sends a message of encouragement and justification for this act." Bill P/18/2742–2010, submitted to the Executive of the Knesset on November 29, 2010. According to the bill, a breach of this prohibition would lead to an obligation to publish an apology and expose the publisher to a potential civil claim vesting the court with the power to award compensation of up to NIS50,000, or approximately US$14,000 as of September 4, 2014, without proof of damages. This bill did not complete the legislative process as it failed to achieve support in the Knesset plenum.

16 See Howe 1999, 2002, 2004. See also Ben Ze'ev and Goussinsky 2008: 79–80. For empirical studies indicating tolerance towards displays of violence and romantic jealousy, and sublimation of violence against the backdrop of the ideal of love, see Henton et al. 1983: 469–474 (describing a study in which a considerable number of high school students who had experienced violence as both aggressor and victim perceived the violent as indicating "love"); Puente and Cohen 2003: 449–451, 457 (describing more tolerant perceptions of violence when it stemmed from jealousy).

17 See Ben Ze'ev and Goussinsky 2008: 63 (arguing that the literature that deals with the murder of women completely disregards the feeling of love, and that disregarding this feeling, per se, reflects the psychological difficulty of linking "love" as a noble emotion to murder).

18 The analogy between separation and death is linked to the perception of love as something eternal, which does not wane and which is not vulnerable to harms. See ibid.: 9–10.

"the dark side of the ultimate expression of lover turns the woman into a hostage – a hostage to the man's life, and, therefore, puts her life at risk."[19]

The social construct of love as a sublime ideal in the name of which, or under the auspices of which, it is justified to show tolerance towards displays of violence and criminal acts has been introduced into the legal discourse of the common law through the legal construct of the doctrine of provocation. The landmark ruling in the context of mitigating criminal liability for murder in circumstances of romantic jealousy was delivered as early as 1859 in the United States, in the *Sickles* case.[20] The case concerned Sickles, a New York City Congressman, who was charged with shooting and killing Barton Key, the District Attorney of New York, who had been having an affair with his wife. Sickles was acquitted upon the court accepting the defense that he had suffered an instinctive temporary loss of control due to intense romantic jealousy.[21] Sickles's defense attorneys managed to persuade the court that it had to recognize the legal presumption of the existence of temporary insanity negating criminal liability for murder, as a result of the human instinct of jealousy[22] (leading, as mentioned, to loss of control followed by deadly violence).[23] This legal construction relied on English precedent, namely, the *Manning* case,[24] which tied provocation to adultery and specifically referred to the feeling of jealousy as a noble manly emotion:

19 Ibid.: 42. The authors also note that, even though the beloved partner is the most important person in their lives, it is not the partner but the man's love for her that is of the utmost importance and the woman herself, her personality and desires, become unimportant.

> The woman as person, with her virtues and weaknesses, actions and failures to act, is not the focus of his consciousness. Paradoxically, the enormous importance attributed to the object of the love is bound up with the object's lack of importance in the sense that the woman's self, her character and personality, desires and feelings play no role.
>
> (Ibid.: 43)

20 Fontaine 2012: 97. See also Keetley 2008: 269–288 (providing a detailed description of the affair and citing Fontaine's account).

21 See Fontaine 2012: 62.

22 Ibid.: 26, 29, 30, 32, 97.

23 Ibid.: 61–63.

24 In a landmark ruling given in 1617 in the *Manning* case, concerning the recognition of adultery as provocation, the accused was acquitted of murder committed in a rage upon finding his wife in a compromising position with the victim. The court held that it would be appropriate to mitigate the conviction from murder to manslaughter because the provocation was "sufficiently great" in the circumstances of adultery and therefore a lesser conviction was justified. Horder 1992: 39 ("It was but manslaughter, the provocation being exceeding great, and … there was no precedent malice.") Subsequently, an important statement was made *obiter dictum* in connection with the socio-legal perception of adultery as serious provocation. The statement was made in England by Mr. Justice Holt in 1707 in *Regina* v. *Mawgridge*, rejecting an assertion of provocation arising during a fight between two men, because the provocation in such circumstances was not as grave as in circumstances of adultery. Ibid.

> When a man is taken in adultery with another man's wife, if the husband shall stab the adulterer, or knock out his brains, this is bare manslaughter: *for jealousy is the rage of the man, and adultery is the highest invasion of property*...[25]

The *Sickles* case therefore further developed the legal link established in eighteenth-century England between adultery and possessive jealousy, and added the elements of love and romantic jealousy as components stirring emotions inherent and natural to man that might subsequently lead to deadly violence through loss of control. This connection was first recognized as creating a legal causal connection for murder in the *Sickles* case, as one of the defense attorneys argued: "To kill *in the name of jealousy* is merely '*obedience to the will of nature.*' "[26]

The acknowledgment of the link between jealousy and murder in the *Sickles* case was not unprecedented, since, as noted, the link had already been created in the eighteenth century in Lord Chief Justice Holt's judgment in the *Manning* case, in the context of jealousy as a strong masculine emotion linked to acts of homicide. However, in the latter case, the court accepted, for the first time, the existence of a legal presumption of romantic jealousy (in contrast to possessive jealousy, in Holt's ruling) being a natural human instinct that could not be controlled through reason and logic.[27] Such jealousy was defined as a mechanism of human passion that had adapted itself to ensure the survival of man, because it helped maintain the "home and love," and the legal recognition of this could only develop against the background of the evolving social and cultural recognition of the emotion of love as the foundation for marriage in the nineteenth

25 Ibid.: 39 (quoting *Regina* v. *Mawgridge*, (1706) 84 Eng. Rep. 1107 (U.K.) 137; Keling 119).

26 Fontaine 2012: 62 (emphasis added).

27 See Horder 1992: 77 (providing another look at this argument). This precedent was preceded by three murder cases (1817 to 1833) that were related to sexual jealousy and established the legal presumption that jealousy was an uncontrollable instinct – and therefore the ensuing violence had to be exempt from criminal liability. The *M'donnough* ruling in 1817 did not yet recognize sexual jealousy as exclusive grounds for negating criminal liability, but for the first time a defendant was acquitted by virtue of the recognition of sexual jealousy (which was associated with a medical defect of the defendant) as negating criminal liability by reason of "loss of control." In 1822 a court recognized the fact that any man would be furious if he saw his wife commit adultery with his best friend (thereby creating a normative legal standard of sexual jealousy, loss of control and lethal violence – even though the defendant himself in that case, Lechler, failed to be acquitted). In 1833 as well, the legal causal connection between love, jealousy, murder and loss of control was considered, and a legal construction was created of love and jealousy that neutralized self-control, resulting in logic and reason being blinded (although in that case again, the defendant failed to obtain an acquittal on charges of killing his partner, who had been murdered for refusing to marry him). Love was recognized as a pure, good, and ideal emotion that was concurrently destructive and violent, and one that could lead to loss of control and murder. See Keetley 2008: 280–282.

century.[28] Until then, marriage had been perceived as fulfillment of a function unconnected to the emotion of love, and cases of uxoricide were attributed to failure of women to fulfill their function as housewives to the satisfaction of men. Thus, the merger of the ideal of love with the institution of marriage in nineteenth-century America also had worrying socio-legal aspects: more violence within the family and an increase in spousal homicides (women were now murdered not only as a result of rage at their failure to fulfill their roles as housewives to the satisfaction of their husbands, but also out of "love" for them).[29] Accompanying the increased incidence of such murders, a hybrid legal doctrine formed and took root, designed to mitigate the criminal liability of the accused, relying both on provocation and the "heat of passion" argument,[30] or, as Sickles's defense attorneys put it: "We propose to prove the *passion*, and the *provocation which led to the passion*."[31]

The legal origins of the American doctrine of provocation

The doctrine of provocation was born in seventeenth-century England,[32] and it was absorbed in almost all the countries governed by Britain in the eighteenth century. The English doctrine perceived provocation by the victim as the factor instigating the intense anger,[33] which thereby diminished the moral guilt of the person accused of the murder.[34] Seventeenth-century English law recognized four circumstances in which the provocation would be regarded as sufficient: where the victim gravely insulted the accused immediately before the killing; where the victim seriously injured a family member of the accused; where the victim had deprived an Englishman of his freedom; and where the victim had committed adultery with the wife of the accused.[35] Subsequently, the case law developed general conditions intended to limit the application of the doctrine of provocation and established objective tests that had to be all satisfied before the defense could be asserted:[36] the existence of "adequate provocation"; the killing have been committed while in the "heat of passion"; the existence of an element of "immediacy" between the provocation and the act of murder; the

28 Ibid.: 272, 276, 288 ("The *Sickles* case, along with trials that came before it, demonstrate that 'instinctive' jealousy was not inevitably there all along; instead, it emerged hand-in-hand with the ideology of romantic love and hallowed domesticity.")

29 Ibid.: 271.

30 Ibid.: 269–271. The fantasy of love aggrandized love, but masked the violence committed in its name, creating, in practice, a dual synthesis between violence and love.

31 See Fontaine 2012: 60; Keetley 2008: 284.

32 See Horder 1992: 23.

33 See Berman and Farrell 2011: 1036–1037.

34 See Pei Lin Chen 2000: 205–206. In effect, this imposes some of the guilt for the act of murder on the victim herself. See Lee 2003: 28.

35 See Pei Lin Chen 2000: 207; Lee 2003: 19; Horder 1992: 24; Berman and Farrell 2011: 1036.

36 See Pei Lin Chen 2000: 205.

existence of a causal connection between the provocation, the passion and the fatal act.

Most jurisdictions in the United States have absorbed the English doctrine of provocation, either expressly or implicitly, including its preconditions and tests. Four key characteristics in the doctrine of provocation are common in all the states.[37] First, the doctrine of provocation is only applicable in the context of homicide (murder); it cannot be applied with respect to other criminal offenses.[38] Second, the doctrine of provocation is not a full criminal defense but only a partial defense, reducing the defendant's criminal liability,[39] and consequently enabling a conviction for manslaughter as opposed to murder.[40] Third, the defendant must have committed the homicide in the "heat of passion."[41] Fourth, the "heat of passion" experienced by the defendant must have originated from the provocation directed at him.[42] Some of the objective tests developed by English case law in the context of the doctrine of provocation are reflected in specific legislation in 11 states in the United States[43] and include the requirements of "severe" provocation, an element of "immediacy" between the murder and the provocation, a causal connection between the provocation and the murder, and the fact that the defendant had not yet "cooled off" or thought better of his response prior to the homicide.[44]

Various jurisdictions in the United States have developed differing versions of the doctrine of provocation; nonetheless, in general, it is possible to identify the existence of three main approaches.[45] There are states that have adopted the English rigid and categorical approach (early common law), states that have adopted the doctrine of provocation based on the approach of a reasonable person (the modern reasonable man approach), and states that have adopted a

37 See Berman and Farrell 2011: 1040–1041.

38 Horder 1992: 134–135.

39 See Berman and Farrell 2011: 1040.

40 Brown 1999: 137, 140. The partial defense reduces the conviction from murder, with its accompanying stigma, lengthy term of imprisonment, and potential death penalty in certain jurisdictions in the United States, to manslaughter, which is not a capital offense and which leads to a significantly shorter term of imprisonment than that imposed for murder. See Lee 2003: 18.

41 Ibid.: 25.

42 See Berman and Farrell 2011: 1040–1041.

43 Mostly in states that have adopted rules developed in English case law, specifically Arkansas, Connecticut, Delaware, Hawaii, Kentucky, Montana, New York, North Dakota, Oregon, New Hampshire and Utah. See Ibid., 1044.

44 See, e.g., *Texas Penal Code Annotated* Section 19.02(2) ("'Sudden passion' means passion *directly caused* by and *arising out of provocation by the individual killed* or another acting with the person killed which *passion arises at the time of the offense* and is not solely the result of former provocation.") (Italics added). See also *Delaware Code Annotated.* Title 11 Section 641 (West, Westlaw through 79 Laws 2014, ch. 437) ("… extreme emotional distress is not reasonably explained or excused … when there is no causal relationship between the provocation, event or situation which caused the extreme emotional distress and the victim of the murder.").

45 See generally, Lee 2003: 18–43.

doctrine of provocation based on the extreme mental and emotional disturbance defense (given statutory effect in Section 210.3 of the Model Penal Code). The two most common approaches are the reasonable man approach and the extreme emotional disturbance approach (as expressed in the Model Penal Code) that, as explained further below, embody the more far-reaching legal applications of the doctrine of provocation. For example, whereas English case law has developed specific and rigid tests for the application of the defense,[46] the two most common American doctrines (the reasonable man approach and the Model Penal Code approach) greatly extended the spectrum of cases allowing the mitigation of the criminal liability of defendants for murder in general, and for the murder of intimate partners in particular.

The American version of the doctrine of provocation based on early English common law

There are only a few jurisdictions in the United States that still adopt the rigid and restrictive English approach, and these are mainly located in the South.[47] Consistent with the doctrine of provocation in nineteenth-century England,[48] these states have confined the application of the doctrine to four exclusive categories and do not allow the mitigation of criminal liability in circumstances falling outside the scope of these categories. The four categories are: where, immediately before the homicide, the deceased severely insulted the accused; where the deceased severely injured a close relative of the accused immediately before the homicide; where the deceased illegally took the defendant's liberty; and where the deceased committed adultery with the wife of the accused.[49] This rigid approach embodies a significant element of the justification approach,[50] which warrants the homicide in such circumstances and occasionally even supports not only mitigating the criminal liability of the accused, but actually acquitting him altogether. Such acquittal greatly extends in fact the scope of the doctrine, which originally allowed only the partial mitigation of criminal liability: "*Homicide is justifiable* when committed by the husband upon one taken in the act of adultery with the wife ..."[51] Under this doctrine, and in accordance with the view prevailing in nineteenth-century England, killing a spouse is not

46 Specific tests that include the requirement to give weight to the personal status of the partner (the wife of the accused), the requirement that the provocation be in real proximity to the act of killing, and allowing a mitigated conviction only in cases where the defendant murdered his wife's lover as opposed to the wife herself. See ibid.: 21.

47 For the conservative cultural characteristics of the southern states of the United States, see Vandiver 1964: 43; Hackney 1969: 906.

48 See Horder 1992: 77–78, 85–89, 100–106.

49 See Pei-Lin Chen 2000: 205 and accompanying text; Berman and Farrell 2011: 1040–1041 and accompanying text.

50 See Berman and Farrell 2011: 1037.

51 *1925 Texas Criminal Statutes* 1220 (repealed 1973).

justified. It is only the murder of a lover that is justified and fully acquitted. In jurisdictions adopting this approach (such as Georgia, Texas and Utah) the defendant is hence not acquitted altogether in cases where the spouse has also been killed, but is only convicted of manslaughter.[52] In the past, this approach was harshly criticized because of its categorical rigidity, which precluded it from being applied in circumstances that deviated from the defined categories and consequently prevented many defendants from enjoying mitigated criminal liability. For example, defendants could not enjoy mitigated criminal liability if they were not married to the intimate partner, if they had not been a direct witness to the act of adultery, or if there had been an admission of adultery but not an actual act of adultery.[53]

The American version of the doctrine of provocation based on the "reasonable person" approach

In light of the criticism voiced against the rigid approach of provocation based on early English common law, in the nineteenth century many jurisdictions in the United States began to develop a more expansive approach to the doctrine of provocation and instilled into it both the concepts of the "reasonable person" and "heat of passion." The "reasonable person" element in the United States (that employed a reasonableness requirement to determine which types of behavior could be considered legally adequate) did not differ significantly from its English counterpart.[54] However, the doctrinal addition of the "heat of passion"[55] was certainly a startling innovation. According to this doctrine of provocation, homicide committed in the heat of passion negates the existence of the mental element of malice aforethought that is required for a murder conviction, and therefore reduces the conviction in such cases from murder to voluntary manslaughter.[56] The "heat of passion" does not completely preclude the control, free choice and awareness of the accused, but is regarded as severely impairing these characteristics due to his extreme emotional or mental distress. In view of this apparent impairment, the doctrine attributes less moral guilt to persons accused of murder in these circumstances.[57] In essence, this approach

52 If the accused murdered both the lover and the spouse, he was not convicted of murder, as the homicide of the lover was categorized as justifiable homicide and the homicide of the spouse was categorized as voluntary manslaughter. See Lee 2003: 21.

53 See ibid.: 24.

54 See Dressler 1982: 428–430.

55 According to this approach, in order to apply the doctrine of provocation, it is necessary to satisfy four requirements: (1) the defendant was actually *provoked into a heat of passion*; (2) the *reasonable person* in the defendant's shoes would have been so provoked; (3) the defendant *did not cool off*; and (4) the *reasonable person* in the defendant's shoes would not have cooled off between the provocative event and the act or acts that led to the victim's death. Lee 2003: 25.

56 See Dressler 1982: 442.

57 See Berman and Farrell 2011: 1048; Dressler 1982: 442–444.

created a hybrid doctrine[58] interweaving provocation with heat of passion. The main problem with this doctrine stems not only from the expanded defense it affords by introducing the concept of "heat of passion" into the doctrine of provocation, but the fact that the legal term "heat of passion" remains obtuse to this day. It lacks clarity[59] and in practice is at the mercy of judicial interpretation, without any statutory restrictions.[60]

As noted, in practice the United States doctrine of provocation based on the reasonable man approach eliminated the rigid categorization of the original English doctrine of provocation, expanded the subjective component in the doctrine and added a broad and vague emotional term as the basis for its application. Consequently (and in contrast to the jurisdictions adopting the rigid English approach), many states in the United States now mitigate the criminal liability of defendants who commit homicide – even when they were not married to the partner, did not personally witness the adultery but only heard about it, or merely suspected adultery.[61]

The American version of the doctrine of provocation based on the "heat of passion" approach

Alongside the doctrine of provocation applying the reasonable person test, 20 jurisdictions in the United States[62] have adopted the doctrine of provocation set out in the Model Penal Code, which in practice is even broader than the doctrine of provocation applying the reasonable person approach. The Model Penal Code approach has further expanded the subjective component of the claim to provocation, and has accorded statutory recognition to the concept of "heat of passion" (and loss of emotional control) as a partial criminal defense in the context of the doctrine of provocation known as extreme mental or emotional disturbance (EMED).[63] Section 210.3(b) of the Code allows the mitigation of

58 See Berman and Farrell 2011: 1042–1043.

59 See Dressler 1982: 431.

60 For an illustration of the statutory lacunae in the context of the term "heat of passion," see ibid.: 431 notes 102 and 104.

61 See Lee 2003: 26.

62 Arkansas, Connecticut, Delaware, Hawaii, Indiana, Kansas, Kentucky, Louisiana, Missouri, Montana, Nebraska, New Hampshire, New York, North Dakota, Oregon, Tennessee, Pennsylvania, South Carolina, Utah and Wyoming. See Lee 2003: 285 note 66.

63 Although the term "loss of emotional control" does not expressly appear in the EMED, in practice it developed within the framework of the interpretation of the concept of "heat of passion," thereby replacing, in essence, the original concept of honor forming part of the English doctrine of provocation. See Horder 1992: 72–75 (discussing the development of the "loss of self-control" in modern law); Rapaport 1996: 1536–1539 (describing the development of the "heat of passion" doctrine). In fact, this term was already introduced into the doctrine of provocation in England in the eighteenth century. See Berman and Farrell 2011: 1037. The term "loss of emotional control" as part of the doctrine of provocation is currently accepted in most jurisdictions in the United States. Dresssler 1982: 422.

criminal liability in respect of a wide range of acts of homicide committed at a time of intense emotional turbulence that would otherwise be defined as murder, and explicitly defines the EMED defense:

> §210.3. Manslaughter: (1) Criminal homicide constitutes manslaughter when: (a) it is committed recklessly; or (b) a homicide which would otherwise be murder is committed *under the influence of extreme mental or emotional disturbance* for which there is reasonable explanation or excuse. The reasonableness of such explanation or excuse shall be determined from the *view point of a person in the actor's situation* under the circumstances as he believes them to be (emphasis added).[64]

The wording of this section of the Model Penal Code provides for a partial criminal defense in the context of the offense of murder, namely the defense of EMED, which although related to the doctrine of provocation is not necessarily linked to it. The introduction of the EMED defense in the context of provocation distances it significantly from the original doctrine of provocation,[65] as the defense is not confined solely to the loss of control ensuing from the provocation. Under this defense, the criminal liability of the accused is mitigated irrespective of the act of provocation, and in general it is not necessary for there to have been any act of provocation,[66] provided that there was an emotional or mental disturbance, or both, that impaired the self-control of the accused. Moreover, this partial defense in turn expands the doctrine of provocation because, if it can be shown that there was provocation that led to extreme emotional or mental disturbance, the homicide need not necessarily have targeted the person committing the provocation, and the provocation itself need not necessarily have been directed against the killer.[67] In other words, contrary to the English doctrine, and significantly expanding the doctrine of provocation applying the reasonable person approach, the Model Penal Code doctrine of

64 *Model Penal Code* 1962. Philadelphia: American Law Institute Section 210.3 (emphasis added). In contrast, according to the definition of murder in the Model Penal Code, a mental element is required, which includes knowledge and purpose, or indifference:

> [C]riminal homicide constitutes murder when: (a) it is committed purposely or knowingly; or (b) it is committed recklessly under circumstances manifesting extreme indifference to the value of human life. Such recklessness and indifference are presumed if the actor is engaged or is an accomplice in the commission of, or an attempt to commit, or flight after committing or attempting to commit robbery, rape or deviate sexual intercourse by force or threat of force, arson, burglary, kidnapping or felonious escape.
>
> (*Model Penal Code* 1962. Philadelphia: American Law Institute Section 210.2)

65 Berman and Farrell 2011: 1044.

66 See Ramsey 2010: 56.

67 See Lee 2003: 31.

provocation greatly extends the range of homicides in which the defendant's criminal liability is mitigated by virtue of this statutory criminal defense.

Another reason why the Model Penal Code doctrine is the most far-reaching among the three main doctrines of provocation in the United States is that the combination of provocation, "heat of passion" and EMED (in addition to the fact that the wording of the statutory provision does not include a requirement of immediacy between the act of provocation and the emotional turmoil) accords this doctrine of provocation an almost exclusively subjective character[68] that, in practice, unrestrictedly extends the range of cases in which it can be applied. Although the specific section in the Code emphasizes that a "reasonable explanation or excuse" must be provided for such emotions, the section subsequently makes it clear that the degree of reasonableness of the explanation or excuse will be judged primarily on the basis of the defendant's own subjective understanding: "The reasonableness of such explanation or excuse shall be determined from *the viewpoint of a person in the actor's situation* under the circumstances *as he believes them to be.*"[69] This expansive approach in effect removes many acts of homicide from the scope of the offense of murder, as the normative threshold of the subjective element is lower than the normative threshold accompanying a requirement that the accused hold a belief like that of *any* reasonable person *as a rule.* It follows therefore that the doctrine of provocation adopted in jurisdictions that have adopted the Model Penal Code is highly forgiving of killers of intimate partners, not only because it applies a partial criminal defense (EMED) for crimes committed under the influence of intense emotions regardless of the existence of provocation immediately before the act of homicide ("heat of passion" crimes), but also because of the broad subjective component operating within it,[70] designed to remove the act of homicide from the scope of the offense of murder.[71]

In fact, the broad legal recognition accorded to the subjective element, combined with the legal recognition of emotions as an element that mitigates criminal liability in the context of acts of homicide, has led to judicial case law that vastly extends the range of cases in which the criminal liability of the killer of an intimate partner is mitigated. Consider for example the brutal and ill-judged circumstances under which Becky was killed by her fiancé, who was eventually awarded by the court mitigation of his murder charge:

> Dixon and Becky had lived together for several months and had decided to get married in the near future. That evening they went to a bar to celebrate and were joined by Dixon's sister and other friends. When Becky asked an

68 See Lee 2003: 38–39; Berman and Farrell 2011: 1044; Dressler 1982: 431.

69 *Model Penal Code* 1962. Philadelphia: American Law Institute Section 210.3(1)(b) (emphasis added).

70 See Lee 2003; Dressler 1982: 431.

71 *Model Penal Code* 1962. Philadelphia: American Law Institute Section 210.3 (defining "murder").

> acquaintance to dance with her, Dixon became jealous and went home. Eventually at Becky's request, Dixon's sister called him and he agreed to return. When he entered and saw Becky dancing with the other man again he charged onto the dance floor and knocked Becky down. One of the waitresses said he hit her with his fist and that it could be heard all over the bar. After Dixon was ejected from the bar his sister left and took Becky home with her. Following several phone calls between Dixon and Becky, he showed up around midnight and proceeded to slap her around. He cursed her, knocked her down several times. One time she hit her head on the coffee table and another time may have hit her head on the stereo. Dixon's 13-year-old niece and her girl friend were in the apartment and testified that Becky had bruises all over her face and that her eyes were black, her jaws were swollen and her nose was bleeding. The friend said she heard Becky beg the appellant to stop hitting her, and she called the police at Becky's request. At one point Becky passed out and Dixon told his sister to call an ambulance. She revived while he was giving her mouth-to-mouth resuscitation, and the ambulance was called off.
>
> Dixon left and took Becky home with him about 1:30 or 2:00 on the morning of January 17th. At 7:30 in the morning Dixon called Becky's place of work and told them Becky had the flu and would not be in for a couple of days. In his written statement, he said he went back to sleep and woke up about three hours later, at 10:00 or 10:30 when Becky wet the bed. When he could not rouse her, he called an ambulance. In response to a question from the ambulance attendant, he said he last hit her about 5:00 in the morning. Becky never regained consciousness, but with the aid of a respirator remained alive for another 12 days.[72]

Twelve days after her brutal and lethal battery Becky died. The Chief Medical Examiner for the State of Arkansas performed an autopsy and testified that she died of cranial cerebral injuries. In addition to three large bruises on her chest, two large bruises on her lower back, and internal bleeding of her eyes, she had bleeding in the muscle that covers the skull. He explained that the contusion of the brain caused it to swell, shutting off the blood supply, and that her brain was dead for at least 10 days before her death.[73] Dixon was charged with murder in the second degree.[74] Despite the abundance of evidence that showed that he

72 See *State* v. *Dixon* 268 Ark. (1980) 471.

73 At p. 473.

74 Ark. Stat. Ann. §41–1503 (1) (Repl. 1977) provides:

> (1) A person commits murder in the second degree if: (a) with the purpose of causing the death of another person, he causes the death of any person; or (b) he knowingly causes the death of another person under circumstances manifesting extreme indifference to the value of human life; or (c) with the purpose of causing serious physical injury to another person, he causes the death of any person.

beat her intermittently over a period of several hours, and continued to beat her even after she had lost consciousness and had been revived by mouth-to-mouth resuscitation, Dixon was not charged with first-degree murder or with first or second-degree felony murder. Perhaps the prosecution felt there was not enough evidence to prove beyond any reasonable doubt that Becky's killing was premeditated.[75]

After entering a plea of not guilty, Dixon was tried before a jury. During the trial, Dixon claimed that he could not be convicted of murder because he caused the death of his fiancée under circumstances of extreme emotional disturbance.[76] Dixon maintained that his unstable emotional and physical condition at the time of the beating rendered him incapable of forming any required culpable mental state.[77] At the trial he was acquitted of the charge of murder in the second degree, found guilty of manslaughter,[78] and received a rather lenient sentence of ten years imprisonment. The court of appeals affirmed his conviction, stating that:

> There was abundant evidence to show that appellant either caused the death of his fiancée under circumstances that would be murder except for extreme emotional disturbance on his part or that he recklessly caused her death, thereby supporting his conviction for manslaughter under either Ark.

75 Such cases of assaultive-femicide should be charged as murder according to the doctrine of the felony murder rule, and thus would not require evidence of premeditation. Lamentably, this doctrine is not applied in such cases because of the "merger doctrine." Further elaboration of the felony-murder-rule doctrine and assaultive-femicide cases is discussed in Chapter 3.

76 Ark. Stat. Ann. §41–1504 (Repl. 1977) provides, in part:

> (1) A person commits manslaughter if: (a) he causes the death of another person under circumstances that would be murder, except that he causes the death under the *influence of extreme emotional disturbance for which there is reasonable excuse.* ... (c) he recklessly causes the death of another person. (Italics added).

77 Ark. Stat. Ann. §41–1503 (1) or §41–1504 (1) (a) and (c). These statutes require in the various subsections conduct of a purposeful, knowing or reckless nature. Ark. Stat. Ann. §41–203 (Repl. 1977) defines these mental states as follows:

> (1) "Purposely." A person acts purposely with respect to his conduct or a result thereof when it is his conscious object to engage in conduct of that nature or to cause such a result.
> (2) "Knowingly." A person acts knowingly with respect to his conduct or the attendant circumstances when he is aware that his conduct is of that nature or that such circumstances exist. A person acts knowingly with respect to a result of his conduct when he is aware that it is practically certain that his conduct will cause such a result.
> (3) "Recklessly." A person acts recklessly with respect to attendant circumstances or a result of his conduct when he consciously disregards a substantial and unjustifiable risk that the circumstances exist or the result will occur. The risk must be of a nature and degree that disregard thereof constitutes a gross deviation from the standard of care that a reasonable person would observe in the actor's situation.

78 *State* v. *Dixon* 268 Ark. (1980) 471, at 471.

> Stat. Ann. §41–1504 (1) (a) or §41–1504 (1) (c) (Repl. 1977). Such a lenient conviction where the evidence showed that he beat her intermittently over a period of several hours, continuing to beat her even after she had lost consciousness and had been revived by mouth-to-mouth resuscitation.[79]

This was only possible because the jury was instructed to decide the reasonableness of defendant's explanations from his own subjective perspective.

Such leniency was expanded to include not only the killing of current non-married intimate female partners, but also even ex-non-married intimate female partners. To take yet another appalling example of expanded legal leniency towards female killers, we can consider Hipolito Martinez's conviction for killing Esther Grazalez, his ex-girlfriend. Hipolito was acquitted from a murder charge despite the fact that Esther had broken up with him seven months beforehand. Furthermore, her killing took place three weeks after he saw her dancing with someone he thought was another man but in fact was the victim's brother. He clearly acted in a premeditated manner by going to her apartment armed with his unlicensed gun. According to the facts stated at the trial, Hipolito had gone out with Esther for approximately four years, even though he was a married man.[80] After Esther told him that she wanted to break up, they had a loud argument and he moved out.[81] Seven months later Esther called to ask if he would like to go dancing at the Calypso. While partying, Hipolito saw Esther dancing with someone he thought was another man, but was in fact Esther's brother, and he told Esther that he would shoot her one day.[82] About ten days later, Martinez was seen lingering in the vicinity of Esther's apartment for two days before the killing, and throwing rocks at her window.[83] On the day of the murder, at 4:00 am, Martinez armed himself with his .32 caliber unlicensed gun and waited in front of Esther's apartment.[84]

> When finally, a car pulled up, Martinez saw Esther in the passenger's seat. Upon seeing him, Esther asked her brother, who had just taken her and her sons to the airport to come up with her to her apartment. As she approached her front door, Martinez grabbed her arm and pointed a gun at her. Esther's brother tried to separate the two but Martinez said: "this isn't between you and me, it's between her and me." Esther's brother backed off and went to the car to call the police. Martinez dragged her from the

79 *Dixon* v. *State* 597 S.W.2d.77 (Ark. 1980), at 77.

80 See case description in Lee 2003: 37 relating to details from police reports and State Appellate Brief in *State* v. *Martinez* 591 A.2d155 (Conn. App. CT. 1991).

81 Op. cit.

82 Op. cit.

83 *State* v. *Martinez* 24 (Conn. App. 1991) 692, at 695.

84 Lee 2003: 37.

> doorway, forced her to walk across the street, muttering repeatedly: "You made me do this." He then struck her in the face and shot her five times. Shortly after the shooting he told the police: "I shot her and I hope she dies."[85]

Hipolito was charged with the crime of murder, but after pleading the affirmative defense of extreme emotional disturbance the jury acquitted him from the murder charge.[86] This acquittal was given despite the facts that implied solid premeditation: arming himself with an unlicensed gun, reaching Esther at her apartment and admitting to the police that he had killed her and telling them shortly after the shooting: "I shot her and I hope she dies."[87] Lamentably, he was not even found guilty of manslaughter with the intent to cause death.[88] A conviction under subsection (a)(2) of §53a–55 would have at least connoted that the trier of fact found that the defendant had acted with the intent to cause death, but under the influence of extreme emotional disturbance.[89] Instead, he was found guilty of manslaughter with intent to cause serious physical injury to another person resulting in that person's death.[90] He was convicted of manslaughter under subsection (a)(1) of §53a–55, which connotes that the trier of fact found that he did not intend to kill Esther, but rather acted with the intent to cause her serious physical injury, at the most.[91] On appeal, his mild conviction of manslaughter was affirmed based on the affirmative defense of extreme

85 Op. cit.

86 As provided in Conn. GEN. STAT. Section 53a–54a:

> (a) A person is guilty of murder when, with intent to cause the death of another person, he causes the death of such person or of a third person or causes a suicide by force, duress or deception; except that in any prosecution under this subsection, *it shall be an affirmative defense that the defendant committed the proscribed act or acts under the influence of extreme emotional disturbance for which there was a reasonable explanation or excuse, the reasonableness of which is to be determined from the viewpoint of a person in the defendant's situation under the circumstances as the defendant believed them to be*, provided nothing contained in this subsection shall constitute a defense to a prosecution for, or preclude a conviction of, manslaughter in the first degree or any other crime (italics added).

87 Op. cit.

88 Under §53a–55 (a) (2), CONN. GEN. STAT. §53a–54a (a) that states:

> (a) A person is guilty of manslaughter in the first degree when: (1) … or; (2) *with intent to cause the death* of another person, he causes the death of such person or of a third person under circumstances which do not constitute murder because he committed the proscribed act or acts under the influence of extreme emotional disturbance. (Italics added).

89 See *State* v. *Chicano*, 216 Conn. (1990), 699, at 709.

90 Under §53a–55 (a) (1), CONN. GEN. STAT. §53a–54a (a) that "(a) A person is guilty of manslaughter in the first degree when: (1) *With intent to cause serious physical injury* to another person, he causes the death of such person or of a third person" (italics added).

91 See *State* v. *Chicano*, 216 Conn. (1990), 699, at 709.

emotional disturbance,[92] a conviction that is extremely disturbing. An acquittal from a murder charge, after the defendant had armed himself with an unlicensed gun, reached the victim at her apartment, waited for days in front of the apartment for the victim to arrive, dragged the victim out of her apartment, shot her five times right in the head at zero range and told the police that he had shot her and wished she died, is eerie. Hipolito's act seems intentional and premeditated murder. How could the appellate court accept his claim of extreme emotional disturbance when he had already been separated from the victim for seven months? Furthermore, how could his claim of EMED have been accepted based on the mere fact of seeing his ex-girlfriend dancing with another man more than two weeks prior to murdering her? Does this timespan mean that his alleged EMED lingered for almost three whole weeks?

Becky's and Esther's murder trials demonstrate, among other things, that under the auspices of this doctrine provocation may be argued even when there is no element of immediacy in terms of the alleged discovery of the adultery,[93] even when the intimate partner is an ex-partner, and even when the partner, from whom he had long been separated, danced with another man.[94] Such judicial rulings have shifted away from the original rigid common law doctrine, and, in fact, are closer to doctrines relating to the mitigation of criminal liability in the context of the murder of women found in Islamic countries.[95]

92 *State* v. *Martinez* 591 A.2d155 (Conn. App. CT. 1991), at 155, 158.

93 Even the element of immediacy has been softened, as according to the wording of the section and the doctrine as it developed in the United States, it is possible to extend the element of immediacy and apply the defense of provocation even if the homicide was not committed immediately after the provocation, provided that at the time of the act of homicide the accused had not yet cooled off or changed his mind. See Lee 2003: 34.

94 See ibid.: 35, 37, 39; Ramsey 2010: 56. For similar case law in Canada, see Fournier et al. 2012: 176–183.

95 See Horder 1992: 192 (asserting that the doctrine of provocation reinforces the ways in which men are perceived and perceive themselves as natural aggressors of women); Lee 2003: 15–45; Ramsey 2010: 35–36, 39, 69 (discussing gender inequality in criminal law). For a more explicit argument relating to the similarity between the doctrine of provocation in circumstances of adultery and Islamic doctrines of murder for reasons of "family honor," see Fournier et al. 2012: 161–164, 182–183, 188–190. In many Moslem countries, there are provisions in the penal code that mitigate or exempt a killer from punishment against the background of violation of the family's honor. See, e.g., Chapter 22 of the Iranian criminal law (the Iranian Law of Hodoud and Qassas), which completely exempts a killer from punishment under such circumstances. Chapter 340 of the Jordanian penal law provides that "he who discovers his wife or one of his female relatives committing adultery with another, and he kills, wounds or injures one or both of them, is exempt from any penalty." The law also states, "he who discovers his wife, or one of his female relatives with another in an unlawful bed and he kills, wounds or injures one or both of them, benefits from a reduction of penalty." Similar laws exist in Bahrain, Egypt, Kuwait, Lebanon, Morocco, Oman, Syria and the United Arab Emirates (for example, Sections 193, 252, 253 of the *Lebanese Criminal Code* and Sections 192, 242 and 548 of the *Syrian Criminal Code*). In practice, in many cases the punishment does not exceed a few months in prison. Regarding the similarity between the doctrine of provocation in the context of adultery and the Islamic doctrines of mitigation of criminal liability in cases of the murder of women, see Spatz 1991: 601–605.

A critical sociological look at the relationship between the doctrine of provocation and the murder of intimate partners

Many researchers have pointed to the masculine cultural foundation of the doctrine of provocation as one that fosters and encourages qualities of materialism, aggression and male jealousy,[96] as well as the problematic moral foundation apparent in a doctrine that displays tolerance and leniency towards violent behavior in general and towards women in particular.[97] Alongside these important criticisms, it is necessary to add a socio-psychological, empirical and concrete critique regarding the application of the legal presumption of loss of

96 See Coss 2006: 51; Horder 1992: 192; Lee 2003: 15–45; Ramsey 2010: 35–36, 39, 69.

97 The moral foundation on which the doctrine of provocation is constructed displays empathy and tolerance towards violent behavior and frames it as a normative aspect of the "reasonable person." See Lee 2003: 20. The tolerance shown toward violent behavior is rooted in the origins of the doctrine of provocation that included aspects of the legal doctrines of "justice" related to the concept of "honor," in light of which homicide was regarded as an appropriate way of preserving honor. Lee points out that the element of "justice" in this doctrine was so prominent that, in the past, a number of states (Georgia, Texas, Utah and New Mexico) did not consider homicide in such circumstances to be a crime at all. Lee 2003: 20. For an analysis of the relationship between the doctrine of provocation and the concept of the "honor" of an Englishman, see Horder 1992: 25–27. Beginning in the eighteenth century, the "justification" element in the doctrine weakened and was replaced by a developing concept of "exemption." See ibid.: 156–185. However, the standard used to examine the nature and characteristics of the provocation remained the standard of the reasonable man, in the light of which the attitude towards violence associated with loss of self-control was softened. For a comprehensive analysis of the reasonable person doctrine as it developed in England in general, and in the context of the doctrine of provocation in particular, see Dressler 1982: 428. For an analysis of the "reasonable person" in the context of the doctrine of provocation as it developed in the United States, see Lee 2003: 25–31, and Dressler 1982: 430. This "tolerance" is related to the moral dimension attributed to the homicide, according to which the guilt of a person who reacts spontaneously and loses control in a situation of intense anger arising from provocation is less than that of a man who has sufficient time to carefully consider the severe ethical implications of his actions. Ibid.: 442. This moral approach enables the development of a legal doctrine which awards the defendant an "exemption" in respect of his actions (as opposed to an acquittal on the basis of "justification," which would mean that the defendant had not committed any criminal offense whatsoever and that his actions were justified not only morally but also, primarily, legally – see Lee 2003: 245) – and in fact sends the message that his actions are "forgiven," though not acceptable. Some researchers argue that, in practice, the doctrine of provocation concurrently contains both the elements of "exemption" (excuse) and "justification," although "justification" is not explicit and is often hidden, concealed and disguised. See Berman and Farrell 2011: 1032–1034, 1057–1070, 1079–1090 (providing an argument concerning the dual structure of the doctrine of provocation as including both exemption and justification); Ashworth 1976: 307; Pei-Lin Chen 2000: 205. Hints of the concept of "justification" may also be found in case law in developed countries, where the courts' rulings are based on the narrative of the defendant (which cannot be verified in view of the physical absence of the murdered ex-partners), and excessive empathy created by the description of the circumstances of the murder as a sudden and personal tragedy for the defendant (a distinction drawn on the basis of a textual analysis of case law concerning the murder of intimate partners in Australia). Coss 2006: 61–68; see also Rapaport 1996: 1524–1527.

control (by which the criminal liability of the accused is mitigated) in the context of the murder of intimate partners.

As noted, the legal leniency or tolerance shown towards the killing of intimate partners stems, not only from the social sublimation of violence in the context of love, but also from the legal presumption regarding the murder of an intimate partner ensuing from a "loss of control." This legal presumption is rooted in the heart of the ideal of love, in the light of which the killing of the loved partner[98] is perceived as a rational paradox: it is not possible to understand how a person could kill his beloved in the name of love. This approach leads to the perception of such a killing as a "rational" accident, analogous to a "hand which has slipped,"[99] and therefore, an act performed by virtue of a loss of control. Nonetheless, recent findings[100] in this context suggest, as could be seen for example in Esther's killing, that murders of intimate partners do not occur in circumstances of emotional turmoil or momentary loss of control, but rather knowingly and deliberately. A study involving in-depth interviews with the murderers of intimate partners,[101] analyzing the dynamics of the emotions that preceded the murders, shows that in most cases the killing of the intimate partner is a "murder that evolves and violence that is meant to end in the death of the woman," and therefore these murders cannot be understood to be "the unintentional or uncontrolled result of powerful anger."[102] In other words, because the acts of murder of the intimate partners cannot be regarded as the result of "loss of control,"[103] it is not correct *empirically* to mitigate the criminal liability of these defendants (whether by applying the doctrine of provocation or the EMED defense).

98 The murder of a woman spurred by the fear of losing her appears on its face to be a fundamentally paradoxical act, as "with his own hands, a man causes the destruction of someone else, because he does not wish to lose that person." Ben Ze'ev and Goussinsky 2008: 84.

99 Ibid.: 80–83. For a description of the development of the legalistic structure legitimizing human weakness and emotional turbulence in relation to outbreaks of violence of men, see Horder 1992: 72–110. See also Coss 2006: 52; Fournier et al. 2012: 175.

100 Ben Ze'ev and Goussinsky's findings indicate that, although the transformation into a killer occurs in an instant (from the legal time perspective, prior to the murder), usually it is not sudden, but the result of a dynamic of progress towards the act over a period of weeks and months. This period is marked by the existence of prolonged emotions, such as jealousy, anger, anxiety, depression and despair, that shape a powerful framework for the emotional perception of reality. Within this emotional context, the idea of murder matures, gains a sense of realism and advances towards realization. Ben Ze'ev and Goussinsky 2008: 110. According to them, understanding the murder as the climax of a dynamic process, culminating in psychological readiness, shows that there is no room for seeing it as local, unplanned violence that "accidentally" exceeded its boundaries. ibid.: 111–114.

101 See generally, ibid.: 39–119.

102 In other words, even though the transformation into a murderer took place in an instant, usually it was not sudden – after all, for the murderer himself, it was not a spontaneous act. Ibid.: 112–113, 119.

103 Ibid.: 114 ("What may often seem to be loss of control is in fact the fruit of premeditation. The murderer had control over his 'loss of control'").

Mitigating the criminal liability of persons accused of the murder of intimate partners is flawed therefore, because of the *moral flaw* entailed in applying a doctrine that encourages tolerance towards violent behavior, the *cultural flaw* entailed in applying an archaic masculine doctrine[104] and the *empirical flaw* entailed in applying a doctrine of "emotional turbulence" (or in its form as a partial defense (EMED) under Section 210.3 of the Model Penal Code) to conscious and deliberate murders. Even if the pattern of killing intimate partners was indeed characterized by a real and substantive loss of control, it would still be worth asking whether it is proper and justified to apply a doctrine of mitigation of criminal liability in the circumstances of the murder of intimate partners[105] since, as noted, in practice this doctrine encourages patterns of violent behavior and, in particular, reinforces gender violence.[106] Moreover, the grant of an exemption (excuse) or forgiveness for murder because of allegations of adultery or because the woman desires to leave, sends a hidden message, legally and morally legitimizing the negation of the woman's right to carry out autonomous personal choices,[107] and consequently killing the woman herself.[108] Similar criticism of this concealed ethical and moral concept in the doctrine of provocation has consequently led to proposals to abolish completely the doctrine of provocation,[109] as well as to its actual abolition in a number of jurisdictions.[110]

Conclusion

The doctrine of provocation practiced in common law countries in general, and in jurisdictions in the United States that have adopted the Model Penal Code in particular, provides a legal shield for gender violence. It enables the mitigation of the criminal liability of men accused of murdering their female partners and might thereby contribute to entrenching and encouraging the murder of these

104 See Howe 1999, 2002.

105 See Lee 2003: 235–245 (describing positivist versus normative reasonableness).

106 Horder 1992: 186 (stating that there is no moral justification for personal retribution to a provocation, and that gender politics might be relevant to the mere existence and operation of the doctrine of provocation).

107 See Ramsey 2010: 72–73 (discussing the report of an Australian Sentencing Advisory Council, explaining that outrage over a woman's decision to leave could not justify murder because it conflicted with her autonomous personal choice); Rapaport 1996: 1524 ("From a feminist perspective separation murder can be seen as the extreme of domestic tyranny – the refusal to acknowledge the independence of a woman from the will of her husband or lover at any price.")

108 In the context of this "forgiveness," see Horder 1992: 71. For understanding and acceptance of these killings accompanied by concealed criticism or attribution of fault to the intimate partner, see also Saunders and Browne 2000: 436; Coss 2006: 70. For empirical support for this argument, see Rapaport 1996: 1516–1517.

109 See Browne et al. 1999: 137; Coss 2006: 71; Horder 1992: 26–33.

110 Australian states, including Victoria (in 2005), Tasmania (in 2003), and Western Australia (in 2008), as well as New Zealand (in 2009), the State of Texas in the United States (in 1994) and even England, the birthplace of the doctrine (in 2009). See Ramsey 2010: 35.

partners. Mitigation of criminal liability on the basis of the American doctrine of provocation, which accords legal significance to loss of control by reason of intense emotion, is based on the legal presumption that the defendant committed the murder in circumstances of loss of control and, according to the expansive doctrine in the Model Penal Code, it is not even necessary to show that the loss of control was connected to any provocative act on the part of the victim. Nonetheless, recent empirical findings concerning the characteristics and motivations for the murder of intimate partners show that such killings do not occur because of loss of self-control, but rather the acts are part of a conscious and deliberate ongoing process, often against the background of the female partner's wish to end the intimate relationship. Mitigation of criminal liability in circumstances of such conscious and deliberate action is inconsistent with the proper doctrinal foundation for mitigating criminal liability. In Israel, for example, judges defined the murder of an intimate partner, which the defendant claimed had been committed as a result of provocation and loss of control, as an intentional act that did not justify mitigation of criminal liability.[111] It goes without saying, of course, that the mitigation of the criminal liability of the murderers of intimate partners is also inconsistent with the fundamental values of the legal system in the United States in the context of gender equality relating to criminal liability, and in the context of the absolute and a-gender value of the lives of the murder victims. These murders should be eradicated by introducing statutory exceptions to the application of the doctrine of provocation and the EMED underlying the Model Penal Code, based on the circumstances and motives common to the murder of intimate partners. A detailed statutory proposal regarding this particular legal fault is further elaborated in Chapter 5.

111 See Criminal Appeal, *Alexander Aliyavev* v. *State of Israel*, Cr/App. 759/97, 1997, 459, 477.

3 "The straw that broke the camel's back"

Assaultive-femicide and the American felony-murder rule

As will be shown, the doctrine's most problematic modification relates to one of its sub-doctrines, the principle of merger. This principle is premised on the fact that homicide is a lesser-included offense within murder.[1] The original purpose of the principle of merger was to exclude the offenses of voluntary and involuntary manslaughter from the felony-murder rule. Lamentably, it was stretched and extended to include lesser non-homicidal offenses such as assault as well. This gross doctrinal extension has in fact created a criminal anomaly whereby blameworthy murderers of women are exonerated and technically exempted from murder convictions. Such legal construction has dire and unjust consequences for women in general and for battered women in particular, since statistics show that a significant share of battered women are eventually killed by their assaultive male intimate partners,[2] in one last lethal assault that was "the last straw that broke the camel's back."

A criminological perspective on assaultive-femicide

Apart from the military and police arenas that are inherently dangerous, the most dangerous and violent arena in the United States is the home.[3] This assertion, though correct, could be stated more precisely: the home is not the most dangerous place for all people; the home is the most dangerous place for women.[4] Indeed, the U.S. Department of Justice estimates that between 90 and 95 percent of domestic violence victims are women:[5]

> Many women in the United States live under siege in their homes, with aggression, including battering and rape, recurrent and pervasive from male

1 See LaFave and Wakeman 1972: 558–559.
2 There are statistical data which show that about half of the women murdered by their partners were, prior to their murder, victims of sustained and routine domestic violence. Downs 1996: 53; Siegel 1996: 2173.
3 Gelles and Straus 1989: 88.
4 Dobash and Dobash 1978: 426–427.
5 Siegel 1996: 2172.

> intimates. Battering of women by their husbands, ex-husbands or boyfriends is the largest single cause of injury to women in the United States.[6]

The criminological significance of these findings is that, in the vast majority of cases, domestic violence is in fact equivalent to violence against women.[7] This phenomenon is by no means marginal. According to reports by the U.S. Justice Department, some four million women suffer from serious or life-threatening violence every year in the United States alone.[8] The empirical findings regarding the extent and characteristics of violence against women are not particularized and do not depend on any specific class, ethnicity or religion, and, in addition to the high frequency of violence against women, the data show that it cuts across all strata and groups in American society.[9]

This violence has five unique characteristics. First and foremost, domestic violence is not gender-symmetrical: it is rare for women to batter or kill their partners.[10] In most cases of domestic violence as well as domestic murders, the perpetrators are men and the typical victims are women. Second, the vast majority of incidents of such violence are directed against woman by their past or present partners, and, in fact, in the United States, three-quarters of all attacks against women are committed by persons who are in or have been in an intimate relationship with these women.[11] Third, the findings relating to attacks on intimate partners show that most of these attacks are likely to include rape and repeated sexual offenses.[12] Fourth, assaults against women in the context of domestic violence are characterized by *severe physical injury that is more hazardous than that caused in the course of attacks committed by strangers in other circumstances.* The U.S. Department of Justice has shown that the injuries suffered by women assaulted by their partners are more serious than those suffered by women assaulted by strangers, and estimates the severity of about one-third of

6 Mackinnon 2001: 715.

7 Violence against women has broader criminological aspects than domestic violence, as female victimology is also a characteristic of crimes committed outside the home environment, for example sexual crimes. In the context of domestic violence, victims of assault and murder are – almost entirely – women. Likewise, patterns relating to the murder of women display empirical proximity to the family arena: women who are murdered are primarily murdered within the framework of "their family," i.e., by their partners.

8 Koss et al. 1994: 44.

9 Mackinnon 2001: 717. The high rate of domestic violence directed against women is similar across different strata and different ethnic groups (albeit the specific expressions and typical responses vary slightly across origin and status).

10 Notwithstanding the absence of a systematic collection of precise data in the context of female perpetrators (the number of women in America who committed murder, those among them who killed their partners, those among them who alleged domestic violence and those among them who alleged homicide in self-defense), the accepted estimate is that each year about 500 women kill their intimate partners. See Maguigan 1991: 397, 400.

11 Siegel 1996: 2172; Browne 1987: 9–10.

12 See Mackinnon 2001: 744, 869; Siegel 1996: 2173.

the attacks against women within the home as *equivalent to the severity of violence accompanying the highest level of crime*: crimes of robbery, felony rape and serious assaults.[13] It also estimates that the vast majority of attacks defined as "common assaults" (i.e., attacks that *prima facie* are not serious), *include serious physical injuries similar to those associated with severe attacks and robberies.*[14] Similarly, the American Medical Association's Council on Scientific Affairs has reported that attacks on women in circumstances of domestic violence are more severe and violent than attacks committed in other circumstances: while approximately half of the attacks committed by strangers end in significant injury, *over 80 percent of the attacks against intimate partners result in real injury, and are characterized by a high rate of serious injury, including damage to internal organs and loss of consciousness.*[15] The fifth characteristic of these attacks is that they constitute a pattern of continuous and escalating assaults that become increasingly severe[16] over time and *result in a greater likelihood of the women being killed.*[17] Taken together, these criminological characteristics lead to the conclusion that, in circumstances of domestic violence, the criminal offense is, at the very least, that of *aggravated assault.* While in most cases these assaults fall just short of homicide, in a significant portion *the aggravated assault eventually leads to homicide.*

The U.S. Model Penal Code (MPC) deals separately with each of the behaviors, ranging from simple assault to the infliction of serious and permanent injury. Offense grading is based on the gravity of harm intended or caused and on the dangerousness of the means used, and ranges from petty misdemeanor to second-degree felony.[18] The offense of aggravated assault is graded as a felony (of second or third degree) as defined in Sections 211.1(2)(a) and 211.1(2)(b) of the MPC. Section 211.1(2) of the Code states that an aggravated assault may be committed in either of two ways: the attempt or the cause of serious bodily injury in a manner that manifests recklessness and indifference to the value of life,[19] or such a knowledgeable or purposeful commission or attempt to commit bodily injury (not necessarily of a serious type) by the mere usage of a deadly weapon.[20] In other words, a person who batters a woman could be convicted of

13 Siegel 1996: 2173.

14 Ibid.: 2173.

15 Ibid.

16 Gillespie 1989: 59–60, 148–149; La Fond 1983: 276–277.

17 For the opposite opinion, stating that "the fact that a battered woman has been assaulted on many occasions in the past but has not been killed might suggest that she is unlikely to be killed by her partner in the future," see Leverick 2006: 91.

18 See *Model Penal Code and Commentaries (Official Draft and Revised Comments)* 1980: 184.

19 The requirement of knowledge or the similar mens rea required for felony-murder rule: recklessness under circumstances manifesting extreme indifference to the value of human life. See *Model Penal Code and Commentaries (Official Draft and Revised Comments)* 1980. Philadelphia: American Law Institute section 211.1(2)(a). See ibid.: 188–189.

20 See *Model Penal Code and Commentaries (Official Draft and Revised Comments)* 1980. Philadelphia:

a felony of aggravated assault if he caused serious bodily injury or if he caused any bodily injury[21] while using a deadly weapon.[22]

The MPC distinguishes between bodily injury and serious bodily injury. The definition of bodily injury in Section 210.0(2) states that it "means physical pain, illness or any impairment of physical condition." In contrast, the definition of serious bodily injury in Section 210.0(3) includes either a risk to the victim's life or bodily injury of a serious permanent nature: "serious bodily injury means bodily injury which creates a substantial risk of death or which causes serious, permanent disfigurement, or protracted loss or impairment of the function of any bodily member or organ." The MPC's definition of bodily injury is restricted to cases involving either the fact or prospect of physical injury or physical endangerment: "bodily injury means *physical pain*, illness or any impairment of *physical condition*."[23] Thus, according to the MPC, mere offensive contact without physical injury,[24] or wrongs based solely upon insult or emotional trauma[25] – are excluded.

While the approach of the MPC towards injury is restricted and only pertains to physical injuries, its approach towards deadly weapons is broad-minded. According to the drafters' commentaries, the section dealing with assault with a deadly weapon "extends liability to negligent infliction of injury with a deadly weapon, despite the general policy of confining penal sanctions to behavior of a higher degree of culpability."[26] The definition of "deadly weapon" in Section 210.0(4) is: "any firearm, or other weapon, *device, instrument, material or substance*, whether animate or inanimate, which in the *manner it is used* or is intended to be used is known to be capable of producing *death or serious bodily*

American Law Institute Section 211.1(2)(b): "attempts to cause or purposely or knowingly causes bodily injury to another with a deadly weapon."

21 As stated, such injury must not necessarily be of a grievous nature because, according to the U.S. Model Penal Code definition in Section 210.0(2), bodily injury could mean any physical pain, illness or any impairment of physical condition.

22 In the case of serious bodily injury, the perpetrator will be prosecuted for an offense that is graded as second-degree felony, and in the case of non-serious bodily injury committed by a deadly weapon the perpetrator will be prosecuted for an offense that is graded as third-degree felony. See *Model Penal Code and Commentaries (Official Draft and Revised Comments)* 1980. Section 211.1(2) and ibid.: 174.

23 See definitions in ibid., Section 210.0(2), emphasis added.

24 According to the drafters, other forms of offensive but not physically endangering behavior can be treated by other provisions in the Code. See *Model Penal Code and Commentaries (Official Draft and Revised Comments)* 1980: 185.

25 See ibid.: 188. Emotional fear is addressed for example in Section 211.1(c), "attempts by physical menace to put another in fear of imminent serious bodily injury," which is a simple assault graded as a misdemeanor (see p. 174).

26 See *Model Penal Code and Commentaries (Official Draft and Revised Comments)* 1980: 191. The drafters also state that "this extension is justified on the ground that any use of an instrument or substance known for its capability of causing death should be accompanied by special care and restraint." Op. Cit.

injury."[27] This approach towards deadly weapons is broad in four main respects: first, it includes not only weapons as such but also all instruments, materials and devices;[28] second, it refers not to the nature of the instrument but to the manner in which it was applied;[29] third, it defines a weapon or instrument as "deadly" not only if it is capable of producing death but also if it is capable of producing serious bodily injury;[30] and fourth, it does not require a high degree of culpability and extends liability for such injury even to cases of mere negligent infliction of injury.[31] Hence, the MPC's approach towards assault with a weapon should have accommodated, in principle, various cases of assaultive-femicide, including those perpetrated by the usage of a non-lethal instrument (as long as it was used in a manner capable of causing serious bodily injury).

Assaults against women typically include elements defined by the MPC as constituting aggravated assault. Conjunct with the MPC's definitions of "bodily injury" and "serious bodily injury" in Section 210.0(3),[32] violence against women could thus be a felony of aggravated assault in three possible ways:

1 if it includes an element of serious bodily injury that substantially *risked the victim's life* [as in the definition of "serious bodily injury" in Section 210.0(3)].
2 if it included a *serious permanent injury* [as in the definition of "serious bodily injury" in Section 210.0(3)].
3 if it included any bodily injury that was *inflicted with a deadly weapon* [as in the definition of aggravated assault with a deadly weapon in Section 211.1(b)].

Since the MPC does not distinguish between inchoate assault offenses and complete offenses,[33] the drafters stretched the offense of aggravated assault to include the mere attempt to cause such serious bodily injury. The Code's grading of the offense of aggravated assault as a felony is consistent with that of

27 Emphasis added.
28 According to the MPC drafters, "this definition is designed to take account of the ingenuity of those who desire to hurt their fellows without encompassing every use of an ordinary object that could cause death or serious injury." See ibid.: 191.
29 The drafters state that the expanded definition "reaches to certain instruments that become deadly weapons only because of the manner of their use," and give an example of the manner in which a car can be used, in ibid.: 191–192.
30 As in *Model Penal Code and Commentaries (Official Draft and Revised Comments)* 1980 Section 210.0(4): "capable of producing death or serious bodily injury."
31 See ibid.: 191.
32 See ibid.: Section 210.0(3): "serious bodily injury" means bodily injury which creates a substantial risk of death or which causes serious, permanent disfigurement, or protracted loss or impairment of the function of any bodily member or organ.
33 See ibid.: 184.

most U.S. jurisdictions[34] and with the American federal criminal law.[35] Hence, the empirically based criminological nature of physical violence against women as including serious bodily injury and risk of death is in line with the legal tendency in the United States to grade such an offense as felonious aggravated assault.

34 Most U.S. jurisdictions (41 jurisdictions) grade the offense of aggravated assault as a felony [see: Alabama, ALA CODE §13A-6-20, §3A-6-20; Alaska, Alaska Stat. §11.41.200; Arizona, A.R.S. §13-1204; Arkansas, Ark. Code Ann. §5-13-204, §5-26-306; Colorado, C.R.S. §18-3-202; Connecticut, CT Gen Stat §53a-59, §53a-70a; Delaware, DEL CODE §613; Florida, Fla Stat. §784.021; Georgia, O.C.G.A. Title 16, §16-5-21; Hawaii, HI Rev Stat §707-710; Idaho, ID Code §18-905, §18-906, §18-111; Indiana, IC §35-42-2-1.5; Kansas, KSA §21-3410; Kentucky, Ky. Rev. Stat. Ann. §508.010, §508.020; Maine, Me. Rev. Stat. Ann - §208, §4, 1252; Maryland, Maryland Criminal Law §3-202, §3-203; Massachusetts, M.G.L. c.265 §13A; Minnesota, MN Statutes §609.02; §609.221; Mississippi, MS Code §97-3-7; Missouri, Miss. Rev. STAT §565.050. 1, §565.072, §565.073; Montana, MONT CODE ANN §5-202; Nebraska, Neb. Stat. Rev. Ann §28-308, §§200.481; New Hampshire, NH. REV. STAT. ANN. §631:1; §28-309; Nevada NRS 631:2; New Jersey, NJ Rev Stat §2C:12-1; New York, N.Y. PEN. LAW §120.10; §120.04-a; §120.11; §120.12; North Dakota, N.D. §12.1-17-01, §12.1-17-01.1; §12.1-17-02; Ohio, O.R.C. §2903.12; Oklahoma, Okla. Stat. §21-646, §21650, §21-650.2, §21-647, §21-5, §219; Oregon, OR Rev Stat §163.185; Pennsylvania, Pa. C. S. A. §2702; Rhode Island, Rhode Island General Laws §11-5-2, §11-5-2.1; South Carolina, S.C. Code Ann. §16-3-600; South Dakota, SD Codified L §22-18-1.1; Tennessee, T.C.A. §39-13-102; Texas, TEX PE. CODE ANN. §22.02; Utah, Utah Code Ann. §76-5-103; Vermont, V.S.A. §1024; Washington, RCW §9A.36.011, §9A.36.021, §9A.36.021; Wisconsin, WI Stat §940.19; Wyoming, WY Stat §6-2-502]. Seven jurisdictions grade such assault as a felony depending on its particular circumstances (see: California, Cal. Penal Code §242, §243; Illinois Criminal Code, 720 ILCS 5/12-3.2; Iowa IA Code §708.1, §708.2; New Mexico, NM Stat §30-3-4, §30-3-3; North Carolina, NC GC §14-32; §14-33; Virginia, VA Code Ann.§18.2-57; West Virginia, W. Va. Code §61-2-9). Only two jurisdictions, Michigan and Louisiana, grade aggravated assaults as misdemeanors (see Louisiana, LSA-R.S. §2, §37; Michigan, Mich. Comp. Laws §750.81a.)

35 See U.S. Code, Title 18, Part I, chapter 51, Section 113:

> (a) (7) *Assault resulting in substantial bodily injury to a spouse or intimate partner, a dating partner*, or an individual who has not attained the age of 16 years, by a fine under this title or imprisonment for not more than 5 years, or both. (8) *Assault of a spouse, intimate partner, or dating partner* by strangling, suffocating, or attempting to strangle or suffocate, by a fine under this title, imprisonment for not more than 10 years, or both. (b) Definitions: In this section—(1) the term "*substantial bodily injury*" means bodily injury which involves—(A) *a temporary but substantial disfigurement*; or (B) a *temporary* but substantial loss or impairment of the function of any bodily member, organ, or mental faculty.

See also definitions of bodily injury in Sections 1365 (3) and 1365(4), that for the definition of serious bodily injury do not require a permanent disfigurement or impairment, and can include risk of death and extreme physical pain. U.S. Code, Title 18, Part I, chapter 51, Section 1365:

> (3) the term "serious bodily injury" means bodily injury which involves (A) a substantial risk of death; (B) extreme physical pain; (C) protracted and obvious disfigurement; or (D) protracted loss or impairment of the function of a bodily member, organ, or mental faculty; and (4) the term "bodily injury" means (A) a cut, abrasion, bruise, burn, or disfigurement; (B) physical pain; (C) illness; (D) impairment of the function of a bodily member, organ, or mental faculty; or (E) any other injury to the body, no matter how temporary.

Assaults against women should thus be classified as *felonious offenses* that are inherently dangerous to human life in general and to women in particular. This socio-legal conclusion appears to provide the two crucial elements necessary for the application of the felony-murder doctrine in cases of assaultive-femicide: the commission of a *felony dangerous to human life*, and the *resulting killing*. Lamentably, with the exception of several U.S. jurisdictions, the vast majority (including the U.S. Model Penal Code) exclude such an offense from the felony-murder rule.[36] The legal exclusion of aggravated assault from the list of predicate felonies for felony-murder creates a perplexing anomaly with regard to assaultive-femicide: it may exonerate blameworthy murderers whose convictions will therefore be downgraded at most to voluntary or involuntary manslaughter. This legal anomaly will be further elaborated below in the context of the discussion about the historical origins and legal principles of the felony-murder doctrine in the United States.

The origins of the felony-murder rule

It is commonly believed that the felony-murder doctrine is rooted in English common law.[37] According to Binder, however, such a doctrine was never really enacted into English law[38] and therefore could not have been transplanted or received into American Law. He anchors his argument on the historical sequence, indicating that America did not receive any felony-murder rules from England for the simple reason that there was no common law felony-murder rule at the time of the American Revolution.[39] Nonetheless, although the doctrine was not legislated[40] or judicially applied in England as such, its sources are most likely anchored in English eighteenth-century legal treatises, commentaries and case law discussions.[41] It is thus plausible that the conceptual origins of the felony-murder rule are rooted in seventeenth-century England, and that these general conceptualizations were enacted, legislated and applied for the most part by U.S. jurisdictions in the eighteenth century.

36 Several recent legislative amendments include such an offense only in so far as the assault is committed against children. The legislative arrangement according to whichassault of a child is a predicate felony murder will be elaborated below.

37 Binder 2011: 60.

38 For a similar argument claiming that the felony-murder rule was not routinely used in the courts of England, see Birdsong 2006: 13.

39 Binder 2011: 63.

40 Although the doctrine appears in Stephen's Digest (article 228), and in England's proposed draft code by the Criminal Code Commission of 1879 [in section 175(a) and (c)]. See Stephen 1883 (3): 80–81.

41 See Birdsong 2006: 4. Fletcher argues that the historical roots of felony murder are "tenuous and ill defined, and that its main sources are not judicial decisions but scholarly commentaries that cast the felony-murder rule as an abstract generalization (and) tell as little about the particular felonies that support the rule." See Fletcher 1981: 421.

The early English conception of criminal homicide derived from the principle that all people who cause death, whether intentionally or accidentally, are liable for murder,[42] and from the principle that an actor is responsible for the unintended harm resulting from an unlawful act, which has its roots in early Christian ethics.[43] It was only towards the thirteenth century that common law legal notions about intention as a conceptual foundation of crime gave rise to the conceptualization of murder as the unlawful killing of another human being with malice aforethought.[44] The exact meaning of "malice aforethought" is unclear, and several meanings were accorded to this notion throughout common law case law.[45] According to the drafters of the MPC, the meaning of malice aforethought had been stretched over time in such an elastic manner that it had become an "arbitrary symbol" used by judges to signify any of a number of mental states deemed sufficient to support liability for murder.[46] Legal scholars have classified malice aforethought into four states of mind:[47] intent to kill (awareness that the death of another would result from one's actions even if the actor did not have a particular desire to achieve such a consequence);[48] intent to cause grievous bodily harm (knowledge that one's conduct would cause serious bodily injury assimilated to intent and deemed as sufficient for a murder conviction if death of another occurred);[49] depraved-heart murder (extreme recklessness regarding homicidal risk that gave rise to an "implied" or "presumed" intent to kill or injure);[50] and an intent to commit a felony (assigning liability for homicide based on the intent to commit a felony.)[51]

It was the fourth "malice aforethought" state of mind, the intent to commit a felony, that gave rise to the subsequent legal doctrine of the "felony-murder rule."[52] However, the doctrine originated in the seventeenth century and rendered the legal excuse of "accidental killing" unavailable to those whose hands were soiled by an "accidental killing" that occurred in the course of an unlawful act.[53] It was this principle of a "killing with soiled hands" which was the conceptual foundation for what would become over time the formal test of criminal liability for felony-murder.[54]

42 See Birdsong 2006: 4.
43 Ibid.: 4.
44 See Birdsong referring to Bracton's ideas – Birdsong 2006: 8–13.
45 See *Model Penal Code and Commentaries (Official Draft and Revised Comments)* 1980: 14.
46 See ibid.: 14.
47 See ibid.: 14, referring to the arguments of Blackstone and Stephen, and see LaFave and Wakeman 1972: 14.
48 *Model Penal Code and Commentaries (Official Draft and Revised Comments)* 1980: 14.
49 See ibid.: 15.
50 See ibid.
51 See ibid.
52 See ibid.
53 The legal excuse of "per infortunium." See Birdsong 2006: 5.
54 See ibid. For an analysis of the initial use of the felony-murder rule in case law, see ibid.: 6–7.

According to the felony-murder rule, the felon's intent in committing the felony is attached to the killing and transformed into the common law's malice aforethought required for murder.[55] A defendant could thus be liable for murder if the killing was connected with an attempted or committed dangerous felony, or while attempting to flee the crime scene. The doctrine seems to be based on the notion that the mere fatal (though accidental) outcome of the felony inherently taints the defendant, whether or not the homicide is culpable.[56] An additional line of thought underlying the doctrine stressed the felonious act preceding the deadly outcome, which therefore dictated that the wrongdoer runs the risk of conviction for accidental killing because his own preliminary wrongdoing lowered the threshold of liability for the resulting death.[57]

The particular conceptualization of the felony-murder rule can be traced back to the early seventeenth century, to Dalton and Coke's commentaries on homicide.[58] Their commentaries introduced the distinction between accidental killing and killing in the course of an unlawful act,[59] with Dalton's approach narrower than that of Coke. According to Dalton, one who caused death in the course of an unlawful act might be guilty of manslaughter or murder, depending on the nature of the unlawful act: only unlawful acts of violence could imply the malice required for a murder conviction.[60] Coke's approach, on the other hand, was more extreme, as it maintained that, while killing accidentally in the course of an unlawful act is excusable as death by misadventure, killing in the course of an unlawful act is not excusable, and is therefore a felonious homicide.[61] This expansive approach did not take into consideration the particular nature of the unlawful act, such that felony-murder according to Coke most likely consisted of a killing occurring in the course of any unlawful act, even if the unlawful act was neither felonious nor dangerous. Subsequent English writers towards the end of the seventeenth century rejected Coke's implication that any unlawful act could serve as the malicious intent required as an element of murder. The most vocal commentator in this regard was Mathew Hale, who insisted that homicide in the course of an unlawful act should be accompanied by the intent to do

55 See Fletcher 1981: 413; *Model Penal Code and Commentaries (Official Draft and Revised Comments)* 1980: 3.

56 According to Fletcher (1981: 426–427), the notion of "tainting" dates back to thirteenth century England, whereby the assumption was that if one person caused the death of another, the killing itself upset the natural order and some response was necessary to expiate the killing and thus to expunge the taint. Fletcher argues that this medieval notion of tainting still haunts the way courts think about criminal homicide, and felons are therefore forced to answer for a human death for no reason other than that they or their accomplice caused it, just because the tainting occurred regardless of fault or blame.

57 See generally, ibid.

58 See Binder 2011: 81.

59 See ibid.: 81–85.

60 See ibid.: 81.

61 See ibid.: 85.

harm,[62] and by the fact that the death was not merely homicide but caused by killing (through battery or other violent act).[63] In other words, Hale's approach restricted the felony-murder rule to unlawful acts of *intentional violence.*

In an effort to reconcile Coke's broad approach with Hale's restricted perspective, Holt and later on Hawkins limited Coke's expansive approach somewhat by proposing to predicate only felonious unlawful acts. According to this approach, all felonies are generally dangerous by their very nature and, as such, a very close causal connection between the danger inherent in the predicate felony and the resulting death should not be required. According to Binder, by the time English courts did apply a felony-murder rule, in the second half of the nineteenth century, the prevailing practice in murder cases appears to have been closer to the views of Hale, predicating the felony-murder rule only to felonies that were considered to be inherently dangerous.[64] Thus, felony-murder in England did not apply to all felons, and did not hold felons strictly liable for purely accidental deaths. Instead, English law conditioned felony-murder liability on causing death through an act of violence or an act manifestly dangerous to human life, in the perpetration or attempt of a felony.[65]

This prevailing approach to felony-murder was the mildest among those proposed by English legal scholars, first and foremost by Hale. In 1879, this approach had been proposed legislatively in England in a detailed bill that stated in Section 175(a) that culpable homicide is also murder:

> if he means to inflict grievous bodily injury for the purpose of facilitating the commission of any of the offenses hereinafter mentioned, or the flight of the offender upon the commission or attempted commission thereof, and death ensues from his violence … (c) … the following are the offenses hereinbefore in this section referred to: piracy, and offenses deemed to be piracy; escape or rescue from prison or lawful custody; resisting lawful apprehension; murder; rape; forcible abduction; robbery; burglary; arson.[66]

As can be seen from the above, by the end of the nineteenth century the proposed English felony-murder statute extended the doctrine to apply not only to the commission of particular offenses, but also to the mere attempt to commit or to flee from the particular foreseeable dangerous enumerated offenses. This expanded approach was led by both Holt and Hawkins, who sought to extend the rule to apply to deaths caused in the course of attempting a felony as well.[67]

62 See ibid.: 86.
63 See ibid.: 87.
64 Ibid.: 93, 98, 99; see also Birdsong 2006: 15–16.
65 Binder 2011: 64.
66 See Stephen 1883 (3): 80–81.
67 Binder 2011: 92.

Throughout case law, several modifications were developed with regard to the felony-murder rule in an effort to limit its scope and adjust its application to notions of moral culpability and fair punishment. These modifications included limitation of the felony-murder rule to inherently dangerous felonies,[68] the requirement of proximate causation between the committed or attempted felony and the occurrence of the victim's death[69] and the principle of merger that excludes lesser offenses of homicide (mainly the offense of assault) considered to be already included within the legal elements of the offense of homicide.[70]

The most substantial legal criticism leveled against the felony-murder rule relates to the assertion that the doctrine divorces criminal liability from blameworthiness.[71] Indeed a common criticism specifically refers to the creation of a *de jure* "heavy handed approximation of malice in killing,"[72] which forms de facto a kind of "strict liability" for homicide.[73] Such strict liability creates, *ipso facto*, an intrinsic injustice that disregards the basic legal criminal requirement of *mens rea*, the question of the felon's moral culpability and individual accountability, and the proportional punishment with regard to the most grievous criminal allegation and its correlated harsh sanctions.[74] This legal criticism has been

68 The limitation of the doctrine to dangerous felonies is rooted in the nineteenth century judicial decision given by Sir James Stephen that implicitly pointed to the notion of human life sanctity while limiting the application of the felony-murder rule in England to: "any act known to be dangerous to life, and likely in itself to cause death, done for the purpose of committing a felony which caused death." See Alderstein 1975: 252 referring to the case of *Regina* v. *Serne*, 16 Cox Crim. Cas. 311 (Central Crim. Ct. 1887). See also Crump and Crump 1985: 391–393.

69 The basic definition of felony-murder implies a causal relationship between the underlying crime and the homicide. This assumption calls for judicial determination of legal questions pertaining to, inter alia, the duration of the felonious act and its proper legal connection to the resulting killing. The common law concept maintains that the act which caused the death must occur "in" or "during" the commission of the felony, and extends the concept to include attempted perpetration of felony and flight or attempted flight after the commission or attempted commission of a felony. Limitation of causation relates to the requirement of a proximate causation between the killing and the felonious act. Therefore, causation doctrines such as "but-for causation," foreseeability and intervening agency are sometimes used to limit felony-murder. See ibid.: 383. For further reading on the limitation of causation applied in the felony-murder rule see ibid.: 383–390.

70 The principle of merger is of utmost relevance to the phenomenon of femicide and will be elaborated further in this chapter. The limitation that refers to the principle of merger disallows use of the felony-murder rule in manslaughter or criminally negligent homicide as underlying felonies (see LaFave and Wakeman 1972: 558–559). Some argue that the purpose of this exclusion is to avoid "bootstrapping," which would allow prosecutors to convert what would ordinarily be a straightforward murder case, involving only one crime, into a felony-murder case, by separating an assault and treating the killing resulting from the assault as murder (see Fletcher 1981: 415–16). Scholars argue that the underlying rationale of this exclusion is to prevent its inappropriate use, because such homicide is an integral part of the said homicide and thus a lesser-included offense within murder (see Crump and Crump 1985: 377).

71 Crump 2009: 1158.

72 See Fletcher 1981: 415.

73 Birdsong 2006: 2.

74 See Fletcher 1981: 428. See also Crump 2009: 1158–1159.

echoed in constitutional legal arguments that state that prosecution for an accidental death squarely denies the equal protection from arbitrary legal procedures in no-fault cases.[75] Roth and Sundby add to this constitutional argumentation, maintaining that recent U.S. Supreme Court decisions suggest that the doctrine's presumption of liability without proof of *mens rea* (as requested for each element of a serious crime) contravenes constitutional rights related to due process and to the Constitution's Eighth Amendment protections guaranteeing against disproportionate punishment.[76] They also suggest that the doctrine's legal presumption of liability operatively shifts the burden of proof to the defendant, thus also violating the defendant's guaranteed constitutional principle of criminal due process and presumption of innocence.[77]

Proponents of the felony-murder doctrine underscore two positive outcomes of the doctrine. The first relates to the proper weight it gives to the *actus reus* as well as to the proper criminal grading of the actual crime committed.[78] According to this approach, a doctrine that includes the result of the defendant's conduct as a relevant determinant of just punishment and of fair criminal labeling is considered morally and socially desirable.[79] The second positive outcome pertains to its influence on societal norms and values in reaffirming and reinforcing the notion of the sanctity of human life. According to this view, the felony-murder rule serves this purpose by distinguishing between and upgrading crimes that cause human death.[80] The most notable argument set forth in favor of the felony-murder doctrine relates to the notion of social deterrence,[81] yet it is still unclear whether the rule deters criminals from committing felonies or influences

75 Fletcher, for example, raises the possibility of equal protection and Sixth Amendment problems with respect to the felony-murder doctrine. For this critique see Fletcher 1981: 425.

76 See Roth and Sundby 1985: 460. (For further reading of U.S. Supreme Court decisions implying that the liability presumption might contravene constitutional rights, see ibid.: 460–471. For further reading on U.S. Supreme Court decisions on the felony-murder rule as possibly contravening the Eighth Amendment guaranteeing against disproportionate punishment see ibid.: 478–485). Somewhat similarly, Canada found the felony murder doctrine to be unconstitutional. See Finkelstein 2005: 218.

77 See Roth and Sundby 1985: 475–477.

78 See Crump and Crump 1985: 366–367.

79 See ibid.: 366–367.

80 See ibid.: 367–368. Crump and Crump further argue:

> Felony murder is a useful doctrine because it reaffirms to the surviving family of a felony-homicide victim the kinship the society as a whole feels with him by denouncing in the strongest language of the law the intentional crime that produced the death.

81 However, FBI crime data used to model the effect of the felony-murder rule suggest that the rule is correlated with higher rates of felonies. This correlation seriously undermines the deterrence logic of such a doctrine. However, Ganz notes that the correlation between higher felony rates and application of the felony-murder rule doctrine may be linked to the fact that states with higher rates of crime would be more likely to adopt the rule. See Ganz 2012: 6.

them to be more careful when carrying them out.[82] In this respect, common criticism leveled against the doctrine relates to the assertion that the rule might not serve positive or intended purposes and might not advance utilitarian concepts such as deterrence.[83]

Only some jurisdictions in the Western world currently rely on the felony-murder doctrine, and no evidence of the rule has been found in French or German law.[84] England itself, the conceptual cradle of the doctrine, abolished the felony-murder rule and all forms of constructive or fictitious malice,[85] and in fact never incorporated the rule in legislation. Still, this doctrine is commonly practiced and legislatively recognized in all U.S. jurisdictions.[86]

The American felony-murder rule

The scholarly commentaries that developed in seventeenth and eighteenth century England most likely had a significant influence on American scholarly writing, among them Blackstone's publication of the *Commentaries on the Laws of England* which became a "standard reference work on the common law of American Colonial lawyers."[87] Blackstone promulgated the general principle that the intent to commit one felony could transfer to an unintended felonious result. According to Birdsong, this notion of transferred intent may have been "the beginning of American jurisdictions' adoption of the felony-murder rule, even though it was not utilized very often in England and certainly was not an 'ancient rule'."[88] From among the three main approaches towards felony-murder that developed in England, American scholars were in accord with the broadest and extended felony-murder upheld by Coke, which viewed death caused accidentally in the course of an unlawful act as murder.[89]

82 According to Ganz,

> one would presume that if a legislature wanted to merely decrease the prevalence of felonies, they would pass laws that prescribe more strict punishments for the felony itself, rather than pass a law that elevates the punishment for something that may or may not happen during the felony."
>
> (See ibid.: 7)

83 See generally ibid.: 3–9.

84 For a description of the French and German laws of homicide, see Fletcher 1978: 321–340.

85 See English Homicide Act of 1957, Chapter 11, Section 1, which provided that a person who

> "kills another in the course or furtherance of some other offense" shall not be guilty of murder unless his act was done "with the same malice aforethought as is required for a killing to amount to murder when not done in the course or furtherance of another offense".

86 Fletcher 1978: 283–284.

87 Birdsong 2006: 14.

88 See ibid.: 14.

89 Binder refers also to George Web who in his treatise of 1736 defined murder as killing with malice aforethought, and argued that this malice aforethought is included in cases where a man is resolved to commit an unlawful act and death ensues. See Binder 2011: 112.

Most American states reformed their homicide laws during the nineteenth century, adopting more detailed statutes that included provisions addressing homicide committed in the course of a crime.[90] By the mid-nineteenth century, most U.S. jurisdictions had a felony-murder rule statute;[91] however, uniform legislation was still lacking. Each jurisdiction had its particular version, yet by and large all versions were limited in scope and no strict liability for all deaths committed in the course of all felonies was applied.[92] The most popular legislative reform to homicide in post-independence U.S. jurisdictions divided murder into degrees.[93] This constituted a major departure from the criminal common law, but as far as the felony-murder rule was concerned, most U.S. jurisdictions still classify all felony murder as murder of the first degree.[94] Some jurisdictions have mitigated the common law rule by which all felony murder is punishable by death and classify felony murder as second-degree murder.[95] Few jurisdictions have mitigated the doctrine by downgrading the offense and its applicable penalty.[96]

There are three main versions, representing three approaches to the American felony-murder doctrine: the enumerating version, the version that requires an additional *mens rea* and the traditional common law version.[97] The enumerating version is the most common among U.S. jurisdictions.[98] Its origins hail

90 Ibid.: 119.

91 By the end of the eighteenth century, more than 80 percent of U.S. jurisdictions had legislated the felony-murder rule in some form. See ibid.: 132.

92 Ibid.: 65–66.

93 This new approach originated with Pennsylvania's 1794 reform statute that restricted capital punishment to first-degree murder, and by the end of the nineteenth century two-thirds of the states had followed suit. See ibid.: 119–120.

94 See Alderstein 1975: 258.

95 See ibid.: 258.

96 See ibid.: 259–260.

97 See Fletcher 1981: 418; Alderstein 1975: 257–267.

98 The vast majority of the U.S. jurisdictions, more specifically 42 jurisdictions, currently apply this version of the felony-murder rule: Alabama, ALA CODE §13A-6–2; Alaska, Alaska Stat. §11.41, §11.41.110; Arizona, A.R.S. §13–1105; Arkansas, Ark. Code Ann. §5–10–101; California, Cal. Penal Code §189; Colorado, C.R.S. §18–3–102; Connecticut, CT Gen Stat §53a-54c; Florida, Fla Stat. Ann. §782.04; Idaho, ID Code §18–4003; Illinois, ILCS §720 ILCS 5/2–8; Indiana, IC §35–42–1–1; Iowa IA Code §707.2; §702.11; Kansas, KSA §21–3401; Louisiana, LSA-R.S. §14:30, §14:30.1; Maine, Me. Rev. Stat. Ann – Title 17-A §202; Maryland, Maryland Criminal Law §2–201; Massachusetts, M.G.L. § chapter 265 §1; Michigan, Mich. Comp. Laws §750.316, §750. 319 §750. 320, §750.327 §750. 328; Minnesota, MN Statutes §609.185, §609.19; Mississippi, MS Code §97–3–27; Montana, MONT CODE ANN §45–5–102; Nebraska, §200.030; New Hampshire, NH. REV. STAT. Neb. Rev. St. §28–303; Nevada NRS ANN. §630:1, §630:1-b; New Jersey, NJ Rev Stat §2C:11–3; New York, N.Y. PEN. LAW §125.25; North Carolina, NC GC §14–17; North Dakota, N.D. §12.1–16–01; Ohio, R.C. §2903.02; Oklahoma, Okla. Stat. §701.7; Oregon, OR Rev Stat §163.115; Rhode Island, Rhode Island General Laws §11–23–1; South Carolina, S.C. Code Ann. §16–3–10, §16–3–20; South Dakota, SD Codified L §22–16–4; §22–16–41; Tennessee, T.C.A. §39–13–202; Utah, Utah Code Ann. §76–5–203; Vermont, V.S.A. §2301; Virginia, VA Code Ann. §18.2–32; Washington, RCW §9A.32.030

back to Pennsylvania's 1794 legislation, which departed from English tradition and classified murder into two degrees (first-degree and second-degree murder), with only first-degree murder punishable by death. In defining the distinct nature of first-degree murder, Pennsylvania statutorily deemed any murder perpetrated by committing or trying to commit arson, rape, robbery or burglary as murder of the first degree.[99] This statute led to the legal interpretation that all other felonies are not, by nature, within the scope of felony-murder. The mere enumeration of these felonies as premising a first-degree murder conviction when causing an accidental killing created a legal presumption of these felonies as inherently dangerous enough to fall within the scope of the felony-murder rule. This classification limited the scope of the common law felony-murder rule and was widely adopted by numerous U.S. jurisdictions, which simply enumerated the felonies that are legally conclusive on the issue of malice. As early as 1829, New Jersey passed a law that specified that sodomy, rape, arson, robbery, burglary, or any unlawful act that has a probable chance of resulting in bloodshed could be the underlying crime that results in a felony-murder conviction.[100] The most notable felonies consistently found in most jurisdictions that adopted the enumerating version are burglary, robbery, rape, arson and kidnapping.[101] Some jurisdictions, such as Illinois, explicitly limit this enumeration to felonies considered inherently dangerous to human life.[102]

Some jurisdictions retained the traditional common law version of the felony-murder rule, which accords criminal liability to death ensuing from any felonious

---

(1)(c); West Virginia, W. Va. Code §61–2–1; Wisconsin, WI Stat §940.03; Wyoming, WY Stat §6–2–101. Four of the above jurisdictions – Illinois, Massachusetts, Ohio and Iowa – enumerate the felonies by way of categorization: Illinois and Iowa enumerate by way of categorizing "forcible felonies," Massachusetts by categorizing "death or life imprisonment felonies" and Ohio by the categorization of "any violent offense."

99 See Alderstein 1975: 251–252 referring to the Pennsylvania statute:

> all murder which shall be perpetrated by means of poison, or by lying in wait, or by any other kind of willful, deliberate and premeditated killing, or which shall be committed in the perpetration or attempt to perpetrate any arson, rape, robbery or burglary, shall be deemed murder of the first degree; and all other kinds of murder shall be deemed in the second degree.
>
> (Quoting from 4J. of Senate 242 (PA. 1794), see ibid.: 251)

100 Act of Feb. 17, 1829 Section 66, 1828–1829 N. J. Acts 109,128: murder killing included "in committing, or attempting to commit sodomy, rape, arson, robbery, or burglary, or any unlawful act against the peace of this state, of which the probable consequence may be bloodshed." (See Binder 2011: 121).

101 See Alderstein 1975: 270–274 (tables containing enumerated felonies by enumerating jurisdictions).

102 See Ill. Ann. Stat. Ch. 38 Section 9–1(a)(3) (Smith-Hurd Cum. Supp, 1976). According to Birdsong, in 1827 Illinois became the first state to pass the first true felony-murder law, which states that an "involuntary killing ... in the commission of an unlawful act which in its consequences, *naturally tends to destroy the life of a human being*, or is committed in the prosecution of a felonious intent ... shall be deemed and adjudged to be murder." This Illinois rule does not apply to all felonies, but rather to those felonies that are inherently dangerous to human life. See Birdsong 2006: 18–19.

act.[103] This version originated in a New York statute enacted in 1829[104] that predicated murder liability upon the commission of any felony.[105] This is the strictest version of the felony-murder rule and only some U.S. jurisdictions recognize any felony as sufficient to classify a related killing as murder.[106] According to this version, the felony-murder rule could be applied upon the commission of any felonious act, without the requirement to prove subjective malice or *mens rea* related to the killing itself. This version of legal liability as part of the felony-murder rule is the closest to "strict liability," as there is no legislative requirement to prove the defendant's actual intent to kill.[107]

The least common version of the felony-murder rule is the version that requires an additional *mens rea* for a felony-murder conviction.[108] This requirement was originally enacted in the Illinois felony-murder statute in 1827,[109] and is currently reflected in the MPC's felony-murder[110] approach. The jurisdictions that add the *mens rea* requirement to the enumerated felonies, limit the application of the felony-murder doctrine by a statutory requirement that the killing be committed with some sort of malice aforethought.[111]

103 Six jurisdictions retain the traditional extended version of the felony-murder rule applied to any felonious act: Delaware, Georgia, Missouri, New Mexico, Pennsylvania and Texas. See Delaware, DEL CODE §635, §636 (a); Georgia, O.C.G.A. §16–5–1; Missouri, Miss. Rev. STAT §565.021.1 (2); New Mexico, NM Stat §30–2–1; Pennsylvania, Pa.C.S.A. §2501; Texas, TEX PE. CODE ANN. §19.02.

104 N.Y.Rev. STAT.pt. 4, Ch. 1, tit. 1 Section 5 (1829): murder killing included "without any design to effect death, by a person engaged in the commission of any felony." (See Binder 2011: 121).

105 Ibid.: 121.

106 See Alderstein 1975: 265–267. New York's 1829 felony-murder statute was the strictest felony-murder rule, specifying that "killing 'without any design to effect death, by a person engaged in the commission of any felony'" could result in a felony-murder conviction. (See Birdsong 2006: 19).

107 According to this version of felony-murder, the intent to commit a felonious act (any felonious act, even if not inherently dangerous), suffices to receive a murder conviction if death occurred while committing or attempting to commit any felony.

108 Additional to either the enumerating version or the traditional common law version. Only four jurisdictions add an additional requirement of *mens rea* to the felonious act requirement for the felony-murder rule application: Arkansas, Delaware, Louisiana and New Hampshire. See Arkansas, Ark. Code Ann. §5–10–102; Delaware, DEL CODE §635(2), §636 (a)(2); Louisiana, LSA-R.S. §14:30; New Hampshire, NH. REV. STAT. ANN. §630:1, 630:1-b.

109 This statute required "felonious intent." See Ill. Rev. Code, Crim. Code sections 22, 24, 28 (1827): "involuntary killing … in the commission of an unlawful act which in its consequences, naturally tends to destroy the life of a human being, or is committed in the prosecution of a felonious intent … shall be deemed and adjudged to be murder" (see Binder 2011: 121).

110 The U.S. Model Penal Code's approach will be elaborated further in this chapter.

111 Such as the requirement of recklessness, indifference towards the value of life and knowledge or malice aforethought. See for example Arkansas that requires "universal malice manifesting extreme indifference to the value of human life generally"; Delaware requiring "criminal negligence"; Louisiana that requires "specific intent to kill or to inflict great bodily harm and is engaged in the perpetration or attempted perpetration of…"; and New Hampshire requiring "knowledge" for capital and first-degree murder and "extreme indifference to the value of

As noted, the enumerating version of the felony-murder rule is the most common among U.S. jurisdictions and is also the version applied by the U.S. Federal Criminal Code.[112] Virtually all U.S. jurisdictions that apply this version limit felony-murder to a list of specified felonies, with the most common enumerated felonies being: arson, robbery, rape, kidnapping and burglary. More in line with Hale's restricted approach to felony-murder, American felony-murder rules predicate murder liability only on felonies dangerous to life, and only on killings in which an intentional act clearly dangerous to human life was performed in the course of a dangerous felony.[113] Consequently, strict liability is not applied to all deaths occurring in the course of felonies, and murder liability is almost always conditioned on causing death with fault.[114] Broadly speaking, the felony-murder rule remains in force in all but three jurisdictions that have completely abolished it either statutorily (Hawaii and Kentucky[115]) or by judicial decision (Michigan).[116]

The U.S. Model Penal Code felony-murder rule

The point of departure of the U.S. Model Penal Code's articulation of the felony-murder rule is most likely anchored in the drafters' criticism of the

---

human life" for second-degree murder. Similarly, U.S. federal codification of the felony-murder doctrine requires "malice aforethought" as an element of the offense of murder, felony-murder included. See Noyes 1994: 537–540.

112 Conjunct with a requirement of "malice aforethought" that must be proved in order to grade the felony-murder as a murder in the first degree. See U.S. Code, Title 18, Part I, chapter 51, Section 1111:

> (a) Murder is the unlawful killing of a human being with malice aforethought. Every murder perpetrated by poison, lying in wait, or any other kind of willful, deliberate, malicious, and premeditated killing; or committed in the perpetration of, or attempt to perpetrate, any arson, escape, murder, kidnapping, treason, espionage, sabotage, aggravated sexual abuse or sexual abuse, child abuse, burglary, or robbery; or perpetrated as part of a pattern or practice of assault or torture against a child or children; or perpetrated from a premeditated design unlawfully and maliciously to effect the death of any human being other than him who is killed, is murder in the first degree.

113 Binder 2011: 72.

114 Ibid.: 66, 68.

115 See Alderstein 1975: 250: Hawaii and Kentucky have abolished the felony-murder rule. Hawaii Rev. Stat. tit. 37 Section 701–04 (1972); KY. Rev. Stat. Section 507.020 (1974). In the relevant commentaries explaining the reason for its abolition, Hawaii drafters argue that:

> if the murder penalty is to be used to reinforce the deterrent effect of penalties imposed for certain felonies (by converting an accidental, negligent, or reckless killing into a murder), it would be more effective, and hardly more fortuitous, to select a certain ratio of convicted felons for the murder penalty by lot. In recognition of the trend toward, and the substantial body of criticism supporting, the abolition of the felony-murder rule, and because of the extremely questionable results which the rule has worked in other jurisdictions, the Code has eliminated from our law the felony-murder rule
>
> (Hawaii Rev. Stat. part II Criminal Homicide, Commentary on 707–701)

116 See Birdsong 2006: 20.

doctrine as a whole. Stating that "principled argument in favor of the felony murder doctrine is hard to find,"[117] the drafters would have probably preferred to abolish the felony-murder rule altogether.[118] Their main argument was that this common law doctrine imposes liability for murder, based on the culpability required for the underlying felony, without requiring separate proof of culpability with regard to the death. Consequently, conviction of murder is not based on any proven culpability with respect to homicide but on liability for another crime. According to the Code's drafters, since the underlying felony carries its own penalty, the additional punishment for murder is therefore "gratuitous – gratuitous, at least, in terms of what must have been proved at trial in court of law."[119] If taken to the extreme, under such general criminal imposition a defendant may carry liability for death occurring while committing a minor misconduct.[120]

The drafters maintain that the criminal law should limit liability to homicide cases whereby death is caused at least "negligently," and indeed Section 210.1.(1) to the Code states that, "a person is guilty of criminal homicide if he purposely, knowingly, recklessly or negligently causes the death of another human being."[121] Thus, literally applied, the felony-murder doctrine embodies a form of strict liability for the homicide, as distinct from the underlying felony, and that form of liability "is inconsistent with the general concepts of culpability on which the U.S. Model Penal Code is based."[122] The Code's general notion of culpability insisted on an element of culpability as a requisite for any valid criminal conviction. Except for crimes of strict liability,[123] it delineates purpose,

117 See *Model Penal Code and Commentaries (Official Draft and Revised Comments)* 1980: 37.

118 See ibid.: 8: "the model code suggestion that the felony murder rule be modified or abandoned."

119 See ibid.: 37.

120 Thus "the application of the ancient rigor of the felony murder rule to such crimes will yield startling results" (see ibid.: 31).

121 See ibid.: 4.

122 See *Model Penal Code and Commentaries (Official Draft and Revised Comments)* 1985: 5. This approach is specified in Section 2.02: "Section 2.02. General Requirements of Culpability: (1) Minimum Requirements of Culpability. Except as provided in Section 2.05, a person is not guilty of an offense unless he acted purposely, knowingly, recklessly or negligently, as the law may require, with respect to each material element of the offense." See *Model Penal Code and Commentaries (Official Draft and Revised Comments)* 1980: 7 for the statement that personal and subjective culpability is the main thrust of the Code's criminal approach.

123 These crimes are limited, according to Section 2.05 of the MPC, to cases where a sentence that is not more severe than a fine may be imposed. Section 2.05 of the Model Penal Code states that:

> When Culpability Requirements Are Inapplicable to Violations and to Offenses Defined by Other Statutes; Effect of Absolute Liability in Reducing Grade of Offense to Violation. cf. Restatement Torts 2d §519: (1) The requirements of culpability prescribed by Sections 2.01 and 2.02 do not apply to: (a) offenses which constitute violations, unless the requirement involved is included in the definition of the offense or the Court determines that its application is consistent with effective enforcement of the law defining the offense; or (b) offenses defined by statutes other than the Code, insofar as a legislative purpose to impose absolute liability for such offenses or with respect to any material element thereof plainly appears. (2)

knowledge, recklessness and negligence as the kinds of culpability that may be called for, and must be proved, in the definition of each specific crime.[124] Therefore, in line with the Code's approach, without a subjective and actual *mens rea* (of at least extreme negligence coupled with indifference), felony-murder should not "provide any basis for imputing to the defendant actual culpability for the homicide."[125] In light of the drafters' inherent rejection of the doctrine's reliance on a form of strict liability without personal culpability,[126] the Code only went so far as to offer a rebuttable presumption with regard to the *mens rea* required for felony-murder conviction on particular enumerated felonies. It was the drafters' contention that, beyond the application of this presumption, "the felony-murder doctrine should be abandoned as an independent basis for establishing the criminality of homicide."[127] Indeed, the gist of the U.S. Model Penal Code's critical view of the doctrine is ingrained in the fact that the felony-murder rule is squarely in conflict with the Code's basic premise that criminal liability should be based on subjective and personal *mens rea*, and on blameworthiness.[128] The Code's approach would thus reject a conviction based on the legal presumption that "a person intends the natural or probable consequences of his acts," and instead would require basing a criminal conviction on the defendant's actual and subjective state of mind, given the circumstances of the case.[129]

In an effort to reconcile the felony-murder doctrine with the U.S. Model Penal Code's basic premise of *mens rea*, the drafters require personal culpability that is greater than recklessness. In doing so, they limited the criminal liability arising from the felony-murder to the actor's subjective and actual extreme recklessness, coupled with an indifference towards the value of life.[130] Such legal

---

Notwithstanding any other provision of existing law and unless a subsequent statute otherwise provides: (a) when absolute liability is imposed with respect to any material element of an offense defined by a statute other than the Code and a conviction is based upon such liability, the offense constitutes a violation; and (b) although absolute liability is imposed by law with respect to one or more of the material elements of an offense defined by a statute other than the Code, the culpable commission of the offense may be charged and proved, in which event negligence with respect to such elements constitutes sufficient culpability and the classification of the offense and the sentence that may be imposed therefore upon conviction are determined by Section 1.04 and Article 6 of the Code.

124 See *Model Penal Code and Commentaries (Official Draft and Revised Comments)* 1985: 227. The code drafters commented on Section 2.2, stating that "the section expresses the Code's basic requirement that unless some element of mental culpability is proved with respect to each element of the offense, no valid criminal conviction may be obtained" (see ibid.: 229).

125 See *Model Penal Code and Commentaries (Official Draft and Revised Comments)* 1980: 5.

126 See ibid.: 5. For further critique of this notion, see ibid.: 30–32.

127 See ibid.: p. 30.

128 See ibid.: p. 20–21. See also Alderstein 1975: 260, quoting Wechsler 1968: 1446 as well as Crump 2009: 1156.

129 See *Model Penal Code and Commentaries (Official Draft and Revised Comments)* 1980: 20–21.

130 See ibid.: 29.

construction was the outcome of the drafters' efforts to retain the doctrine while attempting to compensate for what they perceived to be an inadequate and fictitious connection between the culpability of committing an ordinary felony and the culpability required for murder. Hence, the U.S. Model Penal Code section that refers to the felony-murder rule provides that criminal homicide constitutes murder when it is committed recklessly, under circumstances manifesting extreme indifference to the value of human life. In other words, such killing would not only be committed recklessly, but would also manifest an "extreme indifference to the value of human life."[131] For a murder conviction under the U.S. Model Penal Code, the actor must both act recklessly (a conscious disregard of the risk that grossly departs from acceptable behavior)[132] and also manifest extreme indifference to the value of human life.[133] Section 210.2.(1)(b) to the Code further states that:

> such recklessness and indifference are presumed if the actor is engaged or is an accomplice in the commission of, or an attempt to commit, or flight after committing or attempting to commit robbery, rape or deviate sexual intercourse by force or threat of force, arson, burglary, kidnapping or felonious escape.

According to the Code drafters, "this provision reflects the judgment that there is a kind of reckless homicide that cannot fairly be distinguished in grading terms from homicides committed purposely or knowingly,"[134] but even then such *mens rea* cannot be strictly imposed or concluded. The Code maintains that such *mens rea* is only a rebuttable presumption whereby the prosecution bears the burden of persuasion beyond a reasonable doubt that the defendant acted recklessly and with extreme indifference. Such legal presumption may of course be rebutted by the defendant himself, or simply not followed by the jury.[135] For its drafters, the significance of the Code's legal construction was in

131 See *Model Penal Code and Commentaries (Official Draft and Revised Comments)* 1980 Section 210.2.(1)(b), which states that homicide is murder when:

> it is committed recklessly under circumstances manifesting extreme indifference to the value of human life. Such recklessness and indifference are presumed if the actor is engaged or is an accomplice in the commission of, or an attempt to commit, or flight after committing or attempting to commit robbery, rape or deviate sexual intercourse by force or threat of force, arson, burglary, kidnapping or felonious escape.

132 As stated in the section that defines recklessness, Section 2.02 of the U.S. Model Penal Code: "gross deviation from the standard of conduct that a law abiding person would observe in the actor's situation."

133 See *Model Penal Code and Commentaries (Official Draft and Revised Comments)* 1980: 21.

134 See ibid.: 21.

135 According to Section 1.12(5) of the U.S. Model Penal Code which states that:

> When the Code establishes a presumption with respect to any fact which is an element of an offense, it has the following consequences: (a) when there is evidence of the facts which give

its rejection of felony-murder as a separate basis for establishing liability for homicide while it retained the rebuttable presumption as a concession to the facilitation of proof.[136] Proponents of the U.S. Model Penal Code approach contend that such a legal structure gives a "careful" felon a way out from the harsh strict liability by shifting the burden of proof to the defendant.[137]

The Code's insistence on, and explicit statutory requirement of, *mens rea* for a felony-murder conviction, seems to squarely negate the main legal rationale of the doctrine, which seeks to impose a sort of 'strict liability' for killings perpetrated while committing felonious crimes.[138] Legal scholars argue that a requirement of *mens rea* subverts the rationale of the doctrine to aggravate an unintended killing to murder on the basis of an intended related felony,[139] and that the Code's legal reformulation requiring both recklessness and extreme indifference may seem like a subtle way of abolishing the doctrine.[140] By and large, the U.S. states that reformed their criminal codes since the U.S. Model Penal Code's inception have ignored its recommendations with regard to the required *mens rea* for felony-murder conviction.[141] Only three U.S. jurisdictions have adopted, in some form or another, the Code's proposed reformulation of the felony-murder rule in terms of a required *mens rea* in addition to the commission of the enumerated felony: New Hampshire, Delaware and Arkansas.[142] Nonetheless, these jurisdictions did not go so far as to adopt the Code drafters' *mens rea* requirement: Delaware and Arkansas require either recklessness or extreme indifference to human life (Delaware requiring recklessness and Arkansas

> rise to the presumption, the issue of the existence of the presumed fact must be submitted to the jury, unless the Court is satisfied that the evidence as a whole clearly negatives the presumed fact; and (b) when the issue of the existence of the presumed fact is submitted to the jury, the Court shall charge that while the presumed fact must, on all the evidence, be proved beyond a reasonable doubt, the law declares that the jury may regard the facts giving rise to the presumption as sufficient evidence of the presumed fact.

According to the Code drafters, the jury may regard the facts giving rise to the presumption as sufficient evidence of the required culpability unless the court determines that the evidence as a whole clearly negates the conclusion of the required mens rea. See ibid.: 30.

136 See ibid.: 30.

137 See Alderstein 1975: 261.

138 Legal scholars consider the refusal to transfer legal culpability from an intended felonious result to an unintended homicide to be in square contradiction to the foundations of the doctrine. See Crump and Crump 1985: 391.

139 See generally, ibid.: 390–391, 395.

140 See Crump 2009: 1164.

141 Fletcher 1981: 415.

142 New Hampshire requires "knowledge" for capital felony murder or first-degree felony murder, and requires "recklessness under circumstances manifesting an extreme indifference to the value of human life" for second-degree felony murder (see N.H. Rev. Stat. Ann. Section 630:1). Delaware requires recklessness for first-degree felony-murder or criminal negligence for second-degree felony-murder (see Del. Code. Ann. Tit. 11 section 635–636). Arkansas requires the manifestation of extreme indifference to the value of human life during the commission of any felony for a first-degree felony-murder conviction (see Ark. Stat. Ann. Section 41–1502).

requiring extreme indifference), but do not require both. Currently only New Hampshire comes close to the Code's reformulation in requiring both recklessness and extreme indifference.[143]

The felony-murder doctrine was not only limited by the elaborate and distinctive *mens rea* requirement. It was also limited by the Code drafters' statutory enumeration of the particular felonies whereby such prosecution could be applied. Thus, the Code's felony-murder doctrine is in fact a combination of the enumerating felonies approach and the *mens rea* approach, because the *mens rea* requirement of extreme recklessness and indifference to human life may be presumed from the commission of certain enumerated felonies.[144] The predicated felonies are enumerated in Section 210.2.(1)(b) of the Code and include the following felonies: "robbery, rape or deviate sexual intercourse by force or threat of force, arson, burglary, kidnapping or felonious escape."[145] Oddly, the Code drafters do not comment on their particular choice or on the rationale underlying their decision to include these offenses while excluding others. Perhaps they regarded these felonies as inherently dangerous to human life, and as possibly manifesting the extreme indifference to the value of human life required for felony-murder conviction.[146] In the absence of such comments, we do not really know, for example, why they included the offense of rape[147] as a

143 In New Hampshire, only a second-degree felony-murder conviction can be based on such *mens rea*. This *mens rea* is presumed upon "the use of a deadly weapon in the commission of, or attempt to commit, or in immediate flight after committing or attempting to commit any class A felony." See N.H. Rev. Stat. Ann. Section 630:1–b(1)(b).

144 Fletcher argues that the Code's approach seems to have abolished the felony-murder rule, when in fact it abolished it as a rule of substantive law and reformulated it as a rule of evidence. See Fletcher 1981: 428–429.

145 See *Model Penal Code and Commentaries (Official Draft and Revised Comments)* 1980 Section 210.2.(1)(b), stating that homicide is murder when:

> it is committed recklessly under circumstances manifesting extreme indifference to the value of human life. Such recklessness and indifference are presumed if the actor is engaged or is an accomplice in the commission of, or an attempt to commit, or flight after committing or attempting to commit robbery, rape or deviate sexual intercourse by force or threat of force, arson, burglary, kidnapping or felonious escape.

146 Or perhaps as merely presumptive of the culpability required for homicide (see Fletcher 1981: 414). See also Crump and Crump 1985: 391.

147 A curious case would be the inclusion of the crime of rape in spite of the merger doctrine. Rape is considered by all enumerating jurisdictions to be a predicate to felony-murder in spite of the primarily physical elements of assault. The Code's drafters explain such exclusion of the offense of rape from the merger doctrine in that it is an offense that includes an additional element of "extreme indignity of forced sexual intimacy" (see *Model Penal Code and Commentaries (Official Draft and Revised Comments* 1980: 118). However, perhaps the legislators' willingness to include the crime of rape within the felony-murder doctrine hints at a covert underlying patriarchal approach towards sex and women, coupled with covert leniency towards women's physical battery.

predicate felony while excluding the offense of aggravated assault from the same list.

With respect to femicide, the U.S. Model Penal Code's approach seems problematic for two main reasons. The first pertains to the peculiar *mens rea* requirements by which conviction may be difficult to achieve, particularly in cases of an intimate relationship whereby a basic assumption of love and care could easily rebut the legal requirement to manifest, in the felonious circumstances, an extreme indifference to the value of life. It may be difficult to argue convincingly that the Code's doctrinal approach emphasizing the *mens rea* requirement should be abandoned or altered, in light of the fact that recent U.S. Supreme Court decisions seem to side with the main thrust of the Code's criminal approach requiring personal and subjective *mens rea* for each element of an alleged crime.[148] An additional and more substantial problem relates to the fact that the offense of assault is not listed as a predicate felony. Hence, the Code excludes, categorically and statutorily, any conviction for felony-murder in cases of assaultive-femicide.[149] The deliberate exclusion of assault from the Code's list of enumerated predicate felonies creates a seriously lacking legal structure for

148 Roth and Sundby mention the Supreme Court's decision in the case of *United States* v. *Bailey* [*United States* v. *Bailey*, 444 U.S. 394 (1980)] whereby Justice Rehnquist noted that "'strict liability' crimes are exceptions to the general rule that criminal liability requires an 'evil meaning mind'," and went on to quote the U.S. Model Penal Code proposition that "clear analysis requires that the question of the kind of culpability required to establish the commission of an offense be faced separately with respect to each material element of the crime." For further reading on recent U.S. Supreme Court decisions recognizing substantive limits on legislatures' powers to dispose of *mens rea* elements, see Roth and Sundby 1985: 485–490. In fact, Roth and Sundby argue that the Supreme Court's judicial reliance on the U.S. Model Penal Code's requirement of *mens rea* has been understood by legal scholars as "establishing a constitutional doctrine of *mens rea* against which legislation must be tested." See Roth and Sundby's reference to Erlinder's comment in Erlinder 1981: 163, 188. See Roth and Sundby 1985: 489.

149 The U.S. Model Penal Code drafters abolished the common law doctrine of "murder with intent to injure." They argue that such an offense is treated by the inclusion of the attempt to murder within the current wording of the statute. See *Model Penal Code and Commentaries (Official Draft and Revised Comments)* 1980: 28. The criminal common law accorded to "murder with intent to injure" the express significance of an intent to cause grievous bodily harm and considered such an offense as sufficient for establishing the *mens rea* required for a murder conviction. See common law cases referred to in footnote no. 65 of p. 28 in *Model Penal Code and Commentaries (Official Draft and Revised Comments)* 1980. Philadelphia: American Law Institute. According to the drafters' approach, the offense of murder (as in Section 210.2) accords no express significance to an intent to cause grievous bodily harm (see ibid.: 28). The drafters' removal of the "intent to injure" as an independently sufficient culpability for murder rests on the approach which maintains that it is preferable to handle such cases under the standards of extreme recklessness (see ibid.: 28). Indeed, such recklessness is alleged in U.S. Model Penal Code Section 210.2(1), which deals with felony-murder (as stated, requiring both extreme recklessness and indifference towards the value of life). However, such *mens rea* is legally presumed, according to Section 210.2(1), only with respect to the list of explicitly enumerated felonies from which, lamentably, the offenses of assault or aggravated assault are excluded.

the criminal treatment of femicide, and for the proper conviction of its perpetrators. Consequently, it seems possible to assume that the U.S. Model Penal Code's approach with regard to femicide would be that such cases, along with other cases of assaultive homicide, should be prosecuted for some version of negligent homicide.[150] Such a lenient approach downgrades the severity of the murderer's criminal liability in cases of femicide, who will, at worst, be convicted of negligent homicide with its corresponding lenient sentence. A criminal code that exonerates perpetrators of assaultive-femicide communicates a problematic public message of leniency and tolerance towards lethal violence with the possible result of the victim's killing. Furthermore, such an approach is grossly inadequate from a legal perspective, since it creates an anomalous criminal situation that classifies death resulting from the conduct of an arsonist or a robber as murder, while exonerating femicide perpetrators from the corresponding culpability and the criminal liability for the murder they committed.

Assaultive-femicide and the principle of merger in the felony-murder rule

One limitation that developed within the felony-murder rule seems to have had critical and dire consequences for femicide: the principle of merger. This principle was formulated in order to determine which felonies could serve as predicate felonies. It originally disallowed the use of manslaughter or criminally negligent homicide as predicate felonies according the felony-murder rule[151] because "it would subvert any effort to grade homicide if every felonious homicide aggravated itself to murder."[152] Thus, the basic thrust of the merger principle is that the felony that aggravates the homicide into a murder conviction must be distinct from the resulting killing.[153] Accordingly, the vast majority of U.S. jurisdictions exclude assault from felony-murder convictions, and require an additional actual intent to kill in order to convict a defendant that intended to cause serious injury for murder.[154] Nonetheless, some American judicial

150 See *Model Penal Code and Commentaries (Official Draft and Revised Comments)* 1980: 29.

151 LaFave and Wakeman 1972: 558–559.

152 See Binder 2011: 519.

153 In referring to Hawkins's 1716 treatise (See ibid.: p. 525, referring to Hawkins's 1976 *A Treatise of the Pleas of the Crown* p. 74), Binder argues that the merger problem was recognized as soon as felony-murder rules were first proposed (Binder 2011: 525). He maintains that, in an effort to resolve the merger problem that arises in murder convictions regarding quarrels and arguments that consequently turn violent, Hawkins required that the predicate felony aim at an additional wrong transcending danger to the victim (arguing that "such killing will be adjudged murder, which happens in the execution of an unlawful action, principally intended for some other purpose, and not to do a personal injury to him in particular who happens to be slain." See ibid.: p. 526 (quoting Hawkins).

154 See Leonning 1961: 255. In other words, in addition to the requirement of malice (which refers to the intent to commit the mere act of assault, e.g. knifing, shooting and punching, and not to the intent to achieve the specific result of death), "an actual intent to take life is necessary to

decisions seem to be willing to consider the character and degree of harm inflicted by the assault as the aggravation necessary to raise a simple assault to assault with intent to murder.[155]

The principle of merger limits the inclusion of some predicate felonies by treating certain felonies as inseparable from the homicides to which they give rise. This limitation seems reasonable, as its main purpose is to prevent the "bootstrapping" of a lesser-included offense within murder.[156] A murder conviction based on such "bootstrapping" might contravene the legal statutes and requirements of manslaughter or involuntary manslaughter and disrupt the grading schemes typically found in U.S. homicide statutes.[157] According to Binder, the oft-stated purpose of the merger rule is to maintain the coherence and integrity of a scheme for grading homicide offenses, and it is for this reason the merger limitation requires that a predicate felony have some feature that appropriately aggravates a homicide and relevantly distinguishes it from homicides graded below murder.[158]

Scholars believe that the American roots of the merger principle are ingrained in nineteenth century case law, specifically *State* v. *Schock*.[159] In this case, the Missouri Supreme Court reversed a felony-murder conviction on the grounds that the defendant's acts of personal violence against the deceased were necessary and constituent elements of the homicide itself, and therefore merged with the alleged homicide.[160] Most U.S. jurisdictions avoid the merger problem by limiting predicate felonies and enumerating them statutorily.[161] By explicitly including particular offenses within the statutory provision, legislators provide clear instructions for judges and juries alike, and prevent in advance any possible judicial interpretation that would exclude the predicate offense on the grounds of the merger principle.[162]

As for assaultive-femicide in this regard, the principle of merger has been stretched and grossly extended to include lesser non-homicidal offenses such as assault. Indeed, the central controversy in the legal discourse about the merger principle concerns predicating felony-murder on assault of the deceased: while

establish the offense of 'assault with intent to murder.' It is this intent which the law seeks to punish and prevent, and which distinguishes the offense from a simple assault." Op Cit.

155 See ibid.: 256–258.

156 See Crump and Crump 1985: 377.

157 See Binder 2011: 520.

158 See ibid.: 519, 521.

159 *State* v. *Schock*, 68 Mo. 552 (1878). See Van Zanten 2008: 1573.

160 *State* v. *Schock*, 68 Mo. (1878) 561–562.

161 See Binder 2011: 526, 533.

162 In general, the judicial problem of the interpretation of the merger principle by U.S. jurisdictions is mostly relevant to those jurisdictions that either have a categorical felony-murder rule (like the category of felonies "dangerous to human life" in Alabama, or the category of "forcible felonies" in Iowa), or have a common law felony-murder rule that encompasses all felonies as such, because they transfer the role of defining the limits of the merger doctrine to the judiciary. See ibid.: 526.

some courts preclude felony-murder liability predicated on assault, other courts permit such charges.[163] According to Binder, American judicial decisions that permit felony-murder predicated on assault typically rely on statutory language and structure.[164] However, since most U.S. jurisdictions follow the merger principle, this statutory language and structure excludes assault as a predicate felony-murder offense. This exclusion is based on the argument that assault is a lesser-included offense within murder, and indeed the paradigm case of the principle of merger is a killing that takes place in the course of an assault.[165] The doctrine of merger would argue that, contrary to other predicate felonies, in such cases the prosecutors cannot avoid proving *mens rea* for murder by merely linking both charges: assault and murder. With respect to other felonies, such as robbery or arson for example, the *mens rea* between the felony and the murder is sufficiently distinct and thus does not "merge" into one and the same crime. According to the merger principle, if felonious assault could constitute the predicate felony for felony murder, the predicate felony would be the very act that caused the homicide.[166]

In line with the merger principle, and in order to maintain the grading schemes typically found in American homicide statutes, most U.S. courts decided that the underlying felony that serves as the basis for a felony-murder conviction must be "independent of the homicide and the assault merged therein."[167] According to Finkelstein, it is here that the felony-murder rule encounters its greatest source of confusion, with results that sometimes border on the incoherent.[168] She argues that, in line with the principle of merger, it would be easier to convict defendants of lesser crimes (that appear distinctive enough from homicide) for murder, while defendants who committed more serious crimes would be acquitted from such a murder conviction just because the crime they committed seemed to include elements of homicide:

> felony-murder cannot be charged unless the predicate felony is sufficiently serious, under the inherently dangerous rule. But if the predicate felony is in the class of assault like offenses, the merger doctrine will make felony murder unavailable again.... If the rationale were that such cases are

163 See ibid.: arguing that courts in Texas, Missouri and Massachusetts precluded felony-murder liability predicated on felonious assault while courts in Minnesota, Illinois, Georgia and Iowa permitted such charges. See ibid., footnotes 802 and 803 and related text on p. 533.

164 See ibid.: 534.

165 See Finkelstein 2005: 219–220.

166 U.S. courts contended that, if the felony-murder doctrine were strictly followed, every felonious assault resulting in death would be murder, and any lesser offense (such as voluntary manslaughter, involuntary manslaughter and criminally negligent homicide) would effectively be eliminated. See Barton 1990: 538.

167 See for example *People* v. *Moran*, 246 N.Y. 100, 158 N.E. 35 (1927). See Binder 2011: 519–530 for an analysis of American case law of the principle of merger.

168 See Finkelstein 2005: 219, 221.

particularly serious and so call for putting a thumb on the prosecution's side of the scale, it would not make sense to exempt crimes like assault from the list of predicate felonies.[169]

Curiously enough, the three landmark cases with regard to the principle of merger in assaultive homicide can be traced to decisions of the California Supreme Court in the late 1960s. Moreover, all three decisions were given with regard to defendants who had killed their wife, and all three killings were carried out on the backdrop of the victims' efforts to obtain a divorce and terminate their intimate relationship with the killer. The legal application of the merger principle in these three cases of assaultive-femicide resulted in the defendants' acquittal of murder.[170] The first legal precedent was the case of *People* v. *Ireland* in 1969, which struck down the defendant's conviction of second-degree felony-murder for killing his wife.[171] In this case, Patrick Ireland was charged by indictment with the murder of Ann Lucille Ireland, his wife. Ann Lucille and Patrick had married while he attended college. Several years later, after having two children, they began to experience marital difficulties and Ann entered into the first of a series of secret extramarital affairs.[172] Patrick began to doubt Ann's fidelity and made accusations that resulted in a number of violent physical encounters between them in which Ann sustained injuries. The relationship continued in this turbulent and unhappy state for several years. Ann consulted an attorney and commenced an action for divorce. However, the parties continued to live together and undertook several attempts to revive their marriage that did not result in improved relations between them. Several years later, the Irelands met with a conciliation counsellor who worked with the county conciliation court. As a result of this meeting, the defendant and Ann agreed to seek the services of the Western Behavioral Institute in a last effort to save their marriage. According to the court, on the day of Ann's killing the defendant returned home between 3:30 and 4 pm. Ann was not home, but shortly thereafter she returned and prepared dinner for the family while the defendant had a coffee mug of wine and took a rest until he was called for dinner. After dinner Patrick lay down again and had another coffee mug of wine. Sometime between 7:30 and 8:30 pm he shot and killed Ann by firing at close range at her two .38 caliber bullets from a pistol that he usually kept in his bedroom.[173]

169 Ibid.: 220.

170 If they had committed crimes less serious than and separate from homicide, these could have served as predicate felonies and the defendants would have been convicted of felony murder.

171 *People* v. *Ireland*, 450 P.2d 580 (Cal. 1969).

172 Ibid.: 526.

173 Terry, their six-year-old daughter, in whose presence the shooting took place, testified that after she had gone to bed her parents were

> talking about who was going to leave first; that defendant shortly thereafter got the gun in his pocket, returned to the den, and asked Ann to go outside by the swimming pool and

In court, Patrick Ireland claimed that a second-degree felony-murder instruction may not be properly given when it is based upon a felony that is an integral part of the homicide, and when the evidence produced by the prosecution to prove an offense was in fact included within the offense charged.[174] Therefore, it required that the prosecution prove the defendant's malice aforethought in Ann's killing. In striking down Patrick's convictions of second-degree felony-murder of his wife, the appellate court noted:

> We have concluded that the utilization of the felony-murder rule in circumstances such as those before us extends the operation of that rule "beyond any rational function that it is designed to serve." (*People* v. *Washington* (1965) 62 Cal.2d 777, 783 [44 Cal.Rptr. 442, 402 P.2d 130].) To allow such use of the felony-murder rule would effectively preclude the jury from considering the issue of malice aforethought in all cases wherein homicide has been committed as a result of a felonious assault – a category which includes the great majority of all homicides. This kind of bootstrapping finds support neither in logic nor in law. We therefore hold that a second degree felony-murder instruction may not properly be given when it is based upon a felony which is an integral part of the homicide and which the evidence produced by the prosecution shows to be an offense included *in fact* within the offense charged.[175]

The second landmark case that followed this legal precedent was *People* v. *Wilson*.[176] Similar to the Ireland case, the circumstances of this femicide revolved around the victim's wish to terminate the intimate relationship she had with the killer. In this case, the defendant had been married to Ann Wilson for nine years, but she had left him and filed for divorce. According to the court files, after their separation the defendant attempted to effect a reconciliation and the two occasionally met or talked on the telephone. Based on the court files, the prosecution's evidence can be summarized as follows:

> At about 10:30pm on October 14, 1964, Lewis Champion, Joe Stoglin and William Washington accompanied Ann to her apartment where they ate some food and watched television. Stoglin and Washington fell asleep in

---

> talk; that Ann refused to go and defendant pulled her off the couch where she was lying; that Ann fell to the floor, and she, Terry, then went into the room and began crying; that defendant then sat down in a chair and Ann climbed back upon the couch; that defendant then took the gun from his pocket, and said "Now what, Ann?" and fired three shots at Ann; that the first shot went into the window and the second and third shots struck Ann in the eye and chest.
>
> (Ibid.: 528)

174 Ibid.: 590.

175 Ibid.: 539.

176 *People* v. *Wilson*, 1 Cal. 3d 431 (1969).

> the living room, while Champion continued to watch television. There were several telephone calls within the next hour, which were answered by Ann. Champion answered a later call from the defendant, but Ann told him to hang up. Champion told the defendant that his wife was in the bathroom and the defendant hung up.[177]
>
> A few minutes later, Champion saw automobile lights shining in the driveway to the apartment and immediately thereafter heard the sound of breaking glass from the window on the building door at the bottom of the stairs. Ann ran to the bedroom phone and called the police. She threw a pistol down on the bed along with some bullets, but the bullets were too small and Champion was unable to load the pistol. The defendant broke into the apartment with a shotgun in his hand and pointed it at Champion, who dropped his gun and put up his hands. Champion pleaded that he did not know why defendant had come, but that he had nothing to do with the situation. The defendant said, "All right, let's go." Champion pulled the sleeping Stoglin off the couch, and they left the apartment and started down the stairs. Champion rushed out of the building and fled. Stoglin, who had followed Champion, was shot and wounded as he descended the stairs. Neighbors testified that after two more shots they saw Washington come down the stairs, stumbling over Stoglin and falling behind a bush beside the driveway.[178]

Wilson was convicted of first-degree murder of his wife and second-degree murder of Washington for which he was sentenced to death.[179] However, the court of appeals ruled that his conviction of first-degree felony murder of his wife (with burglary as the underlying felony) and second degree-felony murder of Washington (with assault with a deadly weapon as the underlying felony) were prejudicial error and required reversal of both of the defendant's convictions.[180] In doing so, the Supreme Court rendered that conviction for felony

177 Ibid.: 434.

178 Op. cit.

179 Ibid.: 438.

180 In our recent decision of *People* v. *Ireland* (1969) 70 Cal.2d 522 [75 Cal.Rptr. 188, 450 P.2d 580], we held an identical instruction to bẹ improper on the ground that it went beyond any "rational function" that the felony-murder rule was intended to serve. To allow such use of the felony-murder rule would effectively preclude the jury from considering the issue of malice aforethought in all cases wherein homicide has been committed as a result of a felonious assault – a category which includes the great majority of all homicides. This kind of bootstrapping finds support neither in logic nor in law. We therefore hold that a second degree felony-murder instruction may not properly be given when it is based upon a felony which is an integral part of the homicide and which the evidence produced by the prosecution shows to be an offense included in fact within the offense charged." (Fn. omitted.) (Ibid., 750).... Thus, the felony-murder instruction was based on an underlying felony which was a necessary ingredient of the homicide, and converted the homicide automatically into second-degree murder on a finding of the underlying felony. *This 'bootstrapping' was erroneous in Ireland and is erroneous here.*

(*People* v. *Wilson*, 1 Cal. 3d 431 (1969), 438 (italics added))

murder is relevant only in application to a felony independent of the homicide, stating the following:

> In *Ireland*, we rejected the bootstrap reasoning involved in taking an element of a homicide and using it as the underlying felony in a second-degree felony-murder instruction. We conclude that the same bootstrapping is involved in instructing a jury that the intent to assault makes the entry burglary and that the burglary raises the homicide resulting from the assault to first-degree murder without proof of malice aforethought and premeditation. To hold otherwise, we would have to declare that, because burglary is not technically a lesser offense included within a charge of murder, burglary constitutes an independent felony which can support a felony-murder instruction. However, in *Ireland* itself we did not assert that assault with a deadly weapon was a lesser included offense in murder; we asserted only that it was 'included in fact' in the charge of murder, in that the elements of the assault were necessary elements in the homicide. (70 Cal.2d at p. 539 and fn. 14.) In the same sense, a burglary based on intent to assault with a deadly weapon is included in fact within a charge of murder, and cannot support a felony-murder instruction.[181]

A similar outcome was ruled in the case of *People* v. *Sears*,[182] *a case in which* the defendant broke into his ex-wife's home for the purpose of killing her and ended up killing her daughter and wounding her mother when they intervened. According to the court, upon their marriage Earl Clarence Sears and Clara agreed that she and her three children by a former marriage would continue living in a cottage that she and the children had occupied before the marriage, while Earl would sleep in a nearby garage until he completed an addition to the cottage. Three years later, since the defendant never completed the addition, Clara refused to let him sleep in the cottage even after one of her daughters married and moved out.[183] Earl moved to a hotel. Four days prior to the killing Earl visited Clara. According to her testimony, he threatened to kill her and the children if she obtained a divorce. Four days later he drove to Clara's home and entered together with a friend with whom he had been drinking that evening. They entered the cottage through the unlocked front door, and while his friend stayed in the living room Earl went into Clara's bedroom. He told Clara that he wanted to speak to her, and she put on a robe and accompanied him to the kitchen. Because the floor was cold, Clara returned to the bedroom to get a pair of slippers. According to the court, as Clara re-entered the kitchen the defendant grabbed her robe and said: "If you won't want to come back to me...." Then defendant unbuttoned his shirt and

181 Ibid.: 441.
182 *People* v. *Sears*, 2 Cal. 3d 180 (1970).
183 Ibid.: 183.

drew out an iron bar that he had stuck in his pants before entering the cottage. He struck Clara about the head until she lost consciousness.[184] Clara's daughter, Elizabeth, awakened and approached the kitchen. As she cried out for the defendant to leave her mother alone, the defendant turned on her with the iron bar. Clara regained consciousness and unsuccessfully tried to place herself between Earl and her daughter Elizabeth, but she again became unconscious. Clara's mother Frances Montijo, who lived next door, heard the noise from her daughter's home and decided to investigate. Frances entered to find defendant on top of the screaming child. When defendant saw Frances, he attacked her with a knife he had taken from Clara's kitchen. After cutting her face, defendant threw Frances into a chair, rolled the iron bar against her throat and chest, and stabbed her with a barbecue fork, also taken from the kitchen.[185]

Elizabeth died from a knife wound that punctured her jugular vein. She also suffered numerous other cuts and bruises. Clara suffered multiple lacerations as well as a fractured jaw and a fractured arm. Frances received several wounds on her face, neck, and hands.[186] Earl's felony-murder conviction, with the breaking into his estranged wife's dwelling as the underlying felony, was struck down by the Supreme Court, which rendered that under the merger principle prosecution for felony-murder is unavailable.[187] In doing so the court of appeals reinstated its previous rulings, acquitting both Ireland and Wilson from the felony murder conviction of the murder of their wives (or should we say their wives who had filed for divorce). The Supreme Court stated, among other things, that: "to apply the felony-murder rule to such a situation would extend the doctrine beyond any rational function that it is designed to serve."[188]

184 Ibid.: 184.

185 Op. cit.

186 Op. cit.

187 While the lower court maintained that burglary with the intent to assault was a predicate felony for killing the daughter, the Supreme Court rendered that, under the merger principle, prosecution for felony-murder is unavailable, arguing that:

> To apply the felony-murder rule to such a situation would extend the doctrine "beyond any rational function that it is designed to serve." As pointed out in Wilson, that doctrine can serve its purpose only when applied to a felony independent of the homicide.
>
> (See *People* v. *Sears*, 2 Cal. 3d 180 (1970), 188 (italics added))

188 At p. 189:

> Under *Ireland* and *Wilson*, the instructions of the court on the first degree felony-murder rule and the court's answer to the question asked by the jury must be held erroneous. Those instructions and the answer could reasonably be understood to mean that if defendant entered with intent to assault his wife and stepdaughter he was guilty of burglary and that the first degree felony-murder rule was applicable. To apply the felony-murder rule to such a situation would extend the doctrine "beyond any rational function that it is designed to serve."

The offense of aggravated assault as a predicate felony-murder

According to the merger principle doctrine, there are two prevalent arguments for the exclusion of the offense of assault from predicated felony-murder. The first relates to the *mens rea* of the assaultive-homicide offense and asserts that the predicate felony must be based on an "independent felonious purpose" from the killing.[189] It also contends that the offense of assault merges with the homicide because the purpose of assault is to harm the victim, and it is this intent that produced the victim's death. Hence, no distinctive *mens rea* can be established with respect to the assault. The second argument relates to the *actus reus* of the assaultive-homicide offense, which case law refers to as the "same act doctrine." According to this doctrine, the predicate felony merges with the homicide if it was "the same act" that was clearly dangerous to human life and that caused the death of the victim.[190] In line with this argument, there appears to be no distinctive *actus reus* with regard to the resulting killing, as the same assaultive act perpetrated against the victim was the act that caused the death.

In order to examine the rationale underlying the call for statutory inclusion of the offense of assault within the list of predicate felony murder, the arguments regarding the merging of the assault and the homicide's *mens rea* and *actus reus* should, at the very least, be critically reviewed. Even if the elements of physical assault may seem to be similar to the elements of homicide, they are nonetheless different: while in the case of intent to cause harm the assault would be considered the mere purpose, in the case of intent to cause death the physical assault would be the means to achieve the purpose, the intended death.[191] The intent to harm is thus sufficiently different from the intent to cause death, because the defendant who intends to harm his victim by beating him does not necessarily have the intent to inflict sufficient harm to kill him.[192] The felonious intent in this case (which involves wounding) is thus independent of the homicide. Indeed, recent research about violence against women suggests that perpetrators have different intentions in battering or murdering women: while the purpose of battery is to sustain control over the intimate partner, the purpose of her killing is not to control her, but to eliminate even her existence.[193] This line of reasoning

189 See Finkelstein 2005: 223.
190 See ibid.: 224.
191 See for example Leonning, who argues that "an intent to shoot, knife, etc. is not the same as an intent to murder. Shooting at another is not always done with an actual intent to take life; there may only be an intent to wound or incapacitate." Leonning 1961: 255.
192 See Finkelstein 2005: 224.
193 See Ben Ze'ev and Goussinsky 2008: 90. For elaboration, see Chapter 2.

has in fact been supported by judicial decisions[194] that maintain that an inherently dangerous felony that would otherwise be barred by the principle of merger with regard to assault could nevertheless qualify as the predicate felony if the offender did not intend "to commit an injury which would cause death."[195]

The legal presumption that assaultive-homicide should be excluded from the felony-murder doctrine because the act of causing harm is the same act of causing death should, at the very least, be questioned. Some legal scholars argue that "felony resulting in death is not simply a more serious version of the underlying felony, but *is a qualitatively different crime*, comparable in seriousness to other murders."[196] In other words, the nature of the criminal offense of assaultive-femicide is legally distinct both qualitatively and inherently. Furthermore, even if it is not qualitatively different, the criminal principle of proportionality calls for a distinct and different crime gradation of an assault that results in death. Crump and Crump argue along the same lines that the most important substantial argument to be made in favor of felony-murder is that the doctrine serves the concern for proportionality in offense grading.[197] Hence, the inclusion of assaultive-homicide within the felony-murder rule would serve the substantial socio-legal concern for proportionality in offense grading[198] and would provide "a clear and unambiguous crime definition."[199]

194 For example *People* v. *Robertson* (2004) 34 Cal.4th 156, 95 P. 3d. 872, 17 Cal. Rptr.3d 604 and *People* v. *Mattison* (1971) 4 Cal.3d 177, 481 P.2d 193, 93 Cal. Rptr.185. See Mendez 2010: 259–260.

195 *People* v. *Mattison* (1971), 4 Cal.3d 185, 481 P.2d 198, 93 Cal. Rptr. at 190.

196 Emphasis added, see Crump and Crump 1985: 396.

197 See ibid.: 396. The argument favoring grading and proportionality as a matter of substantial criminal law is in accord with the recent development of the legal doctrine of "fair labeling." This doctrine asserts that the distinctive and fair grading and labeling of offenses is not a mere procedural matter but rather a substantial legal principle underlying criminal law and thus should be followed and applied meticulously. See Ashworth 1981; Williams 1983: 85.

198 For the general argument favoring felony-murder for proportionality as a matter of legal rationality, see Crump and Crump 1985: 396.

199 Crump further argues in this regard that: "This is an important (albeit certainly not the only) value in the criminal law. Ambiguity encourages discriminatory and inconsistent adjudication." See Crump 2009: 1163.

Only a few jurisdictions (Iowa,[200] Illinois,[201] Washington,[202] Montana[203] and Kansas[204]) currently include the offense of assault within the list of predicate

200 In Iowa, the felony-murder statute (section 707.02) enables first-degree murder convictions committed upon "forcible felonies." Iowa Code §707.2: Murder in the first degree: "A person commits murder in the first degree when the person commits murder under any of the following circumstances: The person kills another person while participating in a forcible felony." A reading of the respective list of "forcible felonies" in 702.11 (2007) reveals that assault is listed as a forcible felony (together with murder, sexual abuse, kidnapping, robbery, first-degree arson and first-degree burglary): Iowa Code §702.11 FORCIBLE FELONY: 1. "A 'forcible felony' is any felonious child endangerment, assault, murder, sexual abuse, kidnapping, robbery, arson in the first degree, or burglary in the first degree." The statutory language enabled the felony-murder conviction in the case of *Beeman*, where the merger limitation was explicitly denied based on the clear directive of the legislator (see Barton 1990: 1583, referring to the case, Beeman 315 N.W 2d. at 770).

201 (720 ILCS 5/9–1) (Ch. 38, par. 9–1) Sec. 9–1. First degree Murder – Death penalties – Exceptions – Separate Hearings – Proof – Findings – Appellate procedures – Reversals.

> A person who kills an individual without lawful justification commits first degree murder if, in performing the acts which cause the death: (1) he either intends to kill or do great bodily harm to that individual or another, or knows that such acts will cause death to that individual or another; or (2) he knows that such acts create a strong probability of death or great bodily harm to that individual or another; or (3) he is attempting or committing a forcible felony other than second degree murder.

202 RCW 9A.32.050: Murder in the second degree:

> (1) A person is guilty of murder in the second degree when: (a) With intent to cause the death of another person but without premeditation, he or she causes the death of such person or of a third person; or (b) he or she commits or attempts to commit any felony, including assault, other than those enumerated in RCW 9A.32.030(1)(c), and, in the course of and in furtherance of such crime or in immediate flight therefrom, he or she, or another participant, causes the death of a person other than one of the participants....

203 MONT. CODE ANN §45–5–102: Deliberate homicide.

> (1) A person commits the offense of deliberate homicide if: (a) the person purposely or knowingly causes the death of another human being; (b) the person attempts to commit, commits, or is legally accountable for the attempt or commission of robbery, sexual intercourse without consent, arson, burglary, kidnapping, aggravated kidnapping, felonious escape, *assault* with a weapon, aggravated assault, or any other forcible felony and in the course of the forcible felony or flight thereafter, the person or any person legally accountable for the crime causes the death of another human being.

Binder refers for example to a 2004 Montana court decision [*State* v. *Burkhart*, 103 P.3d 1037, 1046–47 (Mont. 2004)] that rejected the merger doctrine and concluded that the crime of "deliberate homicide" includes causing death in the course of any "forcible felony." See Binder 2011: 540–541.

204 Chapter 21: Crimes And Punishments, PART II.– PROHIBITED CONDUCT, Article 34: Crimes Against Persons, Statute 21–3401: Murder in the first degree.

> Murder in the first degree is the killing of a human being committed: (a) Intentionally and with premeditation; or (b) in the commission of, attempt to commit, or flight from an inherently dangerous felony as defined in K.S.A. 21–3436 and amendments thereto. The

felony murder.[205] However, it seems that not all of these jurisdictions statutorily preclude the merger principle for felonious assault. Kansas, for example, explicitly and statutorily applies the merger principle to such assault and battery, and includes these offenses in the predicate list "only when such felony is so distinct from the homicide alleged ... as to not be an ingredient of the homicide alleged."[206] In the jurisdictions that include assault within the list of predicate felonies without limiting it by the principle of merger (Iowa, Illinois, Washington and Montana), assaultive-femicide perpetrators could probably be prosecuted and convicted for felony murder.[207] The remaining U.S. jurisdictions, which still do not include assault as a predicate offense for felony-murder, should strive for explicit statutory inclusion of such a felonious act.

The statutory inclusion of the offense of assault as a predicate for felony-murder could be supported by the common law's approach that views "the intent to inflict serious bodily injury" as a sufficient intent for the malice aforethought required for a murder conviction.[208] British legal scholars assert

---

> definition of inherently dangerous felony includes aggravated assault and battery as defined in Statute 21–3436: "Inherently dangerous felony; definition ... (b) Any of the following felonies shall be deemed an inherently dangerous felony only when such felony is so distinct from the homicide alleged to be a violation of subsection (b) of K.S.A. 21–3401, and amendments thereto, as to not be an ingredient of the homicide alleged to be a violation of subsection (b) of K.S.A. 21–3401, and amendments thereto: ... (4) *aggravated assault*, as defined in K.S.A. 21–3410, and amendments thereto; ... (6) *aggravated battery*, as defined in subsection (a)(1) of K.S.A. 21–3414, and amendments thereto." (Italics added).

205 Two additional jurisdictions include mayhem as a predicate to felony murder: Maryland [Maryland Criminal Law §2–201: (a)(4)(vii)] and Idaho [ID Code §18–4003(d)]. However, this concept does not explicitly cater to assault and might cater to mutilation, disfigurement and crippling. (For a distinction between the concepts of assault, battery and mayhem see *Model Penal Code and Commentaries (Official Draft and Revised Comments)* 1980: 174–176.)

206 Chapter 21: Crimes And Punishments, PART II. PROHIBITED CONDUCT, Article 34: Crimes Against Persons, Statute 21–3436:

> Inherently dangerous felony; definition ... (b) Any of the following felonies shall be deemed an inherently dangerous felony *only when such felony is so distinct from the homicide alleged* to be a violation of subsection (b) of K.S.A. 21–3401, and amendments thereto, *as to not be an ingredient of the homicide alleged* to be a violation of subsection (b) of K.S.A. 21–3401, and amendments thereto. (Italics added).

207 For examples of case law decisions enabling murder conviction upon assaultive-homicide in such jurisdictions, see Binder 2011: 534–535.

208 See *Model Penal Code and Commentaries (Official Draft and Revised Comments)* 1980: 14. See also Crump and Crump arguing that "since that is the case, assault-homicide closely resembles murder with traditional malice" (Crump and Crump 1985: 379). Crump and Crump further assert that such malice technically requires intent to inflict serious as opposed to mild injury, but in an assaultive transaction that actually results in homicide, "it is ordinarily so difficult to distinguish these intentions that the assault-murder approach may be sensible in terms of proportionality, clear offense definition, and perjury discouragement." See ibid.: 379 footnote 67.

that killings committed while intending to inflict serious injury (even if the perpetrator was unaware of a serious risk of causing death), should be graded as murder.[209] These scholars argue that murder is a fair label for killing while perpetrating a serious injury because:

> to launch an attack of that severity against another person demonstrates a disregard for the vital interests of others deserving of the label "murderous," even if it would not be right to regard the crime as one of first degree murder.[210]

The British approach that labels killings committed while intending to do serious injury as murder is not commonly found in U.S. jurisdictions. Nonetheless, although most U.S. jurisdictions do not follow this approach, and still require establishing a distinct "intent to kill" for a first-degree murder conviction, recent legal scholars as well as some case law decisions seem to be contemplating the notion that the intent or malice requirement for first-degree murder could be fulfilled by an intention on the part of the accused to do "great bodily harm," as a replacement for the "intent to kill."[211]

209 Albeit it would be second-degree murder, if the proposed criminal legislation of the Law Commission for England and Wales were enacted. According to the Commission's legislative proposal, such killings will still be graded as either first or second-degree murder, depending on the perpetrator's awareness of the serious risk of causing death. The Commission's proposal with regard to murder explicitly includes killings committed with the intent to do serious injury as the following wording suggests:

> First-degree murder: (a) intentional killing (b) killing with an intention to do serious injury in the awareness that there is a serious risk of causing death. Second-degree murder: (a) killing with the intention to do serious injury (b) killing with the intention to cause injury or a fear or risk of injury, in the awareness that there is a serious risk of causing death … See Law Commission for England and Wales, Murder, Manslaughter and Infanticide, Law Com. No. 304 (London 2006).

According to the Consultation Paper of the Law Commission for England and Wales in 2006, killings with the intent to do serious injury while being aware of the serious risk of causing death will be graded as first-degree murder. Killings with the intent to cause non-serious injury will be graded as second-degree murder if they were committed with the awareness that such injury could cause death. See definition of second-degree murder proposed by the Commission in Horder 2007: 9.

210 See ibid.: 25. Horder further states that:

> there are sound moral reasons for thinking that killing with intent to do serious injury should be treated as a crime of murder, even if not as first degree murder. The nature of the harm intentionally done will in many cases mean that the defendant has made death a foreseeable consequence of his or her action …
>
> (Op. cit.)

211 See Thomas 1989: 101–102, quoting court decisions from Louisiana, Indiana and Virginia that seem to expand the intent requirement of first degree murder to include the intent to do serious bodily injury. See ibid.: 102 footnote 11 for court decisions in Louisiana and Indiana, and 103–107 for recent court decisions in Virginia.

The statutory inclusion of the offense of assault as a predicate for the felony-murder rule in cases of assaultive-femicide can also be supported by precedent case law decisions that established the application of the felony-murder rule and barred the merger rule in cases in which the homicide occurred while the defendant attacked the victim in her own home. Such circumstances were deemed by the court to be aggravated assaults by definition, leading to the willingness to assert exceptions to the merger rule under such circumstances. These circumstances are highly relevant to cases of assaultive-femicide, because both the victim in said cases, and battered wives in general, share the location of the crime scene: the victim's home. In *People* v. *Miller*,[212] the Supreme Court of New York emphasized the relevance of the location of the assault to cases where the felony that led to the victim's death was committed in the victim's home. Remarking that attacks in such private scenes add special aggravated weight to the committed felony, the court stated:

> It should be apparent that the Legislature, in including burglary as one of the enumerated felonies as a basis for felony murder, *recognized that persons within domiciles are in greater peril from those entering the domicile with criminal intent, than persons on the street who are being subjected to the same criminal intent.* Thus, the burglary statutes prescribe greater punishment for a criminal act committed within the domicile than for the same act committed on the street. Where, as here, the criminal act underlying the burglary is an assault with a dangerous weapon, *the likelihood that the assault will culminate in a homicide is significantly increased by the situs of the assault. When the assault takes place within the domicile, the victim may be more likely to resist the assault; the victim is also less likely to be able to avoid the consequences of the assault, since his paths of retreat and escape may be barred or severely restricted by furniture, walls and other obstructions incidental to buildings.* Further, it is also more likely that when the assault occurs in the victim's domicile, there will be present family or close friends who will come to the victim's aid and be killed.[213]

Taking into consideration the domestic nature of the crime scene in cases of assaultive-femicide,[214] the court ruling in Miller's case could further support the argument set forth for statutory inclusion of the offense of assault as a predicate for the felony-murder rule in cases of assaultive-femicide.

212 *People* v. *Miller* 297 N.E.2d 85 N.Y. 1973. The supreme court of New York rejected Miller's claim that he should be acquitted of a felony murder conviction based on an underlying felony of assault since it was not one of the predicate felonies enumerated in the felony-murder statute. The court rejected his appeal based on its conclusion that the defendant committed an enumerated predicate felony of burglary and not assault.

213 Ibid.: 346 (italics added).

214 Gelles and Straus 1985: 88; Dobash and Dobash 1978: 426–427.

The recent legal approach with respect to child abuse that results in the child's death can provide a further possible approach in the case of intimate partner killing. Intentional felony injury to a child is an assaultive offense, whereby the wording and rationale of the merger doctrine would require its preclusion from the list of predicate offenses for felony murder.[215] While some legal scholars assert that child assault can indeed be a predicate felony-murder offense because it does not totally merge with homicide (in the involvement of an additional and independent felonious purpose of neglect of the duty to care towards the child[216]), others maintain that child abuse is a likely candidate for applying the merger limitation because child abuse that results in death, like an assault that results in death, would not be considered independent of the killing, but rather merged with it.[217] Some case law demonstrates the approach of contemplating that child abuse and assaults merge with the killing: In *People* v. *Smith*[218] for example, the court of appeals reversed the judgment of felony-murder, concluding that Smith's acts of grievous child abuse in that case were an integral part of the homicide, thus merging de facto and *de jure* the offense of battery and abuse into the homicide. In this case, Smith and her two daughters, three-and-a-half-year-old Bethany (Beth) and two-year-old Amy, lived with David Foster. According to the court files:

> On the day the two-year-old Amy died, she refused to sit on the couch instead of the floor to eat a snack. Smith became angry, took Amy into the children's bedroom, spanked her and slapped her in the face. Amy then went towards the corner of the bedroom that was often used for discipline; Smith hit her repeatedly, knocking her to the floor. Foster then apparently joined defendant to "assist" in Amy's discipline. Beth testified that both Foster and defendant were striking Amy, who at that point had been at least partially undressed by Smith. Smith and Foster used both their hands and a paddle on the child, and were also biting her. In addition, Beth testified that Foster put a wastebasket on Amy's head and hit her on the head with his fist. Eventually, Smith knocked Amy backwards and she fell, hitting her head on the closet door. Amy stiffened and went into respiratory arrest. Amy died that evening. Her injuries were consistent with compressive force caused by numerous blows by hands, fists and a paddle.

215 See Barton 1990: 543.

216 The same line of reasoning could be attached to felonies such as rape and robbery, maintaining that in light of the merger principle they should be precluded from the felony-murder rule as they have independent felonious purposes in addition to the felonious act of assault (rape as assault + non-consensual intercourse, and robbery as assault + forced acquisition of money or property). See Bendetowies 1990: 399. See also Binder 2011: 550.

217 Van Zanten 2008: 1588. See also Binder for the argument that "most of the decisions permitting child abuse as a predicate felony also analogized it to assault." Binder 2011: 536.

218 *People* v. *Smith* 35 Cal. 3d 798 1984.

Relying on *Ireland* and *Wilson*, the court concluded that the application of the felony-murder rule is barred: "where the purpose of the conduct was the very assault which resulted in death." More specifically, the court concluded that, in cases in which the violation is a direct assault on a child that results in death (i.e., causing or permitting a child to suffer or inflicting thereon unjustifiable physical pain), "it is plain that the purpose of the child abuse was the very assault which resulted in death."[219] The Court further noted:

> It would be wholly illogical to allow this kind of assaultive child abuse to be bootstrapped into felony murder merely because the victim was a child rather than an adult, as in *Ireland.* In the present case, the homicide was the result of child abuse of the assaultive variety. Thus, the underlying felony was unquestionably an "*integral part of*" *and* "*included in fact*" in the homicide within the meaning of Ireland.[220]

In acquitting Smith from a felony murder conviction, the court mentioned that, despite its deep abhorrence of the crime of child abuse, they see no escape from their duty to apply the merger doctrine they carefully enunciated in *Ireland* and its progeny. In doing so they mentioned Oklahoma's conclusion in a similar case, maintaining that "the felony committed, child beating, is not independent of the homicide and must merge into the homicide."[221] The court further declared its disapproval of the verdict in *People* v. *Northrop*,[222] convicting the defendant of felony-murder in a similar child abuse case resulting in the child's death. Commenting on the inconsistency of such ruling with the *Ireland* decision, the court stated that such conviction was erroneous because the merger doctrine in the felony-murder rule should have barred the defendant's conviction of a felony-murder based on the felonious child abuse.

Contrary to the above case law decisions, many jurisdictions have recently demonstrated, both statutorily and judicially, an explicit willingness to preclude child assault and child abuse from the merger principle and to include them within the list of predicate offenses of felony murder, despite legal approaches that maintain that these offenses should be precluded in line with the merger principle. Fourteen jurisdictions have recently included the offense of assault as a predicate offense to felony-murder, when the victims are children,[223] and even the American Federal Law explicitly includes assault towards children within the

219 *People* v. *Smith* 35 Cal. 3d 798 1984 at p. 807 (italics added).

220 Op. cit. (italics added).

221 *Massie* v. *State* (Okla. Crim. 1976) 553 P.2d 186, 191.

222 *People* v. *Northrop*, *supra*, 132 Cal.App.3d 1027.

223 Currently, 14 jurisdictions explicitly include child assault or child abuse as a predicate felony to felony-murder: North Dakota, Oklahoma, Michigan, Louisiana, Nevada, Iowa, Wyoming, Arizona, Idaho, Oregon, Florida, Utah, Alaska and Tennessee.

list of predicate offenses for first-degree felony-murder.[224] Such an exception was formulated even though these assaultive-homicides do not, as it were, include an additional "act" or an additional "mental state" usually required to preclude the merger principle.[225] The fact that courts and legislators alike demonstrate an increasing willingness to include child assault as a predicate felony for a felony-murder conviction could be at best understood on the backdrop of underlying social norms and values that uphold the sanctity and vulnerability of children, and consider it the moral obligation of their caregivers to deliver such guardianship. This vulnerability is also echoed in assaultive-femicide cases, as the asymmetry of power between the victim and the assailant renders the victims unable to fend for themselves, very similar to cases of assaultive-infanticide: the beating to death of children. Such brutal assaults, occurring in the victim's home where the assailant's power blatantly outweighs the victim's power, and where the victims' withdrawal from the crime scene is practically impossible because of their dependency on the assailant, bear essential similarities to circumstances of battered wives. The legal willingness to include a felonious assault within the list of predicate offenses for felony-murder based on its antisocial nature and society's moral obligation toward its vulnerable members can serve as a model for the inclusion of assaultive-femicide in the felony-murder rule. Legal willingness to regard an antisocial motive as implying part of the malice required for a murder conviction has already been expressed in case law,[226] and could be further applied to assaultive felony-murder.[227] In further establishing the similarity between child assault and women assault, it is worth

224 See U.S. Code, Title 18, Part I, chapter 51, Section 1111:

> (a) Murder is the unlawful killing of a human being with malice aforethought. Every murder perpetrated by poison, lying in wait, or any other kind of willful, deliberate, malicious, and premeditated killing; or committed in the perpetration of, or attempt to perpetrate, any arson, escape, murder, kidnapping, treason, espionage, sabotage, aggravated sexual abuse or sexual abuse, child abuse, burglary, or robbery; *or perpetrated as part of a pattern or practice of assault or torture against a child or children*; or perpetrated from a premeditated design unlawfully and maliciously to effect the death of any human being other than him who is killed, is murder in the first degree. (Italics added).

225 See Barton 1990: 541–545. See also Van Zanten 2008: 1587–1588.

226 Levin mentions that in the case of *Watson* [*People* v. *Watson*, Cal.3d, 290, 637 P.2d 279, Cal. Rptr.43 (1981)], the court indicated two similar tests for determining implied malice for second-degree murder conviction:

> 1. When the defendant intended, with conscious disregard for life, to commit acts likely to kill; or 2. when the defendant, for a base, *antisocial motive* and with wanton disregard for human life, commits an act that has a high probability of causing death. (Italics added).

See Levin 1983: 1303.

227 See for example Bendetowies who supports the inclusion of such an offense within the list of predicate felony-murder offenses because the "felony-murder rule satisfies society's sense of outrage over the killing of a child. Our laws must severely punish those who violate the sanctity of a child's life, in order to preserve the public's trust in a need for justice" Bendetowies 1990: 405.

mentioning some of the arguments in favor of the inclusion of child assault as an underlying felony to felony-murder, and which could be applied to make the case for the inclusion of women assault. For the sake of argument, the following quotation will illustrate (emphasized in added brackets and italics) the same argument set forth for the inclusion of child assault applied to assaultive-femicide within felony-murder:

> Child *(and women)* abuse is most often committed in the privacy of the abuser's home, where there are no witnesses other than the abuser himself. As a result, it is extremely difficult to prosecute child *(and women)* abuse cases, and even more difficult to obtain a murder conviction when death results ... the felony-murder rule will help to protect child*(ren) (and women)* from an abusive situation in which there is a great probability of serious injury or death.[228]

Conclusion

The prima facie exoneration of male intimate partners from a murder conviction on the grounds of the preclusion of assaultive-femicide from felony-murder is ingrained in almost all U.S. jurisdictions.[229] This legal anomaly pertains equally to jurisdictions that enumerate predicate felonies (and preclude assault) and to those that apply the felony-murder rule to all felonious acts while leaving statute interpretation to the judicial authorities. To tackle this problem in jurisdictions that enumerate predicate felonies, it is necessary to persuade legislators in these jurisdictions by proposing to add the crime of aggravated assault to the list of predicate felonies. In jurisdictions that apply felony-murder to all felonious acts without explicit enumeration,[230] there is a need to create an explicit statutory exception to the principle of merger in circumstances of assaultive-femicide. A legislative approach that explicitly includes assault within the predicate felonies will prevent judicial application of the merger limitation to assaultive-femicide. A determined list of predicate felonies that includes assault demonstrates that the legislative body in that jurisdiction has chosen to bar the merger limitation for assaultive-homicide and to exclude this felony from the principle of merger. Some jurisdictions, such as Montana, Illinois, Iowa and Washington, include assault as a predicate for felony murder.

228 See ibid.: 404–406.

229 As noted, currently only Iowa, Washington and Montana include in statutory form forcible assault or aggravated assault as predicate felonies, thus explicitly indicating that the merger principle does not apply to assaultive homicide.

230 Jurisdictions that extend the doctrine to apply to any felonious act. For example, see related statutes in Alaska, Arkansas, Delaware, Georgia, Minnesota, Missouri, New Mexico. See Alaska, Alaska Stat. §11.41.110; Arkansas, Ark. Code Ann. §5–10–102; Delaware, DEL CODE §635, §636 (a); Georgia, O.C.G.A. §16–5–1; Minnesota, MN Statutes §609.19; Missouri, Miss. Rev. STAT §565.021.1 (2); New Mexico, NM Stat §30–2–1.

The crucial importance of explicit statutory wording barring the merger limitation in cases of assaultive-femicide was demonstrated in the *Beeman* case that was ruled in Iowa in 1982. In this case, the State's evidence showed that Beeman took his girlfriend, Michiel, to the park on the night of April 21, 1980. When Michiel refused to have consensual sexual relations with Beeman he kicked her in the head. He later killed her by stabbing her repeatedly 17 times in the chest. Beeman was convicted of Michiel's felony-murder according to Iowa's criminal code Section 707.2(2) by which "A person commits murder in the first degree when he or she kills another person while participating in a forcible felony."[231] Since forcible felony includes any felonious assault and willful injury according to the definitions in §702.11 and section 708.4, Michiel's willful injury by Beeman could have served as the underlying felony in his felony-murder conviction. However, Beeman appealed contending that the trial court erred in giving felony-murder instructions based on the underlying felony of willful injury of Michiel.[232] Indeed, had it not been for the explicit statutory inclusion of the wording "felonious assault" in the 1979 revised legislated list of predicate felonies, Beeman's conviction of Michiel's murder most likely would have been struck down in line with the merger principle.[233] The appellate court rejected his appeal, grounding its ruling on the explicit wording of the revised statute amended by the legislator:

> Any material change in the language of the original act is presumed to indicate a change in legal rights. The legislature is presumed to know the prior construction of terms in the original act, and an amendment substituting a new term or phrase for one previously construed indicates that the judicial or executive construction of the former term or phrase did not correspond with the legislative intent and a different interpretation should be given the new term or phrase.[234]

It is worth noting that in 2006 the Iowa Supreme Court somewhat reversed and retracted its own ruling in the 1982 *Beeman* case. In the case of *Heemstra*,[235] the appellate court ruled that willful injury is a forcible predicated felony only in some circumstances: those that include serious bodily injury creating substantial risk of the victim's death, and are not the cause of the

231 *State* v. *Beeman* 315 N.W 2d. at 770. In Iowa, the felony-murder statute (section 707.02) enables first-degree murder convictions for the commission of "forcible felonies." The list of "forcible felonies" in 702.11 reveals that assault is listed as a forcible felony (together with murder, sexual abuse, kidnapping, robbery, first-degree arson and first degree burglary).

232 *State* v. *Beeman* 315 N.W 2d. at 772.

233 See Van Zanten 2008: 1583, referring to Beeman 315 N.W 2d. at 770.

234 See *State* v. *Beeman* 315 N.W 2d., at 777.

235 *State* v. *Heemstra* 721 N.W.2d 549, 558 (Iowa 2006).

victim's death. Otherwise, willful injury may not serve as a predicate felony despite the legislator's precise words:

> On further reflection, we adhere to the view that willful injury is a forcible felony under Iowa Code section 702.11 and, in *some circumstances*, may serve as a predicate for felony-murder purposes. For example, if the defendant assaulted the victim twice, first without killing him and second with fatal results, the former could be considered as a predicate felony, but the second could not because it would be merged with the murder.... We now hold that, if the act causing willful injury is the same act that causes the victim's death, the former is merged into the murder and therefore cannot serve as the predicate felony for felony-murder purposes. We therefore overrule those cases, insofar as they hold that the act constituting willful injury and also causing the victim's death may serve as a predicate felony for felony-murder purposes.[236]

The dissenting view of Judges Cady and Carter, who insisted that the legislators' explicit wording referring to the inclusion of a willful injury as a predicate felony murder should subordinate any opposing judicial interpretation, came to no avail.[237] This perplexing judicial interpretation is all the more reason to call for a much more explicit and decisive wording of the legislated predicated list within felony-murder statutes, to address circumstances of assaultive-femicide and avoid problematic judicial misinterpretation.

236 *State* v. *Heemstra* 721 N.W.2d 549 (Iowa 2006), at 558.

237 Justice Carter dissented stating that:

> In deciding the case as it does, *the majority of the court disregards the plain meaning of the controlling statutes* in order to obtain a result that is more pleasing to its own sense of justice than *the interpretation of the statute that is plainly evinced by the wording of the legislation and the legislative history*.... The rule of statutory interpretation that is embodied in our rules of appellate procedure insists that *in determining the meaning of statutes "the court searches for the legislative intent as shown by what the legislature said*, rather than what it should or might have said." (Italics added).
>
> (At p. 563)

Corroborating Carter's dissenting view, Justice Cady stated that holding that willful injury may not serve as the predicate felony under the felony-murder rule is not only contrary to established precedents of the court but also contrary to the manner by which the legislature has chosen for the felony-murder rule to operate in Iowa and added that "Under our limited role in government, it is not for us to chart a different course from the legislature" (at p. 569).

4 "To kill or be killed, (when) that is the question"

Femicide and the American criminal doctrine of self-defense

Introduction

As elaborated in Chapter 3, empirical findings assert that domestic violence is characterized by unique patterns.[1] These patterns include the fact that three-quarters of all attacks against women are committed by persons who are in or have been in an intimate relationship with these women; the fact that these attacks are likely to include rape and repeated sexual offenses; the fact that such assaults are characterized by severe physical injury equivalent to the severity of violence accompanying the highest level of crime; and the fact that these assaults constitute a pattern of continuous and escalating assaults that over time become increasingly severe, resulting in a greater likelihood of the women being killed. Of utmost importance for this chapter is the fact that a substantial portion of these battered women are eventually killed by their intimate partners in one last fatal blow, while it is rare for women to kill their intimate partners.[2] If and when women do kill, they are themselves prior victims of ongoing and severe domestic violence by the partner whom they killed.[3]

The significance of the empirical data and the unique characteristics of domestic violence is that, in practice, battered women are at concrete risk of severe physical injury or death, and that risk hovers over them not as a result of a one-time attack but as a result of an ongoing pattern of prolonged and sharply escalating attacks. Unfortunately, the empirical findings concerning the prevalence of violence against women (along with findings about the typical causes and circumstances associated with homicide committed by women), have not yet been appropriately translated into adequate legal presumptions with

1 For elaboration of the empirical findings and the criminological characteristics of domestic violence, see the beginning of Chapter 3.

2 Notwithstanding the absence of a systematic collection of precise data in the context of female perpetrators (the number of women in America who committed murder, those among them who killed their partners, those among them who alleged domestic violence, and those among them who alleged homicide in self-defense), the accepted estimate is that each year about 500 women kill their intimate partners. See Maguigan 1991: 379, 397, 400.

3 About 70 percent of women who used deadly force against their partners in self-defense had previously been consistently and severely battered by them. See Gillespie 1989: xii; Browne 1987: 143.

regard to the use of deadly protective force in circumstances of domestic violence. Consequently, it is almost impossible for a female defendant to obtain justice under the current criminal law doctrine of self-defense. Such battered women are therefore trapped forever in a grim and fatalistic existential dilemma – "to kill or be killed" – between the choice of continuing to suffer severe injury (and even mortal danger) and the choice of using effective protective force (and in an instant turning into defendants to a murder charge.)[4] Such an existential trap (set on one side by the violent perpetrator and on the other by the inadequacy of the current legal doctrine and its structure), may sadly lead battered women to end the unhappy and bitter saga of their lives by committing suicide.[5] Thus, the proper socio-legal handling of the phenomenon of defendants trapped in situations of domestic violence requires, inter alia, a legal arrangement that is well adapted to the unique characteristics of domestic violence in general and those of battered women who use deadly protective force, in particular. In order to promote legal clarity and prevent arbitrary interpretations of the law by fact finders,[6] it is imperative that a clear and explicit legal statutory arrangement is stated and regulated. Therefore, a focused and detailed legislative proposal to amend the Model Penal Code in this respect is articulated in the last chapter of this book.

The American doctrine of self-defense

As stated in previous chapters, American criminal law as a whole[7] is based on its forebear, the English doctrine.[8] The same is true of the legal criminal doctrine

4 Mackinnon 2001: 745; La Fond 1982: 271; Lee 2003: 135. It should be noted that the MPC enables a conviction for an intermediate level of awareness (the *mens rea* of negligence) and creates graduated categories of guilt which enable convictions for offenses less serious than murder (in cases lacking the *mens rea* required for a conviction for murder, where it is not possible to assert the claim of self-defense because of a failure to satisfy the doctrinal requirements). This "intermediate arrangement" is expressed in the text of Section 3.09 of the MPC but it is doubtful whether this legal arrangement is appropriate in cases of battered women who use protective force. For the opinion that an intermediate arrangement (enabling a conviction on the basis of the doctrine of "the defense of mistake") is appropriate in cases relating to battered women, see Sangero 2006: 349.

5 For a discussion of the connection between battered women's sense of "dead end" and their tendency to commit suicide, see Bergman and Brismar 1991: 380–384; Stark et al. 1979.

6 In this regard, see the arguments put by Maguigan 1991: 386–387. Likewise, see Gillespie 1989: 85.

7 The criminal jurisdiction over crimes relating to the federal structure of the United States (crimes relating to military bases, ambassadors, the federal law enforcement agencies or crimes that cross state borders) lies in federal hands (see Dubber and Robinson 1999). However, under the Constitution of the United States, the enforcement of criminal law relating to most crimes (murder, rape, robbery, assault, theft) falls within the jurisdiction of the states (US Constitution, Article 3, Section 2(3); Bill of Rights, 1791, Section 6). The state-level criminal jurisdiction makes it very difficult to shape a uniform federal criminal law that would be applicable to the entire United States (ibid.: 3). The criminal codes of the various states (prior to the drafting of the MPC) were not systematic and lacked comprehensive codification (an outcome of the English common law tradition which focused on the development of substantive law through case law (ibid.: 6], and therefore no federal statutory legislation was available prior to the drafting of the Model Penal Code.

8 In essence, the United States was founded by English colonists who were subject to British rule

of self-defense, which originally developed in medieval Britain.[9] The doctrine comprises an exception to the rule prohibiting the use of force,[10] and is particularly dramatic in the context of its application to acts of homicide that are considered to be justified upon implementation of the doctrine.[11] The traditional rules of the English doctrine of self-defense have hardly changed over the past 900 years[12] and comprise five main requirements:[13] the requirement to *repel an unlawful attack* (under which an act of self-defense is not an attack but a response to an attack unlawfully perpetrated upon the defendant); the requirement to respond to the unlawful attack in an *immediate* manner (under which the defendant has an immediate need to use force and cannot wait for police assistance); the requirement that the defendant's response is *proportional* (under which the damage caused by the defensive reaction of the defendant is not disproportionate to the damage that he is attempting to prevent); the requirement that the defendant's response is *necessary* (under which the defendant does everything he can to prevent the occurrence of the attack, including withdrawing from the scene in so far as possible); and the requirement that *the defendant's behavior prior to the attack is not unlawful* (under which the defendant has not brought about the circumstances in which he is compelled to use protective force, by virtue of his own unlawful behavior).

---

and the English legal system, until the settlers decided to sever themselves from Great Britain, and declared America's independence in 1776.

9 In circumstances where the government was unable to enforce security and the crime rate and numbers of homicides were among the highest in European history, see Gillespie 1989: 35. The English legal principles concerning the application of the claim of self-defense are ancient and are attributed to the Norman invasion in the eleventh century. For a review of the impact of the Norman invasion of England in the eleventh century and the subsequent changes in the English legal system in general and in the doctrine of self-defense in particular, see Leverick 2006: 1; Gillespie 1989: 32–35. For an historical review of medieval England and a cross comparison with America in the nineteenth and twentieth centuries, see Beeghley 2003: 41–77.

10 Herberling 1975: 930–931.

11 The judicial decision to apply the exemption from criminal liability to homicides committed by defendants in self-defense leads in effect to the full acquittal of the defendant. Such acquittals, as a rule, were deemed to be very unusual in light of the accepted Anglo-Saxon view that a defendant who killed a man was guilty of his death irrespective of the circumstances surrounding the killing. Prior to the refinement of the concept of killing in self-defense and its transformation into a principle of Anglo-Saxon law, English law applied a form of "strict liability" to any person who by his act – or even through his property – caused the death of another. The *mens rea* for causing death was completely irrelevant and therefore the particular *mens rea* of the act of homicide (for example, malice, negligence or mistake) had no legal significance in terms of the conviction. See Gillespie 1989: 31.

12 The doctrine developed primarily around two main situations of killing in self-defense: a fight escalating between men and an attack committed by a stranger. While the circumstances of killing by a stranger made almost no contribution to the development of the doctrine of self-defense, many doctrinal principles and rules developed in the context of fights between men. Ibid.: 40.

13 See Fletcher 1990: 18–38; Fletcher 1978: 865–875.

The principles of the American doctrine were codified by the states in the twentieth century and, until then, functioned as common law rulings.[14] As America emerged as an independent socio-cultural and political entity, its criminal doctrine developed into one that was distinct from its English forebear,[15] in so far as it abolished the duty to retreat[16] and softened most of the traditional English requirements for its application. Concurrently with the abolition of the duty to retreat as a pre-condition for asserting self-defense and the softening of most of other traditional English requirements, three additional unique features were later added to the American doctrine: the concept of a separate and distinct category for the use of deadly protective force;[17] the application of the reasonable man doctrine to the requirements of the self-defense doctrine (with the promotion of the subjective elements of reasonableness[18]); and the introduction of the policy permitting the use of force to prevent crime, into the doctrine of

14 The American doctrine that developed in the West was not codified at the time and therefore functioned in the same way as principles of American common law. Likewise, in the eastern states of the United States, in which comprehensive codification of the criminal law had been carried out even before the twentieth century, the doctrine of self-defense did not undergo codification, and therefore there too it was applied as part of the criminal law rules of common law. See Gillespie 1989: 48. Currently, the doctrine of self-defense is regulated in legislation in all but four of the states of the United States (Maryland, Massachusetts, New Mexico and Virginia).

15 The endemic changes to the doctrine are related to unique socio-cultural and geographical characteristics of the British colonists in America of the eighteenth and nineteenth centuries, in the context of which, for example, the prerequisite of retreat was regarded as overly "soft" for the settlers: in the western states of America, the settlements were sporadic and geographically remote from any center of government which could have enforced law and order; retreat in such circumstances was regarded as improper submission. Ibid., 42. Abolition of the duty to retreat requirement and the ethos of "standing one's ground" were reflected in the mythological figure of the sinless cowboy in American culture who expressed the "real American man":

> The figure of the lone hero – be he cowboy, sheriff or outlaw – had reached truly mythic proportions in the popular mind in the last decades of the nineteenth century. He was a "man's man," a two-fisted fighter, never a coward or a bully, never entangled by the Victorian society that his idolizers were tied to, beholden to no one but himself. As Teddy Roosevelt described: "A cowboy will not submit tamely to an insult, and is ever ready to avenge his own wrongs, nor has he an overwrought fear of shedding blood … *he does possess, to a very high degree, the stern, manly qualities that are invaluable to the nation.*"
>
> (Italics added, ibid.: 46)

16 Alongside the general requirement to avoid in so far as possible any involvement in the use of force, exceptions developed to the application of the claim of self-defense (in so far as concerned shooting a person in the back or shooting an unarmed man, or where the act was not an immediate response to the attack. See Gillespie 1989: 42–43, 67). With the end of the frontier era, the expansive doctrine relating to abolition of the duty to retreat prerequisite was gradually narrowed in the western states by means of exacting case law; however, in general the perception that it was appropriate for a man to stand his ground and respond to an attack was broadly accepted in American society, including in particular in the context of the American criminal law doctrine of self-defense. See also Carpenter 2003: 663.

17 Herberling 1975: 933.

18 Sangero 2006: 114–115.

self-defense.[19] These American doctrinal developments were explicitly and statutorily articulated in the American criminal code formulations in the Model Penal Code in the 1950s. The Model Penal Code has had a notable impact on legislative reforms made to subsequent state criminal codes[20] and, in fact, its wording provides the current prototype for the doctrine of self-defense in all the U.S. states.[21]

The doctrine of self-defense in the Model Penal Code has shifted even further away from its British forebear and strengthened the expansive American approach towards the range of applicability of the criminal exception in circumstances where protective force is used. The philosophical and a priori premise of the doctrine in the Model Penal Code sees moral justification in the act of self-defense – justification that is not in any way at the mercy of the legal system in terms of applying the exemption or obtaining forgiveness for the use of protective force.[22] According to the "justification" approach adopted by the Model Penal Code, a person has no need for an exemption from criminal responsibility and is not subject to any criminal liability in circumstances where, not only does he not commit any illegal act, but actually acts in a moral and justified manner.[23] In terms of the moral approach of "justification," the American doctrine of self-defense in the Model Penal Code has expanded the circumstances in which the doctrine applies in relation to four of the main traditional English requirements for the use of protective force. The Model Penal Code has extended the abolition of the duty to retreat by adding to the circumstances in which a person can retreat without danger all other circumstances in which the attack takes place in

19 Ibid.: 115, thereby blurring the distinction between them to some extent.

20 See Herberling 1975: 914–915.

21 Ibid. Dubber and Robinson 1999: 5. In light of the legislative amendments in the various states of the United States, the Model Penal Code had a critical impact on creating certain similarities between the criminal codes of the various states, albeit not all the legal arrangements proposed by the drafters of the Model Penal Code were adopted. For example, many states have still preserved the common law felony-murder rule, even though the drafters of the Model Penal Code abolished this murder offense. Similarly, many states still apply different rules to attempted offenses and completed offenses, whereas the Model Penal Code advocates equivalent punishment for completed offenses and uncompleted offenses. In general, there is still considerable variation between the states on various criminal issues, variation that is entrenched in the absence of effective federal legislation. See Gillespie 1989: 183–184.

22 The text of the Model Penal Code expressly states that this is an exception to criminal liability that takes the form of "justification." See Section 3.02 heading: "Justification Generally: Choice of Evils," Section 3.04(1): Use of Force Justifiable for Protection of the Person. Subject to the provisions of this Section and of Section 3.09, the use of force upon or toward another person is justifiable," and *Model Penal Code Official Commentaries* 1985. Philadelphia: American Law Institute p. 32.

23 For the distinction between "justification" and "excuse," and the approach of the Model Penal Code in this context, see Herberling 1975: 916–925. There are those who argue that a philosophical premise which applies "justification" to all instances of private defense (for example, the defense of necessity) without distinguishing between various instances of private defense which are not justified and require a premise of excuse (for example the "defense of mistake"), is mistaken. See Sangero 2006: 114; Herberling 1975: 919, 923.

the victim's home or workplace.[24] In addition, the Model Penal Code has implicitly loosened the requirement to repel an unlawful assault by substituting the objective standard applied to such requirements. The substitution of the objective standard for a subjective one has expanded the range of circumstances in which the assertion of self-defense may be claimed and accepted.[25] The Model Penal Code has also loosened the traditional English requirement for immediacy by determining that no specific proximity is required.[26] Additionally, it implicitly ameliorated the traditional English requirement for proportionality by articulating

24 The Model Penal Code does not require the defendant to retreat in circumstances in which he believes it would not be effective or would endanger him; in particular, the Model Penal Code does not require the defendant to retreat in his home or place of work: Section 3.04(2)(b)(ii)(A) "the actor is not obliged to retreat from his dwelling or place of work." The Official Commentaries to the text of the Model Penal Code (*Model Penal Code Official Commentaries* 1985. Philadelphia: American Law Institute) state on p. 56:

> The provision also exempts from the duty to retreat a person in his place of work. Because the sentimental factors relevant to dwellings may not apply to one's place of work, it can be argued that this extension is inappropriate; but it was concluded that the practical considerations concerning the two locations were far too similar to sustain distinction.

For further explanation of this position, see *Model Penal Code and Commentaries (Official Draft and Revised Comments)* 1985: 54–55.

25 With regard to the prerequisite of repelling an unlawful act (which is, in effect, a pre-condition for the application of the doctrine as a whole), the Model Penal Code expands the subjective element and states that it is not required that the attack that leads to the use of protective force be indeed unlawful. Instead, it is sufficient if the defendant believes that the attack against which he defends himself is unlawful: "There is no requirement that the force against which the actor defends himself be unlawful. It is enough that he believes it to be so." See ibid.: 40. See also the text of the law: Section 3.04(1)

> ... the use of force upon or toward another person is justifiable when the actor believes that such force is immediately necessary for the purpose of protecting himself against the use of unlawful force by such other person on the present occasion.

The approach of the Model Penal Code greatly strengthens the subjective element found in the requirement of reasonableness, and requires the defendant to act on the basis of his subjective assessment of the danger, and exert the protective force needed in his assessment to repel the attack. See ibid.: 35.

26 According to the provision, no strict proximity is required. Rather, an assessment may be made of time deemed relevant in the context of protective force against an attack. Nonetheless, most U.S. states have chosen not to follow the Model Penal Code's wording "immediately necessary," and instead use the imminence test. See Herberling 1975: 931. The Model Penal Code's terminology in Section 3.04(1) is: "... such force is immediately necessary for the purpose of protecting himself against the use of unlawful force by such other person on the present occasion." Regarding the particular choice of this wording, the MPC Official Commentaries state:

> The actor must believe that his defensive action is immediately necessary and the unlawful force against which he defends must be force that he apprehends will be used on the present occasion, but he need not apprehend that it will be used immediately ... present occasion. The latter words are used in preference to imminent or immediate to introduce the latitude for the attainment of a just result in cases of this kind.
>
> (*Model Penal Code and Commentaries (Official Draft and Revised Comments)* 1985: 39–40)

a distinctive category of protective deadly force[27] that permits the use of such force in circumstances where there is no actual danger to life (e.g., in kidnapping and rape cases).[28] Accordingly, it is safe to argue that four out of the five main traditional English requirements for asserting the claim of self-defense have been made much more flexible by the Model Penal Code.

Prima facie, therefore, the Model Penal Code should have been able to sufficiently accommodate circumstances of domestic violence, within its current doctrine of self-defense. However, as will be demonstrated below, the Model Penal Code has remained unchanged since it was drafted in the 1950s, and is greatly lacking in all gender-related aspects of criminal law.[29] As a result, despite its considerable flexibility, the Model Penal Code contains a distorted legal arrangement with regard to the application of the self-defense doctrine in situations where battered women kill their aggressors.

27 The MPC does not explicitly deal with the prerequisite of proportionality, but rather relates to it implicitly primarily in the context of the use of protective deadly force. See Sangero. 2006: 114; Herberling 1975: 113. The section states as follows: Section 3.04(2) (b): "The use of deadly force is not justifiable under this section unless the actor believes that such force is necessary to protect himself against death, serious bodily injury, kidnapping or sexual intercourse compelled by force or threat" ... The prerequisite of proportionality is dealt with through the exception to criminal liability arising from the use of deadly protective force in circumstances which the legislature deems to be extreme and consequently justify the use of deadly protective force ("Clearly deadly force, as so conceived, should be privileged only in extreme situations." *Model Penal Code and Commentaries (Official Draft and Revised Comments)* 1985: 47). The creation of this legal presumption in the context of the situations referred to in the text of the law also gives rise, in effect, to the prerequisite of proportionality, even though it is not explicitly referred to in this context. In this regard, see the MPC and Official Commentaries, ibid.: 47–48, relating to the common law notion of proportionality: "the formulation rests on the common law principle that the amount of force used by the actor must bear a reasonable relation to the magnitude of the harm that he seeks to avert." For the argument to the effect that the concealed prerequisite of proportionality applies generally in all the criminal codes of the U.S. states which enable the use of deadly protective force in situations of real life threatening danger, see La Fond 1982: 270–275, 239–241.

28 Particularly relevant to this legal conclusion is the situation of rape, which appears in Section 3.04(2)(b) as one that enables the application of deadly protective force even if there is no genuine threat to life. In this context, for example, the drafters of the MPC considered that rape is a situation that justifies the use of deadly protective force even in the absence of real danger to life, if only because of the existence of a social convention (and ancillary legal presumption) that an act of rape harms a supreme social value:

> the premise is, of course, that the discouragement of the infliction of death or serious bodily injury is so high on the scale of preferred societal values that such infliction cannot be justified by reference to the protection of an interest of any lesser pretentions....
>
> (MPC Official Commentaries *Model Penal Code and Commentaries (Official Draft and Revised Comments)* 1985: 48)

29 This area enjoyed considerable development over the past 30 years in the United States and in practice forms one of the most prominent features of American criminal law today. See Sangero 2006: 116; Dubber and Robinson 1999: 7.

The American doctrine of self-defense in circumstances of domestic violence

Though the requirements of the American doctrine of self-defense[30] were greatly eased compared to the traditional English demands, they are still problematic in the context of their application to women in general and, in particular, to battered women who kill their aggressors. Of the five requirements of the doctrine, female defendants facing prosecution for killing their aggressive intimate partners will at most satisfy two of the requirements in terms of their typical conduct and patterns of response: the requirement to behave lawfully prior to their use of force; and the requirement that their use of force be in response to an unlawful assault against them.[31] As the legal requirements for successfully asserting self-defense in this regard are not alternative but cumulative, the significance of merely partial compliance with the legal requirements is fatal. In essence, ***any non-compliance (however partial) with the doctrinal legal requirements suffices to decide the fate of such defendants, namely, their probable conviction for murder***. The critical legal discourse that has taken place over the past 30 years has indeed denounced the incompatibility between the current legal doctrine and its application to women in general[32] and battered women in particular. The critical scholars have highlighted the miscarriage of justice resulting from the failure to adjust at least three of the existing traditional doctrinal requirements to the application of a self-defense claim: the requirements of immediacy, proportionality and necessity (interpreted as the duty to retreat).

Much criticism has been directed at the rigid application of the requirement of immediacy,[33] which inevitably and a priori leads to the rejection of a defendant's

30 Downs 1996: 229–230.

31 For this reason I do not find it necessary to intervene in respect of these two prerequisites in the present legal arrangements.

32 For the masculine foundations of the self-defense doctrine, see Crocker 1985: 121, 123, 126; Fiora-Gormally 1978: 133, 158; Mather 1988: 545, 569; Reece 1991: 53, 55; Gillespie 1989: 31–49, 99–100; Downs 1984: 228.

33 Battered women who killed their assailing partners are most often convicted by reason of a judicial conclusion that the defendants did not comply with the prerequisite of immediacy. See Gillespie 1989: 76. For the opinion that the prerequisite of immediacy should be left intact, even in the context of battered women, see Leverick 2006: 1; Gillespie 1989: 96, 101. See also the arguments put forward by Maguigan generally and in particular Maguigan's assertion that there is no significant discrepancy between the legal doctrine of self-defense and the unique characteristics of battered women who respond in self-defense (Maguigan 1991: 381–382), and that the doctrine of self-defense as formulated is capable of accommodating an examination of the specific social context of the attack (ibid.: 383, 401–405). More specifically, she argues that the existing legislative arrangement allows the application of the doctrine in circumstances of domestic violence in the context of the immediacy prerequisite (as, according to Maguigan, the majority of cases of self-defense engaged in by battered women do not occur during a period of respite or when the partner is asleep – but during the course of unlawful assault (ibid.: 384–385, 391–401)). For criticism of the research methodology and conclusions reached by Maguigan in this context, see Downs 1984: 139; in the context of the prerequisite of proportionality (because there is no explicit prohibition on the use of weapons when defending oneself from an attack, and

claim of self-defense, if and when the protective response takes place during a period of respite or when the immediate danger has seemingly passed.[34] The main argument concerning the requirement for an immediate protective response is its inconsistency with empirical findings regarding the characteristics of domestic violence[35] as well as with findings demonstrating that the requirement to respond while being attacked may actually exacerbate the intensity and severity of the violence directed against such victims.[36] In this context, criticism has also been voiced against the judicial tendency to examine the prerequisite of immediacy from a narrow and concrete perspective that embraces only those events directly linked to the time of the homicide (independently of the continuous, cumulative, cyclical and escalating dynamic of domestic violence). Such judicial examination of the direct events linked to the homicide lead to the incorrect judicial classification of the battered women's responses as mere attacks, hence criminal offenses.[37]

Gender discourse has also criticized judicial decisions, concluding that through their protective response battered women who kill their aggressors grossly overstep the requirement of proportionality,[38] on the ground that the requirement of proportionality, per se, is totally inappropriate in circumstances of predetermined physical asymmetry and inequality.[39] The legal criticism in this

---

because the U.S. states tend to examine compliance with the requirement using contextualization) (Maguigan 1991: 416–419); in the context of the prerequisite of reasonableness (as only a minority of states still employ a strict objective test (ibid.: 409–413)); and in the context of the duty to retreat (as most U.S. states do not require a retreat, and the few that do demand it qualify the requirement where the attack takes place at the defendant's home (ibid.: 419–420)). Similarly, Maguigan asserts that there is no need for legislative reform of the existing procedural law, as in many states in the United States the procedural law allows relevant evidence to be brought regarding the circumstances of the violence (whether through the regulation of expert testimony in general, or by utilizing existing possibilities for adducing evidence in the context of homicide, in particular. Ibid.: 421–423). Maguigan argues that, to the extent that a problem exists in the context of battered women facing criminal charges, that problem does not stem from the wording of the existing legislative arrangements in the substantive and procedural law but rather the manner of their implementation by the judges and members of the jury (ibid.: 386–387, 432–438).

34 Willoughby 1989: 196; Schneider 1980: 623, 634; Mather 1988: 567; Crocker 1985: 145 note 106; Rosen C. 1986: 11, 43; Talbot 1988: 1527, 1528–1529. For the opinion that, empirically, most killings by battered woman can be described as "confrontational" and therefore meet the prerequisite of imminence, see: Maguigan 1991: 384–385, 391–401. For reservations regarding Maguigan's observations, see Downs 1984: 139.

35 Fiora-Gormally 1978: 154; Rosen C. 1986: 34; Gillespie 1989: 68–69, 71.

36 Schneider 1980: 634. Gillespie notes in relation to this requirement: "The imminence requirement can sometimes turn a life and death situation into a macabre game of timing" (see Gillespie 1989: 71.

37 Rosen C. 1986: 11, 31; Gillespie 1989: 72, 81–87.

38 Mather 1988: 587; Gillespie 1989: 93–94.

39 I.e., circumstances where the woman who has been unlawfully attacked is weaker and more inexperienced in the exchange of punches. McColgan 1993: 544; Gillespie 1989: 69, 88, 92, 100–122; La Fond 1982: 250.

regard attests to the fact that compelling a defendant to persuade the court that the use of deadly protective force under the circumstances was proportionate because she faced a real danger to her life is extremely problematic in situations of domestic violence.

Perhaps the case of Judy Ann Laws Norman is the best-known case in the U.S. that rejected the claim of self-defense because the protective response took place during a period of respite or when the immediate danger had seemingly passed. This was the horrific tale of a severely battered woman who was unsuccessful in her claim that she had ultimately killed her batterer in self-defense.[40]

According to the court, at the time of the killing Judy Norman was 39 years old. She had been married to John Thomas for almost 25 years. They had several children and she had been abused by him for more than 20 years. The physical abuse consisted of frequent assaults that included slapping, punching, kicking, striking her with various objects and throwing glasses, beer bottles and other objects at her. Judy also described other specific incidents of abuse, such as her husband putting out cigarettes on her, throwing hot coffee on her, breaking glass against her face and crushing food on her face. She also presented evidence that showed other indignities inflicted upon her by her husband, among them that her husband did not work and forced her to make money in prostitution. As if this was not enough, to family and friends he would make fun of the fact that she made money as a prostitute. He would beat her if she resisted going out to prostitute herself or if he was unsatisfied with the sums of money she made. He routinely called her by degrading names such as "dog," "bitch" and "whore," and on several occasions severely humiliated her by making her eat pet food out of the pets' bowls and bark like a dog. He often made her sleep on the floor. At times he deprived her of food and refused to let her get food for the family. During the years of abuse, Judy's husband threatened to kill her on numerous occasions and to maim her in various ways.[41]

In the early morning hours on the day before his death, Judy's husband, who was intoxicated, went to a rest area off I-85 near Kings Mountain where Judy was engaged in prostitution and assaulted her. While driving home, he was stopped by a patrolman and jailed on a charge of driving while impaired. After Judy's mother got him out of jail later that morning at Judy's request, he resumed his drinking and abuse of Judy. The court noted that Judy's evidence also tended to show that her husband seemed angrier than ever after he was released from jail and that his abuse of her was more frequent. That evening, sheriff's deputies were called to the Norman residence, and Judy complained that her husband had beaten her all day and that she could not take it any more. Judy was advised to file a complaint, but she said she was afraid her husband would kill her if she had him arrested. The deputies told her they needed a warrant before they could arrest her husband, and they left the scene. The

40 *State of North Carolina* v. *Judy Ann Laws Norman*, 324 N.C. 253, 1988.
41 Ibid.: 255.

deputies were called back less than an hour later after Judy had taken a bottle of pills. While the paramedics attended to her, Judy's husband cursed her, called her names and told them to let her die. A sheriff's deputy finally chased him back into his house, as Judy was put into an ambulance. Judy's stomach was pumped at the local hospital, and she was sent home with her mother.[42]

While in the hospital, Judy was visited by a therapist with whom she discussed filing charges against her husband and having him committed for treatment. Before the therapist left, Judy agreed to go to the mental health center the next day to discuss these possibilities. The next day, Judy went to the mental health center to talk about filing charges and possible commitment, and she confronted her husband with that possibility. She testified that she told her husband later that day: "J. T., straighten up. Quit drinking. I'm going to have you committed to help you." He then responded that he would "see them coming" and would cut her throat before they got to him. Judy also went to the social services office that day to seek welfare benefits, but her husband followed her there, interrupted her interview and made her go home with him. He continued his abuse of her, threatening to kill and maim her, slapping her, kicking her and throwing objects at her. At one point he took her cigarette and put it out on her, causing a small burn on her upper torso. He would not let her eat or bring food into the house for their children. That evening, Judy and her husband went into their bedroom to lie down, and he called her a "dog" and made her lie on the floor when he lay down on the bed. Their daughter brought her baby to stay with Judy, and Judy received her husband's agreement to let her babysit. After he fell asleep the baby started crying, and fearing that her husband would wake up Judy took the baby to her mother's house.[43] Judy took a pistol from her mother's purse and walked the short distance back to her home. She pointed the pistol at the back of her sleeping husband's head, but it jammed the first time she tried to shoot him. She fixed the gun and then shot her husband in the back of the head as he lay sleeping. After one shot she felt her husband's chest and determined that he was still breathing and making sounds. She then shot him twice more in the back of the head.[44] When asked at trial why she killed her husband, Judy replied:

> Because I was scared of him and I knowed when he woke up, it was going to be the same thing, and I was scared when he took me to the truck stop that night it was going to be worse than he had ever been. I just couldn't take it no more. There ain't no way, even if it means going to prison. It's better than living in that. That's worse hell than anything.[45]

42 Ibid.: 256.
43 Ibid.: 257.
44 Ibid.: 255.
45 Ibid.: 258.

Judge Martin argued that evidence presented by Judy described a 20-year history of beating and other dehumanizing and degrading treatment by her husband, and repeated the clinical psychologist's testimony that analogized her abuse to the dehumanization process suffered by prisoners of war under the Nazis during the Second World War and the brainwashing techniques of the Korean War.[46] However, the evidence about Judy's atrocious, severe, prolonged and escalating physical, emotional, economic and mental abuse by her husband was to no avail. The trial court did not find Judy's tormenting abuse fit for jury instructions to consider whether her case was a self-defense case. Though the jury acquitted her of the first-degree murder indictment of her husband, Judy was found guilty of manslaughter.[47] Judy appealed her conviction, based on evidence presented about the battered wife syndrome and her genuine belief that she could not escape her husband without him hunting her and beating her to death for doing so, and also based on her sound prior experiences that she could not expect help from others, and on her husband's continuous and escalating threats and abuse that worsened in the two days preceding the killing. Notwithstanding the uncontroverted evidence that she shot her husband three times in the back of the head as he lay sleeping in his bed, Judy claimed that she was rightfully entitled to have her jury instructed to consider whether the homicide was an act of perfect self-defense.[48] The court of appeals found Judy's unspeakable abuse worthy of self-defense consideration and granted a new trial.[49]

Judy was not granted the chance to have her claim of self-defense considered. The prosecution filed for a review of the appellate judgment, and the second appeal's ruling stated that the trial court properly declined to instruct Judy's jury on the law relating to self-defense. The second court of appeals' main argument in reversing the first court of appeals decision awarding Judy a new trial in which the jury would be instructed to consider whether she acted in self-defense was based on the requirement of imminence, to which they ruled that Judy did not adhere. According to the court, the evidence in Judy's case did not tend to show that she reasonably believed that she was confronted by a threat of imminent death or great bodily harm. To the contrary, grounding their decision on the uncontroverted evidence that Judy's husband had been asleep for some time when she walked to her mother's house, returned with the pistol, fixed the pistol after it jammed and then shot him three times in the back of the head, the second court of appeals ruled that the evidence tended to show that no harm was "imminent" or about to happen to Judy when she shot her husband. In trying to explain their ruling the second court of appeals stated:

46 In his dissent, ibid.: 268.
47 Ibid.: 253–254.
48 Ibid.: 259.
49 Ibid.: 254.

> The defendant was not faced with an instantaneous choice between killing her husband or being killed or seriously injured. Instead, all of the evidence tended to show that the defendant had ample time and opportunity to resort to other means of preventing further abuse by her husband. There was no action underway by the decedent from which the jury could have found that the defendant had reasonable grounds to believe either that a felonious assault was imminent or that it might result in her death or great bodily injury. Additionally, no such action by the decedent had been underway immediately prior to his falling asleep ... We are not persuaded by the reasoning of our Court of Appeals in this case that when there is evidence of battered wife syndrome, neither an actual attack nor threat of attack by the husband at the moment the wife uses deadly force is required to justify the wife's killing of him in perfect self-defense.... The reasoning of our Court of Appeals in this case proposes to change the established law of self-defense by giving the term "imminent" a meaning substantially more indefinite and all-encompassing than its present meaning. This would result in a substantial relaxation of the requirement of real or apparent necessity to justify homicide. Such reasoning proposes justifying the taking of human life not upon the reasonable belief it is necessary to prevent death or great bodily harm – which the imminence requirement ensures – but upon purely subjective speculation that the decedent probably would present a threat to life at a future time and that the defendant would not be able to avoid the predicted threat. As we have stated, stretching the law of self-defense to fit the facts of this case would require changing the "imminent death or great bodily harm" requirement to something substantially more indefinite than previously required and would weaken our assurances that justification for the taking of human life remains firmly rooted in real or apparent necessity. That result in principle could not be limited to a few cases decided on evidence as poignant as this. ***The relaxed requirements for perfect self-defense proposed by our Court of Appeals would tend to categorically legalize the opportune killing of abusive husbands by their wives*** solely on the basis of the wives' testimony concerning their subjective speculation as to the probability of future felonious assaults by their husbands. ***Homicidal self-help would then become a lawful solution, and perhaps the easiest and most effective solution, to this problem.***[50]

Eventually, and lamentably, Judy was not awarded a new trial where her claim for self-defense could be truly and legally considered. Judy's conviction of voluntary manslaughter was affirmed and she was sent to prison.

Consider Theresa's case, yet another example where the battered wife considered the abuser's killing necessary because her life was in real danger.[51]

50 Italics added, ibid.: 262–264.

51 See *THE PEOPLE, Respondent*, v. T*HERESA JONES, Appellant*, Crim. No. 7470, Court of Appeal of California, Second Appellate District, Division Two, 191 Cal. App. 2d 478; 12 Cal. Rptr. 777; 1961 Cal. App. LEXIS 2076.

During their married life, Theresa's husband LeRoy had beaten her on numerous occasions (480). The homicide occurred on the evening of March 21, 1960, at their home. They were arguing for quite some time prior to LeRoy leaving the house at 9 o'clock, and resumed the argument upon his return. It seemed as if LeRoy had been drinking. *Theresa recounted that LeRoy cursed her and threatened to beat her when the children went to bed. Later he picked up a table knife, with which he had been eating, held it up and said, "I will throw this knife at you." Finally, he threatened to kill her. He stood up with the knife in his hand, raised it, and took some steps.*[52] At that point Theresa recalls turning to the buffet, near where she was sitting, and procuring a .22 caliber pistol purchased by her about six weeks before. Theresa testified that she shot toward the ceiling and admonished LeRoy not to come close to her. But he kept advancing, and as Theresa further testified, "I was afraid he was going to jump on me or kill me or beat me or something, and I just couldn't take no more beating." It was then that she shot him.[53]

The court of appeals ruled out justifiable homicide. The court rejected Theresa's claim of self-defense and ruled that she did not meet the traditional common law doctrine requiring reasonableness, real life danger or great bodily injury, imminent danger, necessity and proportionality. According to the court, Theresa was not in real and tangible danger even at the time when her husband kept approaching her and threatened to kill her while holding a knife because, according to the court, unless proven otherwise battered wives do not seem to be in and of themselves in a situation of great bodily harm while being assaulted:

> To justify a homicide committed by one in resisting or repelling an assault or battery committed or attempted to be committed upon his person by another, it must appear to the slayer as a reasonable man that a threatened danger is immediate, and such appearance of danger must be sufficient to excite the fears of a reasonable person, if in like position, that he was in danger of receiving death or great bodily harm, and the slayer must act under the influence of such fears and not in a spirit of revenge; and further, the degree of resistance must not be clearly disproportionate to the nature of the injury offered or given; the force used in repelling or resisting the assault or battery must not be clearly greater than is apparently necessary.[54]

52 Italics added.

53 Ibid.: 779.

54 The court further stated:

> A homicide is justified and not punishable when committed by a person in the lawful defense of himself, when he has reasonable ground to apprehend that he is in danger of death or great bodily injury and that there is imminent danger of such a design being accomplished. The acts which a person may do in self-defense and justify under a plea of self-defense depend upon the conduct of those involved in the encounter and the circumstances attending it. No fixed rule is

Clearly the appellate court deemed Theresa's shooting in relation to the threat towards her with a knife as disproportionate, and ruled that her reading of the situation when she was under a knife attack against her as an imminent deadly or great bodily harm threat as unreasonable. Even more bizarre was the court's interpretation and blunt disregard of even the statutory wording with respect to the felonious legal definition of a wife assault, according to which Theresa claimed that the homicide statute itself accords battered wives legal justified use of deadly protective force. Theresa argued that the wording of the statute defines homicide as justifiable and not unlawful "when committed by any person when resisting any attempt to murder any person, or to *commit a felony*, or to do some great bodily injury upon any person."[55] Nonetheless, inexplicably the court deemed that, even though the California Penal Code[56] provides that homicide is justifiable when resisting an attempt to commit a felony, the correct legal application of such wording should not be literal, and should not refer to any felony as such, but rather should be "limited to the commission of felonies that involve a danger of great personal harm, or some atrocious crime attempted to be committed by force."[57] Thus, strangely enough, the court concluded that Theresa's physical assault by her husband with a deadly weapon should not be

> applicable to every case, but certain general principles are established as guides for the jury's determination. The law of self-defense is founded on the principle of necessity, either actual or apparent, and in order to justify the taking of human life on this ground the slayer, as a reasonable man, must have reason to believe and must believe that he is in danger of receiving great bodily harm; and further, the circumstances must be such that an ordinarily reasonable person, if he were in those circumstances and if he knew and saw what such person in real or apparent danger knows or sees, would believe it was necessary for him to use, in his defense and to avoid great bodily injury to himself, such force or means as might cause the death of his adversary. A bare fear that a person's life or limb is in danger is not sufficient to justify a homicide. To justify taking the life of another in self-defense, the circumstances must be such as to excite the fears of a reasonable person placed in a similar position, and the party killing must act under the influence of such fears alone. The danger must be apparent and must be present and imminent, or must so appear at the time to the slayer as a reasonable person, and the killing must be done under a well-founded belief that it is necessary to save one's self from death or great bodily harm.
>
> (At p. 480)

55 The Penal Code of California, Section 197, subdivision 1.

56 Ibid.

57 The court further stated that the section:

> does no more than codify the common law and should be read in the light of it. Taken at face value, and without qualification, it represents an oversimplification of the law today. The authorities generally rely on Blackstone for the earliest expression of the rule. He rationalized it in terms of no killing being justified to prevent crime unless the offense was punishable by death. (4 Blackstone's Commentaries, pp. 180–182.) But in those days all felonies were capital offenses. Perhaps the leading American case on the point is *Storey* v. *State*, 71 Ala. 329, 336–341, where the early law is reviewed and rejected, and the application of the rule limited to the commission of felonies that involve a danger of great personal harm, or "some atrocious crime attempted to be committed by force." This limitation is today generally recognized. (Perkins on Criminal Law, 1957 ed., pp. 880–883; 1 Wharton's Criminal Law, Anderson, 1957 ed., pp. 453–456; 1 Warren on Homicide, 1938 ed., pp. 634–637.) Any

equated with a felony. Such a judicial interpretation is in contrast to the explicit literal wording of the relevant statute in section 273d of the California Penal Code at the time, which clearly instructs that "Any husband who willfully inflicts upon his wife corporal injury resulting in a traumatic condition is guilty of a felony." The court went even further when it stated that the legal interpretation of such physical assault by her husband as a felonious crime was an "unrealistic and artificial interpretation" of the statute:

> The legislative purpose in enacting section 273d, Penal Code, was to reduce domestic conflict, not to promote resort to violence in the household.... In creating the statutory felony of wife-beating the purpose of the legislature was not to issue a license for a wife to kill her husband, but to provide a means of dealing with a particular family situation. The punishment provided by a statute is not necessarily an adequate test as to whether life may be taken for in some situations *it is too artificial and unrealistic.*[58]

Regrettably, Theresa's motion for a new trial was denied. Her conviction of manslaughter was thus affirmed and she was sentenced to the state prison.

In addition to criticism of the requirement of real and substantial danger to life and the proportionality between the attack and the protective act, the demand that battered women retreat from their own home in order to avoid being attacked (and thus satisfy the traditional doctrinal requirement of necessity that is translated into the duty to retreat) has been criticized as incompatible with the concrete circumstances of battered women.[59] Consider for example the

---

> civilized system of law recognizes the supreme value of human life, and excuses or justifies its taking only in cases of apparent absolute necessity.
>
> (*State* v. *Nodine*, 198 Ore. 679 [259 P.2d 1056, 1067–1071], at p. 482)

58 Italics added. The court of appeal further stated:

> We must look further into the character of the crime, and the manner of its perpetration.... When these do not reasonably create a fear of great bodily harm, as they could not if defendant apprehended only a misdemeanor assault, there is no cause for the exaction of a human life. A misdemeanor assault must be suffered without the privilege of retaliating with deadly force.... *The fact that the assault is committed by a husband should not alter the rule. The existence of the matrimonial status should be an additional reason to forego resort to a homicide.*
>
> (Italics added, at p. 481)

The court further argued that their interpretation of the non-felonious nature of wife-beating is further implied in line with the language of the homicide statute:

> (Pen. Code, §197, subd. 1) lends support to this view. It states that homicide is justifiable in resisting an attempt to murder, or to commit a felony, or to do some great bodily injury. *By implication, the felony contemplated by the statute is one that is more dangerous than a personal assault.*
>
> (Italics added. Op cit.)

59 In the case of battered women, this demand is often translated into a question that troubles many: "why don't they leave?" Gillespie 1989: 77–81. For the opinion that, in cases of battered women,

horrific and unbearable abuse that Betty[60] suffered at the hands of her husband, coming close to dying on several occasions before ultimately shooting and killing him. The following is Betty's prolonged battery as recounted by Dubin:[61]

> Betty and Carl Hundley had been married for ten years. Betty's accounts of the marriage sound more like that of a prisoner of war than a blissful wedlock. During their marriage, Carl knocked several of Betty's teeth loose, broke her nose many times, and threatened to cut her eyes out and cut off her head. Betty suffered from diabetes which laid a fertile ground for Carl to play his sadistic games. He would often hide her insulin or, if he was feeling particularly playful, would dilute it with water. Needless to say, Betty drifted into diabetic comas on numerous occasions. Six weeks before Carl's death, Betty moved to a local motel in an attempt to escape the abuse. Carl immediately began harassing her with death threats directed at her and her family. Betty, fearing for her life, began carrying a gun. On the day of the shooting, Carl warned Betty he was going to kill her that night. That evening, he broke into Betty's motel room while she was in the bathroom. He forced her into the shower with him where he proceeded to shave her pubic hair in a rough and brutal manner, severely cutting her. This sadistic gesture was followed by a brutal rape. Afterward, Carl threw a dollar bill at her and while holding a beer bottle in his hand, demanded she go fetch him some cigarettes. In the past, Carl had severely beaten Betty with a beer bottle. She retrieved the gun from her purse believing another beating, or worse, was forthcoming. Carl responded, "You are dead, bitch, now!" As he reached for the beer bottle, Betty closed her eyes and slowly squeezed the trigger.[62]

Betty's claim of self-defense was unsuccessful. The jury did not find that she was in "immediate" danger, therefore not meeting the necessity requirement. In this respect, the Kansas Supreme court stated that, since Betty's last attack did not occur in an isolated area where help was unattainable, Betty's protective act did not appear reasonably necessary: "At the very least, defendant would have had a five minute head start on the defendant had she failed to return with the cigarettes."[63] Unfortunately, this false presumption that a battered woman is free to leave safely in the heat of an attack undermines her credibility and ultimately her chances of a successful claim of using deadly protective force. Under such circumstances the real, life-threatening danger to Betty was not the outcome of a one-time or concrete sadistic shaving and brutal rape but persisted as a constant danger, shaped by the unique characteristics of the violence she had been

retreat from home should not be exempted from the retreat rule, because of the aggressor's rights to life, see Leverick 2006: 83–85.

60 *State* v. *Hundley*, 693 P.2d 475 (Kan. 1985).

61 Dubin 1995: 238–239.

62 *State* v. *Hundley*, 693 P.2d 475 (Kan. 1985) at 475–476.

63 *State* v. *Hundley*, 693 P.2d 475 (Kan. 1985), 481.

experiencing from her husband:[64] it was the gradual, inevitable and objective escalation of real life-threatening danger, characteristic of the cyclical pattern of domestic violence that she had suffered from and tried to prevent by moving into the local motel, only to be hunted down once again by her abusive husband.[65]

Scholars studying battered wives argue that staying at home despite being attacked testifies more to the many practical difficulties involved in abandoning the home (including, inter alia, concern for the children, economic dependence on the partner, lack of alternative locations, incompetence of the law enforcement agencies, etc.) than to a positive choice to remain with the violent partner.[66] Critical legal discourse has pointed to the futility of such a legal requirement as it is a well-known fact that retreat will not halt an attack perpetrated against a battered woman (at most, it will postpone it[67] but possibly even exacerbate it[68]). The requirement to retreat in circumstances where the aggressor and the victim live together in practice negates the possibility of asserting the doctrine of self-defense in cases of domestic violence where battered women do not retreat from their own home.[69] This legal requirement disregards the fact that the "arena" from which the battered woman is required to retreat is none other than her own home, and the demand per se therefore violates her fundamental human right to live freely and not by mercy, in her own home.[70]

Contrary to criticism in relation to the incompatible legal interpretation of the doctrine's requirement in circumstances of domestic violence described above, an initial sense of compatibility between the requirements of the doctrine and the typical circumstances of battered women on trial for killing their partners arises when reviewing the self-defense doctrine set out in the Model Penal

64 For a psychological account of the battered women syndrome in this respect, see Walker 1979: 55–70; Downs 1984: 53–70. For an overall account of the reasonableness of battered women, see Gillespie 1989: 123–144.

65 For the importance of considering the entire web of abuse and violence as relevant when examining the immediate background to the attack, see Nicolson and Sanghui 1995: 1122; Downs 1984: 96. Accordingly, even though it is not always possible to point to a critical and acute event immediately before the response of the battered women, it is also not possible to talk seriously of a transient danger that may not take place. See Gillespie 1989: 60. Likewise, see McColgan 1993: 508–529.

66 Schneider 2000: 77–79; Mahoney 1991: 10–23; Gillespie 1989: 144–156; Carpenter 2003: 680–681; Leverick 2006: 8.

67 Rosen R. 1993: 371, 405. For recent case law decisions, see Carpenter 2003: 654 note 3.

68 Mahoney 1991: 53–92; Gillespie 1989: 151; Carpenter 2003: 682, 694.

69 Gillespie 1989: 187–188.

70 Mackinnon 2001: 762. Likewise, scholars have argued that it is not proper for this right to be negated even if the scene is none other than the home of the person being attacked by her partner, since he too has property rights in the joint home. Moreover, such judicial rulings reflect an inappropriate preference for property rights over the interest in life and bodily integrity. Gillespie 1989: 84–87. Even states that do not make retreat a requirement for asserting self-defense offer no remedy for battered women, as some of these states explicitly require the defendants to retreat in the case of co-dwellers – for example, in Alabama (Ala. Code 13A-3 §23); Florida (Fla. Stat. §776.013); Pennsylvania (18 Pa. Cons. Stat. §505); South Carolina (S.C. Code Ann. §16-11-440) and Tennessee (Tenn. Code Ann. §39-11-611).

Code. To begin with, the moral approach emerging from the MPC is compatible, prima facie, with its application in circumstances of severe and sustained domestic violence. In contrast to the moral approach of "excuse" that implicitly attributes moral failure and lack of reasonableness to battered women,[71] the "justification" approach adopted by the MPC does not regard the actions of the battered woman as being morally or legally flawed.[72] Instead, the moral and legal approach identifies protective acts of domestic violence as being a priori justified.[73] In contrast, the moral approach adopted within the concept of "excuse"[74] essentially leaves the criminal conviction for murder with its myriad social and emotional implications intact,[75] even if, at the conclusion of the judicial process, it ultimately negates the criminal liability of the battered woman for her "unlawful acts."[76] Legal scholars might argue that any sophistry regarding which doctrine is appropriate ("excuse" or "justification") is unnecessary, since the defendant is acquitted and goes free on either ground.[77] However, the

71 The attribution of a moral failure stems from the premise that the act of self-defense in such situations is neither proper nor justified. It is argued that the excuse doctrine ascribes to these women a pathological deviation from the standard of the reasonable person by reason of the existence of symptoms of mental disturbance that on one hand do not amount to a psychological illness but on the other hand certainly temporarily or permanently impair their ability to reach a "reasonable and rational" decision (for example, to leave the aggressive partner). In practice, according to the excuse approach, situations of domestic violence entrench the "substantive failure" of battered women to make autonomous and prudent decisions (in contrast to a reasonable man who is capable of being responsible for his actions and choosing appropriate reasonable behavior even in situations of severe crisis). For details, see Coughlin 1994: 37–47, 55–57; Schopp et al. 1994: 45, 92–93, 95–97; Burke 2002: 211.

72 For an approach that analyzes and defines the behavior and choices of a battered woman as rational and reasonable both on the subjective and on the objective level, see ibid.: 214–216.

73 In this regard, there would be no need for recourse to an exemption from criminal liability or exemption from punishment for one reason or another.

74 The "excuse" approach a priori defines the battered woman's act of repelling an attack as an unlawful act, and consequently as a crime in itself. For the preference given to the "excuse" doctrine in connection with battered women accused of killing their partners, see Rosen C. 1986: 31 and Sangero 2006: 350. See also Byrd 1991: 169.

75 It follows, therefore, that the very application of the excuse doctrine to battered women, while ensuring the woman's liberation from physical imprisonment, stigmatizes her as a morally defected person and perpetuates gender-based stereotypes that allow the continued discrimination against and subjugation of women in general and battered women in particular. For a general discussion of this issue, see Coughlin 1994: 7, 14, 28, 54, 62, 67, 87–88, 92.

76 The "excuse" approach is concerned with whether the battered women are indeed liable for their unlawful act, and excuse is based, therefore, on the ground that the defendants committed their unlawful act by reason of the special situation in which they found themselves at the time. See Rosen C. 1986: 12, 17, 42–44.

77 See Rosen R. 1993: 408–409, who argues, for example, that the insistence on distinguishing between justification and excuse in this regard, is "much ado about very little." Similarly, Kinports argues:

> Although the distinction between justification and excuse may have some academic or theoretical importance, it makes no practical difference to the defendant whether the jury determines that her use of protective force was justified or excused. In either case, she is acquitted and goes free.
>
> (See Kinports 1988: 393, 460)

distinction between a judicial acquittal on the grounds of "excuse" and a judicial acquittal on the grounds of "justification" has substantive legal and practical significance. For these reasons, the Model Penal Code's choice of the "justification approach" should be applied to circumstances of domestic violence.

Prima facie, the expansions found in the Model Penal Code doctrine seem to create a proper and flexible basis for accommodating the legal application of the doctrine of self-defense in circumstances of domestic violence. Unfortunately, however, further scrutiny of the Model Penal Code reveals that it contains legal rules that create fundamental obstacles when applying the doctrine in circumstances of domestic violence. To begin with, a critical review of the Model Penal Code requirement of retreat reveals that, despite the abolition of this requirement with regard to the home of a person and his place of work, it has not been abolished in circumstances where the aggressor is a co-dweller.[78] Particularly puzzling in this regard is the Model Penal Code drafters' explicit decision to retain the retreat requirement when the aggressor is a co-dweller[79] while

78 In other words, the duty to retreat has been abolished in respect of the home arena only when the attack is carried out by a stranger. A perusal of the Official Commentaries of the drafters of the Model Penal Code reveals that they chose not to abolish the retreat prerequisite (as they did in respect of the workplace) in respect of attacks at the home, and stated that in so far as concerned situations of domestic violence a duty existed to retreat from the home. Indeed, the requirement to retreat from the home in situations where the aggressor is a co-dweller is not expressly stated in the law (it is only implied) but it is expressly clarified in the Official Commentaries to the law, see *Model Penal Code and Commentaries (Official Draft and Revised Comments)* 1980: 56.

79 A hint of the gender bias leading to the abolition of the requirement to retreat at the workplace but not at the home may perhaps be seen in the fact that in the explanatory comments provided by the drafters of the Model Penal Code there is a reference to the fact that the legislative proposal of 1958, which suggested abolishing the requirement of retreat both at the workplace and at home, was not accepted. The explanatory remarks also contain strict gender terminology regarding characteristic domestic violence, which may indicate masculine bias resulting in the rejection of the 1958 proposal in the context of the home: in the explanatory comments, the typical victim of an attack at the home is the "wife," whereas the terminology used to describe the typical aggressor at the home is the "husband":

> The provision also exempts from the duty to retreat a person in his place of work ... a second, and also difficult issue, is whether the right to stand one's ground should be when the attack is by a co-dweller or co-worker. The proposal originally submitted to the Institute did not extend the exception in either instance; a wife was compelled to retreat from the attack by her husband in their common home ... as was one partner from an attack by another partner at their place of work. The institute voted to require retreat from attacks at one's place of work in such context, but not from attacks at one's dwelling. The language of Subsection (2)(b)(ii)(A) states that provision.
>
> (Ibid.: 56)

This arbitrary decision is actually dangerous when explicitly adopted in the explanatory comments of the Model Penal Code, since, as noted, the Model Penal Code and its explanatory comments comprise a legislative model and source of judicial interpretation in many states in the United States. Thus, even states that have explicitly abolished the retreat requirement (Alabama, Florida, Tennessee, Pennsylvania and South Carolina) may apply an exception relating to the home front, when referring to women assaulted by their partners.

completely abolishing it in the workplace when the attack is carried out by a co-worker.[80] In effect, since most attacks on women are carried out by intimate partners while they are at home (which is usually also the place of residence of the aggressive partner in domestic violence cases)[81] the requirement to retreat in so far as the aggressor is a co-dweller, completely **nullifies de facto** the doctrine of self-defense whenever the battered woman does not retreat from her own home.[82]

Apart from the requirement to retreat in cases where the aggressor is a co-dweller, the Model Penal Code explicitly requires the woman to surrender to the aggressor's demands prior to resorting to the use of deadly protective force.[83] In this regard, the Model Penal Code draws a strange technical distinction between the aggressor's positive demands (to perform certain acts) and his negative demands (to abstain from performing certain acts). The Model Penal Code subsequently states that a person must comply with the aggressor's demands to abstain from taking certain action, before using deadly protective force.[84] The legal (and bizarre) requirement that an intimate partner must

80 For criticism of the particular abolition of this requirement, see Herberling 1975: 939.

81 See Carpenter 2003: 669. Carpenter argues that the characteristics, identity and property rights of the aggressor are not relevant to determining the degree to which the use of deadly force in self-defense is necessary. Ibid.: 661–662, 700. Furthermore, Carpenter argues that an assault at the home is equivalent to a legal determination that the defendant satisfied the requirement of retreat, because the home – as a "place of last resort" – is similar to the "wall of retreat", exactly as was required in the Middle Ages when applying the doctrine of self-defense. Ibid.: 667.

82 Ibid.: 660.

83 Section 3.04(2)(b)(ii):

> the actor knows that he can avoid the necessity of using such force with complete safety by retreating or by surrendering possession of a thing to a person asserting a claim of right thereto or by complying with a demand that he abstains from any action that he has no duty to take. As follows from the text of the law, the Model Penal Code distinguishes between lawful and unlawful demands in terms of the requirement of compliance, so that a person is not obliged to comply with unlawful positive demands, such as during a robbery, but he must comply with positive demands so long as they are not unlawful.
>
> (*Model Penal Code and Commentaries (Official Draft and Revised Comments)* 1980: 58)

Likewise, in relation to the requirement of compliance, the MPC distinguishes between demands to perform an act and demands to avoid an act and, as clearly emerges from the comments of the drafters, this arbitrary legal arrangement was chosen merely for technical reasons relating to drafting difficulties (see ibid.: 60).

84 As noted in Section 3.04(2)(b)(ii), the requirement of compliance with the demands of the aggressor does not apply to the aggressor's positive demands to perform any act (for example, the daily positive demand made of Norman to engage in prostitution, bark like a dog, eat from the dog's plate and more. See *State* v. *Norman*, Courts of Appeals of North Carolina, 378 S.E.2d 8 (N.C.1989)), as, according to the text of the section, a battered woman is entitled to refuse to perform such acts. However, according to the language of the section, the requirement of compliance applies, with strange and broad generalization, to an entire range of possible demands on the part of the aggressor to abstain from performing certain acts, whether large or small, marginal or significant (provided only that the defendant is not under a lawful duty to perform them, or in the language of the provision: to abstain from any action that he has no duty to take).

comply with all the aggressor's demands so long as they are negatively stated (i.e. that she must avoid certain actions) ***is equivalent to the legalization of a full repertoire of demands that together might create a horrible and permanent pattern of severe domestic violence***, including offensive, strange, arbitrary, humiliating and depressing demands, provided however that they direct the victim to abstain from performing certain actions.[85] Even if we assume that such an odd legal arrangement is appropriate in principle in the context of the self-defense doctrine as a whole, it certainly and patently cannot be applied in circumstances of domestic violence that, by their nature, are ***continuous, repetitive and escalating***. Furthermore, even if we accept that such a legal arrangement might be appropriate in certain circumstances of domestic violence, its practical application shifts the judicial focus towards ***marginal and insignificant issues relating to the particular classification*** of the type of violence committed against the women standing trial. In such trials, the judicial decision is based solely on the ***technical classification*** of the kind of domestic violence committed against the battered women prior to their use of protective force (i.e., demands to perform certain acts or demands to abstain from certain acts). Thus, when considering the need to use deadly protective force the applicability of the exception permitting the use of such force is examined in a technocratic manner, without taking into account the most significant elements of the demands made of the defendant in the context of domestic violence, namely, the content, nature, extent and duration of these demands.[86] This bizarre legal arrangement creates a situation whereby defendants who are victims of domestic violence must found their claim to self-defense on an entirely technical classification of the patterns of violence adopted by their abusive partners.[87] Such a legislative arrangement would be tolerable if it were merely cumbersome and technocratic, but in fact it is fundamentally harmful and dangerous in the context of domestic violence, since

85 A terrible and permanent pattern of violence may take place under the auspices of this law, all of which is based on demands to abstain from certain acts, including but not only to abstain from eating at the table in company, to abstain from watching television, to abstain from talking to people, to abstain from meeting friends and family, to abstain from reading books, and similar outrageous and abusive demands. Such macabre possibilities would have been avoided had the Model Penal Code adopted language qualifying the demand to comply with the demands of the aggressor so long as the interference with the victim's freedom was minimal. An example would be the terms adopted in North Dakota in this context: N.D. Section 12.1–05–07(2)(b) "The use of deadly force is not justified if it can be avoided, with safety to the actor and others, by retreat or other conduct involving minimal interference with the freedom of the individual menaced." Regrettably, no such clarification exists in the present version of the MPC.

86 I.e., whether the aggressor's demands fall within the positive category (demands to perform certain acts) or the negative category (demands to abstain from doing certain acts).

87 In other words, if the violent demands are positive (for example, a demand that the defendant perform a certain act (large or small) following which she responds with deadly protective force) a claim of self-defense is more likely to succeed than where such a claim is raised in circumstances where deadly protective force is used in response to the partner's demand to abstain from an act, even if the nature of the demand to abstain is humiliating, violent, abusive and outrageous.

the legal arrangement *legitimizes de jure an entire range of abusive patterns of domestic violence.*

In addition to the problems involved in the categorical requirement to comply with the aggressor's (avoidance) demands, the language of the MPC creates a substantive problem in relation to the exercise of deadly protective force in circumstances where there seem to be no concrete and provable threats to life. Although some might argue that the legal arrangement in the Model Penal Code does in fact enable its application in circumstances that do not pose a tangible threat to life or body (relying on an interpretive analogy to other circumstances contained in this section, for example, circumstances of rape[88]), a strict reading of the wording of the section reveals that a legal interpretation of this type cannot be extracted from the statute and applied to circumstances of domestic violence because – incredibly – the MPC *explicitly permits "marital rape."*[89] The Model Penal Code statutorily and categorically exempts men's criminal liability for a variety of sexual offenses, as long as they are committed against their female partners.[90] Such immunity from legal culpability for sexual

88 The current legislative arrangement permits the use of deadly protective force in circumstances of rape. The reference is to rape using force or threats (a circumstance equivalent to the rape definition in Section 213.1 (a) of the Model Penal Code, without the inclusion of the other circumstances of rape, found in subsections (b) and (c); for example, interfering with the victim's ability to refuse to engage in sexual relations through the use of drugs or when the victim is unconscious). The significance of this is that rape is considered to be a circumstance justifying the use of deadly protective force even if there is no tangible threat to life or threat of serious bodily injury. Although some researchers believe that rape inherently involves serious bodily injury (see the description of these claims in Leverick 2006: 150) if, in fact, rape involved a real danger to life and/or serious bodily injury, it would have been included for that reason in the legislative categories already existing in the section, and no separate legislative reference would be required in relation to this circumstance. Indeed, from a state-level perspective in the United States, rape is considered a circumstance that justifies the use of deadly protective force. (For a review of the legal regulations in the U.S. states concerning the use of deadly protective force in circumstances of rape, see Gillespie 1989: 62–67.) It is interesting to note that, historically, rape was considered a circumstance justifying deadly protective force, even if it was not accompanied by violence or great physical injury, probably not because of the serious physical injury aspect, but because it was detrimental to a woman's respectability and the moral conventions of society. For this argument, see also ibid.: 33, 38; Leverick 2006: 150, 155. (For the arguments of scholars to the effect that rape strikes a mortal blow to the humanity and human dignity of the victim, see ibid.: 156–157). For a comprehensive analysis of the connection between the social subjugation of women and their objectification in terms of the offense of rape, see Mackinnon 2001: 772–897.

89 For further details regarding marital rape at common law, see ibid.: 856–871.

90 The definition of sexual offenses in the Model Penal Code provides for the inherent immunity of the spouse from criminal liability in respect of such offenses – in the various grades of rape: "Section 213.1 (1) Rape: A male who has sexual intercourse with a female not his wife is guilty of rape"; "(2) Gross Sexual Imposition: A male who has sexual intercourse with a female not his wife commits felony of the third degree"; "Corruption and Seduction: 213.3 A male who has sexual intercourse with a female not his wife, or any person who engages in deviate sexual intercourse"; "Sexual Assault: 213.4 A person who has sexual contact with another not his spouse"; "Indecent Exposure: 213.5 A person commits a misdemeanor if, for the purpose of arousing or gratifying sexual desire of himself or of any person other than his spouse … " See also the *Model Penal Code*

violence accordingly negates any successful assertion on the part of a battered woman regarding the legitimacy of the use of deadly protective force in domestic circumstances, where the woman cannot point to a concrete and tangible danger to her life.

Thus, despite the overall seemingly greater flexibility of the doctrine of self-defense in the Model Penal Code, its explicit and implicit provisions within the context of the application of the doctrine in the particular circumstances of domestic violence together and separately[91] create a legal arrangement that it is doubtful can properly be applied in cases of battered women who kill their aggressor partners.

Conclusion

Though advanced and enlightened, the American legal system has not yet offered any effective solutions to the problems faced by battered woman. Today, there is a much deeper awareness of the socio-legal problems faced by battered woman, as well as greater scientific knowledge of their behavior. Still, American legislators seem to be unwilling to adjust the legal approach to this disturbing issue. Only upon the emergence of such willingness will it be possible to find the appropriate legal remedy, either by creating a new defense or by extending

---

and Commentaries (Official Draft and Revised Comments) 1980: 275: "... the central notion has always been unlawful sexual intercourse committed upon a female by imposition. The term 'unlawful' served the function of excluding cases where the actor and the victim were married to each other." According to the commentaries of the drafters, it is still possible to prosecute a man who forcibly rapes his partner, albeit for assault (by virtue of the use of force) and not for rape. If the rape is also accompanied by serious injury, then the man can also be prosecuted for causing serious injury, although not for the offense of rape (see ibid.: 344–345). In the Official Commentaries of the Model Penal Code, the drafters refer to the criminal exemption applying to spouses and explain it with a number of well-known arguments in this field. See in this regard, for example, Rumney 1999: 243–270. The reasons cited by the drafters of the Model Penal Code to explain this legal arrangement are: marriage as an irrevocable consent to sexual intercourse (see *Model Penal Code and Commentaries (Official Draft and Revised Comments)* 1980: 342); the home as a private arena which should not be interfered with in general or through the criminal law in particular (ibid.: 345); the woman's oath of marriage to obey the husband's demands (ibid.: 343); and the claim that the element of breach of intimacy (that exists in relation to the offense of rape between strangers) does not exist between spouses because of the alleged intimacy already constituted in their relationship (ibid.: 346). The law indeed uses the terminology "husband"; however, the definitions section clarifies that this exception also applies to unmarried couples who live together: Section 213.6 (2) spouse relationships ... the exclusion shall be deemed to extend to persons living as man and wife, regardless of the legal status of their relationship." Moreover, according to the Official Commentaries of the drafters, this criminal exception applies even if the couple have already separated (without a formal procedure of divorce), as long as no judicial separation order has been given. The legal implication of such an arrangement is that men are immune from criminal liability in respect of sexual violence, even against former partners (see ibid.: 342).

91 Because of the cumulative characteristic of the doctrine requirements for the successful application of the claim of self-defense.

the applicability of existing defenses so as to enable fair consideration to be given to battered women's responses expressed by the use of protective force. Current legal insights on the issue of battered women who kill their assailant partners should be translated into a suitable and focused legal arrangement with respect to the application of the American doctrine of self-defense as set out in the Model Penal Code, in order to allow its proper application to women accused of killing their partners in circumstances of severe and continuous domestic violence.

5 Preventing femicide

Proposed statutory amendments to the American Model Penal Code

The proposed legislative amendments include unique and innovative features, as well as a legal formula that provides a socio-legal response targeted at and tailored to issues central to the phenomenon of femicide, that have not been adequately addressed by legislative proposals in this context to date. This chapter will articulate a focused and detailed legislative proposal to amend the MPC with regard to the three criminal doctrines most relevant to the phenomenon of femicide: the doctrine of provocation, the felony-murder rule and the doctrine of self-defense. These legal doctrines were critically reviewed in the previous chapters and legal and criminological insights were drawn. This chapter will translate these insights into detailed legislative amendments for proper socio-legal treatment of the grievous phenomenon of femicide.

The chapter will propose detailed amendments to the doctrine of provocation in circumstances of intimate partner femicide as per section 210.3(b) of the Model Penal Code, to the doctrine of the felony-murder rule in circumstances of assaultive-femicide as per section 210.2(b) of the Model Penal Code and to the doctrine of self-defense in circumstances of domestic violence as per section 3.04(2)(b) of the Model Penal Code.

Proposed amendments to the doctrine of provocation in circumstances of uxoricide

As noted in Chapter 2, among the various doctrines of provocation applied in the United States, the statutory doctrine of provocation in the MPC, which is followed by the majority of states, is the most expansive and therefore the most forgiving towards the murder of female intimate partners. By retaining intact the legal doctrine that allows broad judicial legislation and statutory protection in the context of emotional crime (EMED), and in the light of the criminological characteristics of the killing of women, a real and terrible risk is faced by women seeking to make autonomous decisions about their intimate relationships. This expansive doctrine sends a social message of forgiveness towards such murders,[1] and might inadvertently even encourage such acts.[2]

It is therefore proposed to categorically define, in statute, the circumstances in which it will not be possible to assert a claim of provocation and/or EMED. The aim is to strengthen the objective test in the doctrine of provocation, which has been eroded and diminished, particularly in the doctrine of provocation applied in U.S. jurisdictions that have adopted the MPC. This objective exclusion would meet the criticism commonly voiced against the excessive subjectivity of both the doctrine of provocation and the partial EMED defense that accompanies it.[3] A normative limitation applied through a categorical exclusion within the framework of the objective test in the doctrine of provocation is supported by researchers[4] who favor limiting the incidence of the mitigation of criminal liability for anti-social acts[5] and is consistent with the frequent criticism voiced about the inadequacy of the law in the context of the murder of intimate partners.[6]

The strategy of setting limits on the application of the doctrine of provocation is not new and, in fact, has existed for centuries in tests developed by both the original English case law and by common law countries, as preconditions for its application.[7] Even the strategy of setting statutory limits based on the objective element of the doctrine of provocation is not new and can be found in various U.S. jurisdictions, albeit not always with respect to the specific circumstances surrounding the murder of intimate partners.[8] Recommendations and proposals for categorically and statutorily excluding the application of the doctrine of provocation in the context of the murder of women have already been set forth by other researchers in the field,[9] and have been incorporated in

1 See Ramsey 2010: 81–82. See also Howe 1999: 127–137; Howe 2002.

2 It is perhaps possible to learn of the potential risks from empirical findings regarding the increased incidence of murder of intimate partners following such case law in Brazil: in 1980, a judgment significantly reduced the punishment of a defendant who had murdered his partner after she had decided to leave him after the court accepted the defendant's claim that the murder had been committed because of the "violation of his honor." That same year, in San Paulo alone, 722 cases of murders of partners took place in which the men claimed diminished criminal liability. Spatz 1991: 597, 618.

3 See Dressler 1982: 421, 431; Lee 2003: 34–35; Ramsey 2010: 144.

4 See Horder 1992: 144.

5 For the didactic notion regarding the social treatment of violence against women, see Rapaport 1996: 1507, 1509; Spatz 1991: 626.

6 See Rapaport 1996: 1546. See also Howe 1999: 127–137.

7 See Lee 2003: 39–40.

8 For example, there are limitations concerning the application of the claim of provocation in the context of the crying of an infant or in the context of verbal provocation. See, e.g., Tasmanian Criminal Code Act 1924 (No. 69 of 1924) (subsequently repealed in 2003) (providing that "[n]o one shall be held to give provocation to another only by doing that which he had a legal right to do, or by doing anything which the offender incited him to do in order to provide the offender with an excuse for killing or doing bodily harm to any person.")

9 See, e.g., Horder 1992: 92–94; Brown 1999: 140 (arguing that there is room to qualify the doctrine of provocation in circumstances where the very recognition of these circumstances encourages anti-social attitudes). See also Riley 2008: 55, 73.

legislation that has completed the legislative process, for example, in the state of Maryland.[10] Parallel legislative amendments to include objective tests and limitations within the doctrine of provocation have been enacted in other common law countries such as Australia, Canada and even the England, the cradle of the common law doctrine of provocation.

In Canada, for example, the defense of provocation as codified in Section 232 of the Canadian criminal code[11] was amended in 2015. Prior to the amendment, in order to be entitled to such legal defense the accused had to prove, in addition to two separate subjective tests,[12] two objective tests: the occurrence of a wrongful act or insult, and the response resulting from the wrongful or insulting act. While the previous subjective tests remained in place,[13] the legislative amendment restricted the defense of provocation by adding two additional explicit objective tests regarding the provocative act to which the accused responded. The two new objective requirements are that the wrongful act would be clearly an unlawful act (at least a five-year indictable offense) and that it is capable of causing an ordinary person to lose self-control. These objective tests aim to encourage self-control and "conduct that complies with certain societal standards of reasonableness and responsibility."[14]

The first objective test refers to the victim's "wrongful or insulting" conduct that should amount to an indictable offense of five or more years. By limiting the judicial interpretation of "wrongful acts" that may lead to a successful claim of the partial defense of provocation only to situations in which the victim's conduct constituted an indictable offense under the Canadian Criminal Code that is punishable by five or more years in prison, mere or minor wrongful acts or insults would no longer be sufficient for a claim of provocation.[15] In referring to the

10 Md. Code Ann., Criminal Law, §2–207.

11 The official title of Canada Criminal Code is "An Act respecting the criminal law" (R.S.C. 1985, c. C-46, as amended). The original wording states:

> Murder reduced to manslaughter: 232. (1) Culpable homicide that otherwise would be murder may be reduced to manslaughter if the person who committed it did so in the heat of passion caused by sudden provocation. (2) A wrongful act or an insult that is of such a nature as to be sufficient to deprive an ordinary person of the power of self-control is provocation for the purposes of this section if the accused acted on it on the sudden and before there was time for his passion to cool.

12 The two subjective tests relate to having committed the killing while being in the heat of passion, and killing while being in the heat of passion caused by a sudden provocation.

13 That is, that the accused prove he acted in response to the provocative act, and that he prove that he acted on such circumstances "on the sudden and before there was time for their passion to cool" [as the wording in Section 232(2)].

14 See *R.* v. *Singh*, 2016 ONSC 3739 (CanLII), at paragraph 61.

15 See Section 2.3.2 in Legislative Summary of Bill S-7: An Act to amend the Immigration and Refugee Protection Act, the Civil Marriage Act and the Criminal Code and to make consequential amendments to other Acts, Parliament of Canada, Library of Parliament Publications, Publication Number 41–2–S7-E.

reasons for which "wrongful acts" and "insults" were statutorily and objectively limited, the Canadian Parliament explicitly referred to a Court of Appeal for Ontario case of femicide that prescribed a narrow judicial interpretation of "wrongful acts" that can amount to provocation.[16] In the Legislative Summary of the bill, the Canadian Parliament introduced the legislative amendment by linking it to the domestic violence circumstances of that femicide case, whereby a man killed his wife after she made comments he took to mean she was having an affair.[17] In that case, the court of appeals rejected the accused's claims that his Islamic religion and culture valued family honor, that a wife's infidelity would be a source of great stigma for her husband and that the defense of provocation should be applied in his case.[18] In explaining the socio-legal and moral reasons for the legislative limitations to the doctrine of provocation, the Canadian Parliament found the Court of Appeal's statement in this ruling worthy of quoting:

> *Provocation does not shield an accused who has not lost self-control, but has instead acted out of a sense of revenge or a culturally driven sense of the appropriate response to someone else's misconduct.* An accused who acts out of a sense of retribution fueled by a belief system that entitles a husband to punish his wife's perceived infidelity has not lost control, but has taken action that, according to his belief system, is a justified response to the situation.... *These beliefs are antithetical to fundamental Canadian values, including gender equality.* It is arguable that as a matter of criminal law policy, the "ordinary person" cannot be fixed with beliefs that are irreconcilable with fundamental Canadian values.[19]

In addition to the objective definition of "wrongful acts" that may constitute provocation, the amendment included a second objective requirement that further restricted the circumstances whereby a victim's felonious acts would constitute adequate provocation. The second test was introduced by legally constructing the defense within an objective standard of the "reasonable person." Therefore, only those five-year sentencing indictable acts and insults that are capable of causing an ordinary person to lose self-control are open for consideration as provocation.[20] Such an objective test further limits the application of the accused's claim to provocation because it does not simply require that an ordinary person would commit

16 The parliament debate protocol referred to *R.* v. *Humaid*, [2006] O.J. No. 1507, 208 C.C.C. (3d).

17 See section 1.1.4, Legislative Summary of Bill S-7: An Act to amend the Immigration and Refugee Protection Act, the Civil Marriage Act and the Criminal Code and to make consequential amendments to other Acts, Parliament of Canada, Library of Parliament Publications, Publication Number 41–2–S7-E.

18 *R.* v. *Humaid*, [2006] O.J. No. 1507, 208 C.C.C. (3d).

19 Italics added. The parliament refers to *R.* v. *Humaid*, [2006] O.J. No. 1507, 208 C.C.C. (3d) 43, paras 85 and 93, and also to *R.* v. *Tran*, para 34.

20 As stated in the explicit wording: "of such a nature as to be sufficient to deprive an ordinary person of the power of self-control" in Section 232(2) in Canada Criminal Code.

the offense, but "whether the ordinary person would lose self-control to the degree that he formed the intention for murder."[21]

In a similar effort, two states in Australia, Victoria and Queensland, statutorily limited and restricted the doctrine of provocation by adding objective tests. In Victoria, for example, despite the abolition of the provocation doctrine as a partial defense in 2005,[22] in 2014 the parliament introduced an additional provision to ensure that provocation claims would not re-emerge in later stages of the trial. The amendment was required despite the fact that the provocation defense had been repealed in 2005, because it remained as a factor for consideration by judges in the sentencing stage. Concerned that problems that led to the abolition of the provocation defense would re-emerge at sentencing by way of blaming the victim for inciting her own death,[23] the additional legislative amendment aimed to restrict any such claims at the sentencing stage[24] by allowing the exclusion of evidence "if its probative value is substantially outweighed by the danger that it might unnecessarily demean the deceased in a homicide trial."[25]

The state of Queensland in Australia also amended its provocation law in 2011 to limit provocation claims in circumstances of intimate partner relationship in general and femicide cases in particular.[26] Accordingly, the offense of murder cannot be reduced to manslaughter if the deceased and the accused had been in an abusive domestic relationship, or if there were acts of serious

21 See the Court's interpretation of this enacted objective test in *R.* v. *Singh*, 2016 ONSC 3739 (Can LII), at paragraph 49.

22 See Section 3B of Crimes (Homicide) Act 2005 (Vic.).

23 Provocation claims could re-emerge in the sentencing stage in the form of blaming the victim for inciting her own death "because of her conduct and perpetuating along family violence and archetypal defendants' responses to alleged insults to their 'male honor'." See Domestic Violence Resource Centre Victoria Discussion No. 10, 2016. "Out of Character? Legal Responses to Intimate Partner Homicides by Men in Victoria 2005–2014": 18–19.

24 See ibid.: 18–19.

25 By adding a new Subsection 135 (d) to the Evidence Act 2008. Vic. Subsection 135(d) was inserted by No. 63/2014 s. 9(1)(b): PART 3.11 – Discretionary And Mandatory Exclusions 135 General discretion to exclude evidence:

> The court may refuse to admit evidence if its probative value is substantially outweighed by the danger that the evidence might – (a) be unfairly prejudicial to a party; or (b) be misleading or confusing; or (c) cause or result in undue waste of time. ***(d) unnecessarily demean the deceased in a criminal proceeding for a homicide offense.*** (Italics added).

At the same time, recognising that a victim who killed an abusive partner would need to introduce family violence evidence, the amendment includes a note specifically exempting family violence evidence from this principle: "Note: This section does not limit evidence of family violence that may be adduced under Part IC of the Crimes Act 1958." The note exempts the use of family violence evidence in such cases, even though such allegations may be considered offensive to the deceased. See Domestic Violence Resource Centre Victoria Discussion Paper No. 10, 2016. Out of Character? Legal Responses to Intimate Partner Homicides by Men in Victoria 2005–2014: 24.

26 See section 304B of Queensland Criminal Code. These changes are based on the Queensland Law Reform Commission Report: "A Review of the Excuse of Accident and the Defence of Provocation," 2008.

domestic violence committed by the deceased in the course of that relationship.[27] Such objective limitations were further restricted in 2016, instructing that fact finders should take into consideration any evidence of domestic violence in circumstances of provocation claims whereby the deceased and the accused were in an intimate relationship at the time of the killing.[28]

Furthermore, and in order to ensure that defendants do not raise the claim of provocation if the female partner wanted to end the intimate relationship, three explicit and particular categories of behavior were introduced by Queensland's legislative amendment. All three categories of behavior essentially concern ending or changing the relationship and cater to sexual and personal autonomy of each partner within an intimate relationship. Subsection (3)(c) of Section 304 provides that provocation claims do not apply if:

> 3. (c) the sudden provocation is based on anything done by the deceased or anything the person believes the deceased has done
>
> (i) to end the relationship; or
> (ii) to change the nature of the relationship; or
> (iii) to indicate in any way that the relationship may, should or will end, or that there may, should or will be a change to the nature of the relationship.

Even England, the cradle of the common law doctrine of provocation that statutorily legislated the doctrine in the Homicide Act of 1957, repealed it in 2010.[29] The partial defense of provocation was abolished and substituted with a partial defense of diminished criminal responsibility accorded to

27 Ibid.: 225:

> Studies over the years consistently demonstrate that men and women kill under different circumstances. Speaking generally, in the context of intimate partner homicides, men who kill their intimate partners (or their love rivals) are more likely to kill out of jealousy, to maintain control, in response to losing control of another person or to defend their "honour."... It is not uncommon for men who kill their intimate partners to raise the defence of provocation on the basis that they were provoked to kill by their partner's infidelity, insults or threats to leave the relationship.

28 The amendment to Section 304(4) of the Criminal Code legislated through Criminal Code and Other Legislation Amendment Act 2011 states: "Section 304: (4), regard may be had to any history of violence, or of sexual conduct, between the person and the person who is unlawfully killed that is relevant in all the circumstances." See Recent Developments in the Criminal Law in Queensland, 3–6. https://portal.barweb.com.au/Upload/FCK/Cummings.Greg.pdf.

29 The doctrine was abolished by The Coroners and Justice Act 2009. Under the partial defence of provocation enacted in 1957, a defendant who would otherwise be guilty of murder will be guilty of manslaughter instead if he or she was provoked by things said or done (or both) to lose self-control, and in the opinion of the jury the provocation was enough to make a reasonable person do as the defendant did. The original text of the provocation partial defense was legislated in Section 3 of the Homicide Act 1957 which read as follows:

defendants that successfully claimed killing while being under loss of self-control.[30] The new partial defense for murder limits the circumstances by which a defendant's murder conviction may be reduced to manslaughter, particularly in the realm of intimate partner relationships.[31] The new partial defense to murder of "loss of control" sets forth the cumulative requirements that must be met for the new partial defense to be successful. According to the explanatory notes submitted by the Ministry of Justice,[32] the defendant's claim for loss of self-control will be accepted only if a person of the defendant's sex and age with an ordinary level of tolerance and self-restraint and in the defendant's circumstances may have acted in the same or similar way toward the defendant. This means that the reasonable person doctrine in such claim prescribes "an ordinary level of tolerance and self-restraint" and excludes claims of defendants that do not meet the objective standard of tolerance and self-restraint.

In addition, the legislative amendment limits the range of circumstances that may qualify for a claim of loss of control, by setting two objective cumulative requirements with regard to the "qualifying trigger" for the defendant's "loss of control."[33] According to the explanatory notes to the legislative amendment, whether a defendant's sense of being seriously wronged is justifiable will be an objective question that sets a very high threshold for the circumstances under which a partial defense is available to the effect that it substantially narrows the potential availability of a partial defense in cases where a loss of control is attributable to things done or said compared to the partial defense of provocation

---

> Where on a charge of murder there is evidence on which the jury can find that the person charged was provoked (whether by things done or by things said or by both together) to lose his self-control, the question whether the provocation was enough to make a reasonable man do as he did shall be left to be determined by the jury; and in determining that question the jury shall take into account everything both done and said according to the effect which, in their opinion, it would have on a reasonable man.

30 The Coroners and Justice Act 2009.

31 The new partial defence to murder as introduced in section 54 of the Coroners and Justice Act 2009 states:

> Partial defence to murder: loss of control (1) Where a person ("D") kills or is a party to the killing of another ("V"), D is not to be convicted of murder if – (a) D's acts and omissions in doing or being a party to the killing resulted from D's loss of self-control, (b) the loss of self-control had a qualifying trigger, and (c) a person of D's sex and age, with a normal degree of tolerance and self-restraint and in the circumstances of D, might have reacted in the same or in a similar way to D.

32 Coroners And Justice Act 2009, Explanatory Notes, UK Ministry of Justice, 52–55.

33 See Section 55 of the Coroners and Justice Act 2009:

> Meaning of "qualifying trigger." (4) This subsection applies if D's loss of self-control was attributable to a thing or things done or said (or both) which – (a) constituted circumstances of an *extremely grave character*, and (b) caused D to have a *justifiable* sense of being seriously wronged. (Italics added).

(where no threshold exists in relation to the provoking circumstances).[34] Particularly relevant to the empirical findings with regard to femicide is Subsection 6(c), which explicitly excludes any sexual infidelity circumstances from being a qualifying trigger for a successful claim of loss of control.[35] According to the explanatory notes of the legislative amendment, this subsection provides that, in determining whether a loss of self-control has a qualifying trigger, the fact that a thing done or said amounted to sexual infidelity is to be disregarded. Thus, if a thing done or said amounts to sexual infidelity, that fact is disregarded in determining whether the qualifying trigger for the defendant's loss of control applies. The result is that if a person kills another because they have been unfaithful, he or she will not be able to claim the partial defense of loss of control.[36]

In light of these legislative steps adopted in common law countries such as Australia, Canada and England, I propose adding to Section 210.3(b) a categorical limitation on its application in circumstances relating to the killing of intimate partners against the backdrop of their desire to end the intimate relationship. The text of the proposed limitation is consistent with previous approaches that recommended a strategy for creating statutory categorical exclusions to the application of the claim of provocation in circumstances where intimate partners are murdered.[37] Similar and more detailed strategies[38] have been proposed, explicitly defining the range of circumstances in which it would not be possible to claim provocation, such as expressly mentioning the circumstances of terminating the intimate relationship or engaging in sexual relations with another person.[39]

34 See Coroners And Justice Act 2009, Explanatory Notes, UK Ministry of Justice, section 347 at 54.

35 Subsection (6):

> In determining whether a loss of self-control had a qualifying trigger … (b) a sense of being seriously wronged by a thing done or said is not justifiable if D *incited the thing to be done or said for the purpose of providing an excuse to use violence;* (c) *the fact that a thing done or said constituted sexual infidelity is to be disregarded.* (Italics added).

36 See Coroners And Justice Act 2009, Explanatory Notes, UK Ministry of Justice, section 349 at 54.

37 See e.g., Riley 2008: 70–71, 73 (describing such a strategy).

38 See Brown 1999: 140; Ramsey 2010: 92–94 (proposing to categorically and statutorily qualify the claim of provocation in cases where it is not legitimate to assert it – for example, in the context of homosexuals, in the context of verbal expressions only, in the context of the conduct of children and in the context of intimate partners).

39 In essence a statutory qualification such as this (relating to the circumstances of separation of the partners as an exception to which the norm is not applied) was already enacted in 1857 in the state of Texas in the United States, which expressly limited the application of the doctrine in circumstances where the spouses had already separated prior to the discovery of the adultery. Tex. Penal Code Ann. §1220 (repealed 1973). This law is not used here as a model, except in relation to the qualification provision, because it contains the partial defense of provocation for murders committed in circumstances of adultery. The relevant qualification was enacted in the Texas Penal Code as early as 1857, and finally repealed in 1973: "A homicide is justifiable when committed by the husband upon a person of any one taken in adultery with his wife; *provided the killing takes place before the parties to the act of adultery have separated.*" Ibid. (Italics added). In any event, this

Proposed amendments to Section 210.3(b) of the Model Penal Code

§210.3. Manslaughter: (1) Criminal homicide constitutes manslaughter when: (a) it is committed recklessly; or (b) a homicide which would otherwise be murder is committed under the influence of extreme mental or emotional disturbance for which there is reasonable explanation or excuse. The reasonableness of such explanation or excuse shall be determined from the viewpoint of a person in the actor's situation under the circumstances as he believes them to be. *Notwithstanding, the discovered, suspected or confessed will of an intimate partner to terminate an intimate relationship or begin one with someone else shall not constitute extreme mental or emotional disturbance for which there is reasonable explanation or excuse, for the purpose of this clause.*

Explanations accompanying the proposed statutory amendments to Section 210.3(b)

The proposed wording contains five unique features: *First*, for the sake of fairness and despite statistics showing that for the most part the murderers are men and the female partners are the victims,[40] the wording uses gender-neutral terminology and therefore applies to all partners, irrespective of gender.

Second, in contrast to Brown's proposal[41] or the provision enacted in England that uses terminology possessing negative connotations (by using the word "infidelity"), the proposed wording is careful to use terminology devoid of negative moral, social or religious connotations. The use of negative terminology that in itself describes the alleged sexual choices that the victim made connotes a negation and restriction of women's privilege to exercise autonomous choices over the kind of sexual intimacy they desire. Such negative legal and statutory wording might serve to strengthen current social attitudes and beliefs that accord social legitimacy to violence against women. Therefore, our proposed amendment does not employ words such as "sexual infidelity," "adultery," "unfaithfulness" or "betrayal," but rather the neutral term "intimate relationship."

Third, the proposed wording uses the broad term "intimate relationship" to refer to the typical characteristics of the type of relations between the murderer and the victim. Such broad terminology is consistent with the

---

statutory qualification was never enforced in practice. Notwithstanding the specific legislation, the courts in Texas continued to apply the partial defense of provocation to defendants, even in cases where they had murdered their spouses after they had already separated. See Lee 2003: 22.

40 As with the murder of men, women are almost always murdered by men (i.e., most murderers are men). U.S. Department of Justice, Bureau of Justice Statistics *Homicide in the U.S. Known to Law Enforcement 2011*. 2013: 4. www.bjs.gov/content/pub/pdf/hus11.pdf.

41 See Brown 1999: 140 ("(I) Where a defendant alleges provocation where the deceased has left, attempted to leave or threatened to leave an intimate sexual relationship. (II) Where the defendant alleges provocation because of suspected, discovered or confessed infidelity.")

recommendations of the Queensland Law Reform Commission set up in Australia that proposed to explicitly qualify the doctrine in circumstances when the partner seeks to terminate the "intimate relationship."[42] The term "intimate relationship" may refer to a sexual relationship, a romantic relationship or a marital relationship, and therefore covers the entire spectrum of possible relationships in this context. The decision to include a broad term that refers both to the circumstances of intimate relationships and to the circumstances of sexual relationships is grounded in the statistics that show that the murder of female partners is closely linked to the victim's desire to terminate the intimate relationship or to the partner's claims of the victim's sexual relationship with another man.[43] The empirical findings indicate that women are frequently murdered based on claims of their engaging in other sexual relationships, and that there is often a proximity of time between the desire of the female partner to end the intimate relationship and go her separate way and the defendant's claim of provocation stemming from the woman's other sexual relations.[44] Accordingly, it is important to word the qualifying provision to cover the widest possible range of circumstances in this context. The term "intimate relationship" is not rigid in terms of the type of sexual relations embraced by the qualifying provision and extends the boundaries of the provision to include any type of sexual relationship, without any requirement for actual sexual relations to have taken place in order to qualify for the exclusion within the doctrine of provocation. This contrasts with proposals that use the rigid terminology "to have sex"[45] or, as in the state of Maryland in the United States, "sexual intercourse,"[46] thereby limiting the applicability of the legal exception to circumstances of full sexual relations. Since violence against women occurs even in intimate relationships that do not include sexual relations, it is crucial to use expansive terminology that can be properly applied to all intimate relationships, including those with little or no sexual relations.

Fourth, the proposed wording includes a reference not only to real and factual intimate relations but also to the attribution of such a relationship, an admission in respect of such a relationship and a desire for such a relationship. A broad provision of this type would also embrace cases of murder committed simply because the woman indicated that she desired an intimate or sexual relationship with another person, or even because the defendant attributed

42 See Queensland Law Reform Commission (QLRC), *A Review of the Excuse of Accident and the Defence of Provocation*. Report No. 64: 481. 2008: "the Commission recommends a limitation on the circumstances in which the *deceased's exercise of choice about a relationship* may provide a sufficient foundation for the defence of provocation." (Italics added).

43 See ibid., chapter 2, footnotes 61–62 and related text.

44 See ibid., chapter 2, footnotes 63–64 and related text.

45 See Ramsey 2010: 94: "a decision by the victim to terminate or decline to begin a romantic or sexual relationship with the defendant or *to have sex* with another person." (Italics added).

46 Md. Code Ann., Criminal Law, §2-207.

such a desire to his intimate partner.[47] Therefore, the proposed qualification will apply not only in circumstance of the actual physical discovery of an intimate relationship with another but also in circumstances whereby there was only a verbal reference to a desire for such a relationship, including circumstances in which such a desire was ***attributed*** to the intimate partner by the defendant without any physical or verbal evidence of such desire actually existing. In this way, the proposed wording extends even further the formula approved in England: "a thing done or said,"[48] to include not only the discovery or admission of the existence of such a relationship, but also the very ***attribution***, even if only fictitious, of such a relationship.[49] This categorical expansion of the qualification reflects the notion that the law does not accord any importance or relevance to evidence or claims about the existence of a physical or other type of intimate relationship, but considers it important to protect every person's right to make autonomous decisions concerning his or her own intimate desires.

Proposed amendments to the doctrine of felony-murder rule in circumstances of assaultive-femicide

In order to properly treat assaultive-femicide perpetrators, it is of extreme importance to advance an explicit legislative and statutory inclusion of the offense of aggravated assault in circumstances of domestic violence. Such explicit legislation will prevent arbitrary judicial interpretations that exonerate defendants,[50] in line with the current exclusion of the offense of assault from the felony-murder doctrine.[51]

The proposed statutory amendment is based on the most commonly held version of the felony-murder rule in the United States: the enumerating version. This version enumerates the felonies that are formally conclusive on the issue of

47 For the connection between pathological jealousy (and psychological terms such as "delusional jealousy" or "Othello syndrome") and the murder of intimate partners, see Leong et al. 1994: 1445–1446.

48 According to the amended Section 55 in the Coroners and Justice Act 2009.

49 A result attained by using the term "suspected" in the proposed wording.

50 As noted in Chapter 3, in the case of *Beeman* (see Beeman 315 N.W 2d. 770) for example, the court rejected the defendant's argument that the merger limitation should preclude his use of assault against his former girlfriend as a predicate felony, solely based on the applicable statute's plain meaning and the legislature's clear intent that assault may operate as a predicate felony. See Van Zanten 2008: 1584. Iowa's jurisprudence took a marked turn in 2006. In *State* v. *Heemstra*, 721 N.W.2d 549 (Iowa 2006), in spite of its explicit language (categorizing forcible felonies as predicate to felony murder) the Iowa Supreme Court overruled its decision regarding Beeman (in *Beeman* 315 N.W 2d. at 770), and held that an assault causing the victim's death cannot be a predicate for felony murder. The implications of such a judicial decision for assaultive-femicide cases have yet to be seen.

51 The exclusion is based on the grounds of the "merger principle" sub-doctrine. For an elaborated analysis of the merger principle and its dire consequences for the phenomenon of assaultive-femicide, see related discussion in Chapter 3.

malice required for a murder conviction. As noted in Chapter 3, the mere enumeration of felonies as premising first-degree felony-murder conviction when causing an accidental killing is widely used by numerous U.S. jurisdictions. As the majority of state criminal codes in the United States have adopted the enumerating felony-murder version, the proposed legal arrangement is compatible with both the current felony-murder version in the MPC and (*mutatis mutandis*) with most U.S. jurisdictions. Such a legislative amendment prevents, *de jure*, any judicial exclusion of such an offense on the grounds of the merger principle,[52] and enables proper prosecution of assaultive-femicide perpetrators.

The proposed inclusion of the offense of aggravated assault within the MPC's list of predicate felony-murder follows the Model Penal Code's approach, which creates a legal rebuttable presumption concerning the defendant's criminal liability for the killing he committed in such circumstances. In line with the MPC drafter's approach, such legal presumption can be rebutted by the defendant.[53]

The proposed amendment abolishes the existing legal exception from criminal liability of men for assaultive homicide of female partners by adopting gender-neutral terminology in relation to the gender identity of both the perpetrator and the victim. The proposed definitions adopt gender-neutral and egalitarian legislative terminology, and pertain to domestic violence in general (not just to violence against women) so as to include potential male victims. In doing so, the proposed arrangement adjusts the legal harmony required for the proper conviction of assaultive-femicide perpetrators who are, lamentably, still exonerated from a murder conviction on the grounds of the application of the merger principle in the context of assaultive offenses.

The proposal includes direct amendments to Section 210.2 of the Model Penal Code. In addition, and if only for reasons of legal harmony, the proposal includes indirect amendments to Section 210.6, which addresses aggravating circumstances for death penalty upon first-degree felony-murder convictions. The wording of the proposed amendments to the MPC's felony-murder doctrine in circumstances of assaultive-femicide is as follows.

52 For an analysis of the merger principle sub-doctrine and its implications for the felony murder rule and assaultive-femicide, see Chapter 3.

53 For further analysis of the rebuttable legal presumption of criminal liability promoted by the felony-murder doctrine of the Model Penal Code, see Chapter 3.

Proposed direct amendments to Section 210.2 of the Model Penal Code

§210.2 Murder.

(1) Except as provided in Section 210.3(1)(b), criminal homicide constitutes murder when:

   (a) it is committed purposely or knowingly; or
   (b) it is committed recklessly under circumstances manifesting extreme indifference to the value of human life. Such recklessness and indifference are presumed if the actor is engaged or is an accomplice in the commission of, or an attempt to commit, or flight after committing or attempting to commit robbery, rape or deviate sexual intercourse by force or threat of force, arson, burglary, kidnapping, felonious escape, *or aggravated assault perpetrated as part of a pattern of domestic violence.*

For purposes of this section—

(1) *The term "aggravated assault" has the same meaning as given that term in Section 211.1(2).*[54]
(2) *The term "pattern" means assault engaged in on at least two occasions;*
(3) *The term "domestic violence" has the same meaning as given that term in (the proposed)*[55] *Section 3.11 (4).*[56]

54 Section 211.1(2):

> Aggravated Assault: A person is guilty of aggravated assault if he: (a) attempts to cause serious bodily injury to another, or causes such injury purposely, knowingly or recklessly under circumstances manifesting extreme indifference to the value of human life; or (b) attempts to cause or purposely or knowingly causes bodily injury to another with a deadly weapon.

55 This amendment relies on the proposed definition of Section 311.(4) within the proposal to amend the self-defense doctrine to apply to circumstances of domestic violence, as will be suggested further along in this chapter.

56 The wording of the proposed Section 3.11 (4) is as follows:

> "Domestic violence" means – the occurrence of any of the following acts by a person, which is not an act of self-defense: (i) Causing or attempting to cause physical or mental harm to a family or household member. (ii) Placing a family or household member in fear of physical or mental harm. (iii) Causing or attempting to cause a family or household member to engage in involuntary sexual activity by force, threat of force or duress. (iv) Engaging in activity toward a family or household member that would cause a reasonable person to feel terrorized, frightened, intimidated, threatened, harassed or molested. (v) Causing or allowing a child to see or hear violence directed against a person by a family or household member: or putting the child, or allowing the child to be put, at real risk of seeing or hearing that violence occurring.

Proposed indirect amendments to Section 210.6 of the Model Penal Code

> §210.6. Sentence of Death for Murder; Further Proceedings to Determine Sentence.
>
> (1) Death Sentence Excluded. When a defendant is found guilty of murder, the Court shall impose sentence for a felony of the first degree if it is satisfied that:...
>
> (3) Aggravating Circumstances:
>
> ... (e) The murder was committed while the defendant was engaged or was an accomplice in the commission of, or an attempt to commit, or flight after committing or attempting to commit robbery, rape or deviate sexual intercourse by force or threat of force, arson, burglary, kidnapping ***or aggravated assault perpetrated as part of a pattern or practice of domestic violence.***

Explanations accompanying the proposed statutory amendments to Sections 210.2(b) and 210.6(3)(e) of the Model Penal Code

The wording of the proposed legal arrangement adds the offense of "aggravated assault" to the enumerated felonies of the present category that lists and regulates predicate felony-murder in Section 210.2(2)(b) of the MPC. The expansion of this category is consistent, in particular, with the legal arrangements in the states of Washington and Iowa, which explicitly include assault within the list of predicate felony-murder,[57] and the legal arrangements in the states of Montana and Illinois, which explicitly include aggravated assault within the list

57 See Iowa statute in Iowa Code §707.2: "Murder in the first degree: A person commits murder in the first degree when the person commits murder under any of the following circumstances: 'The person kills another person while participating in a forcible felony'..." A reading of the respective list of "forcible felonies" list in 702.11 (2007) reveals that assault is listed as a forcible felony (together with murder, sexual abuse, kidnapping, robbery, first-degree arson and first-degree burglary): Iowa Code §702.11 FORCIBLE FELONY: 1. "A 'forcible felony' is any felonious child endangerment, assault, murder, sexual abuse, kidnapping, robbery, arson in the first degree, or burglary in the first degree." See also Washington's statute in RCW 9A.32.050:

> Murder in the second degree: (1) A person is guilty of murder in the second degree when: (a) With intent to cause the death of another person but without premeditation, he or she causes the death of such person or of a third person; or (b) He or she commits or attempts to commit any felony, including assault, other than those enumerated in RCW 9A.32.030(1)(c), and, in the course of and in furtherance of such crime or in immediate flight there from, he or she, or another participant, causes the death of a person other than one of the participants....

of predicate felony-murder.[58] The expansion of the list of predicate felonies to cater explicitly to homicide within circumstances of domestic violence is also consistent with the legislation in the states of Minnesota and Illinois, which includes particular legal instructions for the prosecution of homicide in circumstances of domestic violence.[59]

Apart from the proposed amendment that includes the offense of aggravated assault within circumstances of domestic violence, the proposal contains three additions that provide statutory definitions of the particular terms required for the application of the proposed amended arrangement. The first, added as subsection 210.2(2)(b)(1)to the MPC, is designed to provide a legal clarification of the term "aggravated assault" and refers to the existing definition in Section 211.1(2) of the MPC.[60] By referring to the existing definition of aggravated assault in the Code, the amendment includes as predicate felonies both assaults that caused serious bodily injury and assaults that caused injury with a deadly weapon.[61] The second addition, added as subsection 210.2(2)(b) to the MPC,

58 See Montana's statute in MONT. CODE ANN §45–5–102:

> Deliberate homicide. (1) A person commits the offense of deliberate homicide if: (a) the person purposely or knowingly causes the death of another human being; (b) the person attempts to commit, commits, or is legally accountable for the attempt or commission of robbery, sexual intercourse without consent, arson, burglary, kidnapping, aggravated kidnapping, felonious escape, assault with a weapon, aggravated assault, or any other forcible felony and in the course of the forcible felony or flight thereafter, the person or any person legally accountable for the crime causes the death of another human being.

See also Illinois statute in 720 ILCS 5/9–1) (Ch. 38, par. 9–1) sec. 9–1.

> First degree Murder – Death penalties – Exceptions – Separate Hearings – Proof – Findings – Appellate procedures – Reversals. (a) A person who kills an individual without lawful justification commits first degree murder if, in performing the acts which cause the death: (1) he either intends to kill or do great bodily harm to that individual or another, or knows that such acts will cause death to that individual or another; or (2) he knows that such acts create a strong probability of death or great bodily harm to that individual or another; or (3) he is attempting or committing a forcible felony other than second degree murder.

59 See Minnesota's statute in MN Statutes section 609.185 (murder in first degree) and Section 609.19 (murder in second degree). See also Illinois' statute in 720 ILCS 5/9–1 (b) (Aggravating Factors).

60 See Section 211.1(2) of the Model Penal Code:

> Aggravated Assault: A person is guilty of aggravated assault if he: (a) attempts to cause serious bodily injury to another, or causes such injury purposely, knowingly or recklessly under circumstances manifesting extreme indifference to the value of human life; or (b) attempts to cause or purposely or knowingly causes bodily injury to another with a deadly weapon.

61 As noted in Chapter 3, according to the current wording of the definition of aggravated assault in Section 211.1(2) of the Model Penal Code, an assault with a deadly weapon will be graded as a felonious aggravated assault even if the injury was not serious, and even if the weapon used was not inherently deadly. For further analysis of the definition of assault, see Chapter 3.

is designed to provide a legal clarification of the term "pattern" and follows the current definition of the term within the circumstances of domestic violence, as worded in the felony-murder section of the U.S. criminal Code[62] and in the section that addresses felony-murder in Minnesota's criminal code.[63] The third addition, added as subsection 210.2(2)(b)(3) to the MPC, is designed to provide a legal clarification of the term "domestic violence," and refers to a proposed definition that will be added to subsection 311.(4) of the MPC as will be elaborated below.

Along with the extended approach that includes the offense of aggravated assault within the predicate felony-murder, the proposed amendment is limited in relation to two main legal principles. *First*, the criminal inclusion of the offense of assault is explicitly limited to "aggravated assault," and thereby prevents excessive expansion of the felony-murder doctrine to simple assaults. *Second*, the proposed text restricts the application of the criminal offense of aggravated assault by introducing two cumulative preconditions: the aggravated assault must be committed in circumstances of domestic violence, and the inclusion of such offense is restricted to the precondition of a "pattern" of domestic violence. Such a legal arrangement follows the approach reflected in the U.S. Criminal Code that restricts criminal liability for such assaults provided they are preconditioned on a prior pattern.[64] These two circumscribed yet cumulative requirements create a balanced legislative arrangement: on the one hand it includes in its consideration elements and characteristics of assaultive homicide within circumstances of domestic violence, and on the other hand it does not unduly expand the scope of the felony-murder doctrine to simple assaults or to aggravated assaults that are not preconditioned on a previous pattern of domestic violence.

62 See U.S. Code, Title 18, Part I, chapter 51, Section 1111(b)(4): "the term 'pattern or practice of assault or torture' means assault or torture engaged in on at least two occasions."

63 See Minnesota's legislation that states for example that an assaultive homicide would be graded as a first degree murder if the perpetrator:

> causes the death of a human being while committing domestic abuse, when the perpetrator has engaged in a past pattern of domestic abuse upon the victim or upon another family or household member and the death occurs under circumstances manifesting an extreme indifference to human life.
>
> (MN Statutes §609.185)

64 See U.S. Code, Title 18, Part I, chapter 51, Section 1111:

> (a) Murder is the unlawful killing of a human being with malice aforethought. Every murder perpetrated by poison, lying in wait, or any other kind of willful, deliberate, malicious, and premeditated killing; or committed in the perpetration of, or attempt to perpetrate, any arson, escape, murder, kidnapping, treason, espionage, sabotage, aggravated sexual abuse or sexual abuse, child abuse, burglary, or robbery; or perpetrated as part of a pattern or practice of assault or torture against a child or children; or perpetrated from a premeditated design unlawfully and maliciously to effect the death of any human being other than him who is killed, is murder in the first degree.

In addition to the direct amendments proposed to Section 210.2 of the Model Penal Code, the proposal takes note of indirect amendments with regard to aggravating circumstances for a death penalty sentence within the felony-murder rule, as worded in Section 210.6 and necessary for legal harmony in regulating aggravating circumstances within the felony-murder doctrine. In this respect, the proposed amendment suggests amending subsection 210.6(3)(e) so as to include the offense of aggravated assault in circumstances of domestic violence within its list of aggravating circumstances for the death penalty. As noted in Chapter 3, the legislative arrangement of the State of Illinois somewhat resembles the proposed indirect amendment of section 210.6(3)(e) of the Model Penal Code: Illinois enacted a section catering to murder in circumstances whereby there was a restraining order under a domestic violence statute, and included such circumstances as aggravating factors for the death penalty upon first-degree murder conviction.[65] Similar legislation viewing femicide as an aggravating factor was also legislated in Minnesota, and such legislation should be further tailored to the particular phenomenon of lethal violence against women. In this respect, is it is worth mentioning jurisdictions that legislated statutes catering to homicide in circumstances of domestic violence, intending to frame domestic violence circumstances as aggravating factors. For example, Minnesota's statutes state that an assaultive homicide will be graded as a first-degree murder if the perpetrator:

> causes the death of a human being while *committing domestic abuse,* when the perpetrator *has engaged in a past pattern of domestic abuse upon the victim* or upon another family or household member and the death occurs under circumstances manifesting an extreme indifference to human life.[66]

Following this legal construction of lethal domestic violence as an aggravating factor, Minnesota grades as second-degree murder any unintentional assaultive homicide if committed under domestic violence circumstances, while the perpetrator had been restrained under an order for protection. Minnesota's statute states that whoever:

> causes the death of a human being without intent to effect the death of any person, while intentionally inflicting or attempting to inflict bodily harm upon the victim, when the perpetrator is restrained under an order for protection and the victim is a person designated to receive protection under

65 720 ILCS 5/9-1 (b):

> Aggravating Factors: A defendant who at the time of the commission of the offense has attained the age of 18 or more and who has been found guilty of first degree murder may be sentenced to death if: (19) the murdered individual was subject to an order of protection and the murder was committed by a person against whom the same order of protection was issued under Illinois Domestic Violence Act of 1986.

66 MN Statutes Section 609.185.

> the order, is guilty of unintentional murder in the second degree and may be sentenced to imprisonment for not more than 40 years.[67]

Illinois enacted a similar statute catering to murder in circumstances whereby there was a restraining order under a domestic violence statute, and included such circumstances within the aggravating factors for a death penalty sentence upon first-degree murder conviction.[68]

Proposed amendments to the doctrine of self-defense in circumstances of domestic violence

The highly polemic debates surrounding the circumstances of battered women who kill their batterers and eventually cannot claim the self-defense doctrine led to legislative reforms in various common law countries. The most comprehensive amendments to the doctrine were legislated by Victoria State in Australia both in 2005 and in 2014,[69] and equally impressive were the relevant provisions legislated by Canada in 2012.

Victoria State in Australia made major legislative reforms to the doctrine of self-defense in 2005, aiming to cater, among other things, to circumstances of domestic violence. The amendment explicitly states that in alleged family violence circumstances a person may believe and may have reasonable grounds to believe that his conduct was necessary even if his response to a harm was not immediate and/or proportional.[70] By this the legislation de facto abolished the

67 See MN Statutes 609.19 Murder In The Second Degree: whoever:

> (2) causes the death of a human being without intent to effect the death of any person, while intentionally inflicting or attempting to inflict bodily harm upon the victim, when the perpetrator is restrained under an order for protection and the victim is a person designated to receive protection under the order. As used in this clause, "order for protection" includes an order for protection issued under chapter 518B; a harassment restraining order issued under section 609.748; a court order setting conditions of pre-trial release or conditions of a criminal sentence or juvenile court disposition; a restraining order issued in a marriage dissolution action; and any order issued by a court of another state or of the United States that is similar to any of these orders.

68 See 720 ILCS 5/9–1 (b) Aggravating Factors:

> A defendant who at the time of the commission of the offense has attained the age of 18 or more and who has been found guilty of first degree murder may be sentenced to death if: the murdered individual was subject to an order of protection and the murder was committed by a person against whom the same order of protection was issued under Illinois Domestic Violence Act of 1986.

69 Through the Crimes Amendment (Abolition of Defensive Homicide) Act 2014 (Vic.).

70 See Crimes (Homicide) Act 1958 (Vic.) Section 9AH:

> Family violence (1) Without limiting section 9AC, 9AD or 9AE, for the purposes of murder, defensive homicide or manslaughter, *in circumstances where family violence is alleged a person may believe, and may have reasonable grounds for believing, that his or her conduct is necessary* – (a) to defend himself or herself or another person; or (b) to prevent or terminate the unlawful deprivation of his or her liberty or the liberty of another person – *even if* – (c) he or she is

two common law requirements that were the most challenging for battered wives who killed their batterers. Furthermore, the legislative reform instructed fact finders with regard to the evidence that may be relevant to establish the need and the reasonableness of the accused's conduct by explicitly including a wide range of social, cultural, economic, historical and psychological aspects of the alleged family violence that may be adduced.[71]

In 2014 the self-defense doctrine in Victoria was reformulated once again to instruct fact finders to focus on the situation faced by the accused in the context of family violence.[72] In these circumstances the Parliament's explanatory notes state that the new section provides a statutory subjective test that enables a defendant to claim self-defense if he or she *believed* that the conduct is necessary and the conduct was a *reasonable response in the circumstances as the person perceives them.*[73] The wording of the amendment does not focus on whether the person had objective "reasonable grounds" for his or her belief that it was necessary to act in self-defense – rather, on the way the accused himself perceived the circumstances. The reform further indicates how self-defense provisions should be interpreted in circumstances of domestic violence by instructing that defendants under such circumstances may claim self-defense even if their conduct did not meet the common law's requirements of immediacy and proportionality. In this amendment Victoria's Parliament recognizes that family violence may affect how a person acts in self-defense, stating that: "For example, a person may act in self-defence in response to an ongoing

---

> responding to a harm that is *not immediate*; or (d) his or her response involves *the use of force in excess* of the force involved in the harm or threatened harm. (Italics added).

71 See amended Section 9AH(3):

> Evidence of – (a) the *history of the relationship* between the person and a family member, including violence by the family member towards the person or by the person towards the family member or by the family member or the person in relation to any other family member; (b) the *cumulative effect, including psychological effect,* on the person or a family member of that violence; (c) *social, cultural or economic factors* that impact on the person or a family member who has been affected by family violence; (d) the *general nature and dynamics of relationships affected* by family violence, including the possible consequences of separation from the abuser; (e) the *psychological effect of violence* on people who are or have been in a relationship affected by family violence; (f) *social or economic factors* that impact on people who are or have been in a relationship affected by family violence. (Italics added).

72 See Domestic Violence Resource Centre Victoria Discussion Paper No.10, 2016. "Out of Character? Legal Responses to Intimate Partner Homicides by Men in Victoria 2005–2014": 23, referring to Victoria, Legislative Assembly 2014: 2835.

73 Italics added. The legislative amendment was recommended by the Victorian Law Reform Commission in its Defences to Homicide: Final Report (2004) and states that:

> in circumstances where self-defence in the context of family violence is in issue, a person may believe that the person's conduct is necessary in self-defence, and the conduct may be a reasonable response in the circumstances as the person perceives them, even if – (a)the person is responding to a harm that *is not immediate*; or (b) the response involves the *use of force in excess* of the force involved in the harm or threatened harm. (Italics added).

threat of violence, rather than an immediate attack, or when their physically stronger partner has their guard down."[74]

Canada also introduced legislative instructions with regard to the self-defense doctrine in circumstances of domestic violence.[75] The most relevant provisions for battered women claiming self-defense are those instructing fact finders to consider three relevant aspects: the extent of imminence in the defensive conduct of the accused; potential disparities in the physical capacities of the sides; and any history of domestic violence between the sides.[76] In addition, the amendment instructs to consider the extent to which the use of force was imminent and whether there were other means available to respond to the potential use of force.[77] According to the Parliamentary debate over this legislative reform,[78] the wording codifies the precedent ruled by the Supreme Court of Canada in one of the most well-known cases of a battered wife who killed her batterer, the case of *Lavallee*.[79] In this ruling the imminence of an attack, long thought to be a determinative required element of self-defense, was ruled to be considered as only one of the overall possible relevant factors to be considered. According to the bill's drafters, codifying the amendment was intended to ensure that the courts would not deny battered women a claim of self-defense solely on the basis of the immediacy of their defensive response.[80] It also statutorily stated that, although the common law

74 See Crimes Amendment (Abolition of Defensive Homicide) Act 2014, No. 63 of 2014: 8.

75 The amendment changed the self-defense doctrine as worded in Section 34 of Canada's Criminal Code. The new legislation reads as follows:

> (1) A person is not guilty of an offense if (a) they believe on reasonable grounds that force is being used against them or another person or that a threat of force is being made against them or another person; (b) the act that constitutes the offense is committed for the purpose of defending or protecting themselves or the other person from that use or threat of force; and (c) the act committed is reasonable in the circumstances. (2) In determining whether the act committed is reasonable in the circumstances, the court shall consider the relevant circumstances of the person, the other parties and the act, including, but not limited to, the following factors: (a) the nature of the force or threat; (b) the extent to which the use of force was imminent and whether there were other means available to respond to the potential use of force; (c) the person's role in the incident; (d) whether any party to the incident used or threatened to use a weapon; (e) the size, age, gender and physical capabilities of the parties to the incident; (f) the nature, duration and history of any relationship between the parties to the incident, including any prior use or threat of force and the nature of that force or threat; (f.1) any history of interaction or communication between the parties to the incident; (g) the nature and proportionality of the person's response to the use or threat of force; and (h) whether the act committed was in response to a use or threat of force that the person knew was lawful.

76 As in Subsections 2(b), 2(e) and 2(f) of Section 34 in Canada's Criminal Code.

77 As in Subsection 34(2)(b) of Canada's Criminal Code.

78 See Government of Canada, Department of Justice, Bill C-26 (S.C. 2012 c. 9), Reforms to Self-Defence and Defence of Property: Technical Guide for Practitioners. www.justice.gc.ca/eng/rp-pr/other-autre/rsddp-rlddp/p5.html

79 *R.* v. *Lavallee*, [1990] 1 S.C.R. 852.

80 Senator Fraser quotes the Senior Counsel in the Criminal Law Policy Section of Canada's Department of Justice in the Senate debate over the bill, stating that the Supreme Court ruled in the

requirement to retreat may be relevant to a person's claim of self-defense, it should not be determinative and rigidly interpreted. The drafters of the amendment took note of Senator Joan Fraser's[81] remarks on the relevance of such provision to battered wives who kill their batterers, quoting the following paragraph from her speech in the bill's explanatory notes:

> in the *Lavallee* case … the Supreme Court addressed many of the myths about spousal abuse, spousal violence and self-defence arguments that could be brought in those cases by the abused spouse. Ms. Lavallee was a woman who had been repeatedly and severely abused, and one night her partner told her that later that night he was going to kill her, and she believed him, so she shot him, dead. This case went all the way to the Supreme Court, and it was a landmark judgment instructing courts to take into account expert testimony about the effect of being an abused spouse, a feeling of having nowhere to go, nowhere to turn, no escape, and sometimes being driven to commit very serious violence in order, one believes, to defend oneself, even if that defence is not specifically necessary because one is not being abused at that precise moment.

Aware that when legal doubts arise in court reference is sometimes made to the Senate debate, Senator Fraser insisted inserting into the formal record of the Senate the explanatory notes forwarded by the Department of Justice in Canada with regard to the purpose of the legislative amendment:

> For the first time, the Supreme Court gave an interpretation to the existing self-defence laws such that the situation of the battered woman could be taken into account. Essentially the court said that where battered women's cases had previously not resulted in a successful self-defence plea was because the jury could not appreciate how a reasonable person in that woman's situation would not have left the relationship sooner, or how they might have perceived they were at risk. The most important thing the Supreme Court determined in that case was that whenever there is an aspect of reasonableness in the law of self-defence, it is important to consider the particular circumstances of an abused person – and the nature of their relationship – and attribute that to the reasonable person. That is essentially what 34(2)(*f*) is trying to get at; in determining what is reasonable you would have to consider the history of the relationship.

---

case of Lavallee that a battered spouse situation is exactly one where the assault might not be imminent, but nonetheless the person would reasonably feel himself taking into account the history of the relationship in considering whether they have any option but to do what they did. See Canada Senate Debates, June 12, 2012.

81 Op. cit.

Another relevant amended provision relates to the statutory instruction to consider the size, age, gender and physical capabilities of the parties to the incident when evaluating a person's claim of self-defense.[82] Such explicit instruction ensures that, in determining the battered wife's claim of imminence and proportionality, her physical capabilities in relation to her perpetrator would be duly noted and considered. Yet another provision of utmost relevance to the battered woman's perception of tangible danger, imminence and proportionality was introduced. The provision explicitly instructs that, in addition to the physical disparities of the sides, additional consideration should be given to the nature, duration and history of any relationship between the parties to the incident, including any prior use or threat of force and the nature of that force or threat.[83] This provision codified de facto and *de jure* the legislators' recognition that evidence about the relationship and history between the parties is crucial for placing the conflict in its proper context. It is of particular interest that the drafters found the circumstances of domestic violence particularly relevant to this amended provision and referred once again to the precedent case of Lavallee:

> *In the Lavallee case, the Supreme Court of Canada made clear that evidence of an abusive history between the parties, and expert evidence about the dynamics of domestic abuse on the victim, contextualize the accused's experience so as to allow their actions to be viewed and understood as objectively "reasonable" in the circumstances.* Paragraph 34(2)(f) makes clear that the history of the relationship, and any abuse within it, are relevant to assessing the reasonableness of the accused's defensive actions, and thereby signals that *courts should continue to apply the principles from Lavallee under the framework of the new law.*[84]

Even England, the cradle of the common law self-defense doctrine, enacted legislative reforms in 2010, seemingly accommodating battered wives who killed their batterers if and when they are unsuccessful in claiming self-defense. The legislative amendment to the Homicide Act of 1957 provides an optional route for battered women who killed their perpetrators, through the partial defense of loss of control, setting forth that when the defense is successful the defendant will be guilty of manslaughter instead of murder.[85] The new partial defense enacted in section 54 of the Coroners and Justice Act 2009 implicitly accommodates circumstances of domestic violence because the partial defense can be

82 As in Subsection 34(2)(e) of Canada Criminal Code.
83 As in Subsection 34(2)(f) of Canada Criminal Code.
84 Italics added. Section 55(3). See Government of Canada, Department of Justice, Bill C-26 (S.C. 2012 c. 9), Reforms to Self-Defence and Defence of Property: Technical Guide for Practitioners. www.justice.gc.ca/eng/rp-pr/other-autre/rsddp-rlddp/p5.html.
85 See Section 54(7), the Coroners and Justice Act 2009.

granted even when the loss of control was not sudden.[86] Furthermore, and with relevance to femicide, the amendment instructs to admit a subjective test of the defendant's loss of control due to their fear of a serious violent attack.[87] The Parliament's notes placed this amendment in the context of circumstances of domestic violence by stating that the legal requirement in such circumstances "will be a subjective test and the defendant will *need to show that he or she lost self-control because of a genuine fear of serious violence, whether or not the fear was in fact reasonable.*"[88] This implicit statutory inclusion of domestic violence circumstances is further structured along the legal requirement to consider the defendant's history of abuse at the hands of the victim by stating that:

> a defendant that killed while loss of control is not to be convicted of murder if a person of defendant's sex and age, with a normal degree of tolerance and self-restraint and *in the circumstances of the defendant*, might have reacted in the same or in a similar way to the defendant. (Italics added).

Following the legal framework set forth in the above legislative reforms, I propose a reform to the self-defense doctrine in the Model Penal Code to cater adequately to battered women indicted for the killing of their batterer. The proposed amendment to the self-defense doctrine in circumstances of domestic violence is in line with the current structure of the American doctrine that precisely and distinctly regulates the conditions for using deadly protective force, and proposes to expand the category of deadly protective force as it is currently formulated in Section 3.04(2)(b) of the MPC. As such, the proposed amendment, *ipso facto*, creates a legal presumption whereby circumstances of severe and prolonged violence in the family pose a real danger to the victim's body and life. The proposed amendment also caters to the specific legal requirements that, according to the MPC, victims of domestic violence must meet as they relate to circumstances prior to the use of deadly protective force. In this regard, the proposed amendment offers unique adjustments to the current legal structure in relation to the duty to retreat applicable to victims of domestic violence (where the perpetrator is a co-dweller), as well as to their duty to comply with the perpetrator's demands prior to using deadly protective force.

In addition, and if only to ensure legislative harmony, the amendment proposed in this book suggests criminalization of acts of sexual violence committed against intimate female partners, acts that, unfortunately, are currently explicitly

86 According to Section 54(2) of the Coroners and Justice Act 2009: For the purposes of Subsection (1)(a), it does not matter whether or not the loss of control was sudden.

87 "This subsection applies if D's loss of self-control was attributable to D's fear of serious violence from V against D or identified person."

88 Italics added. See Coroners and Justice Act, Explanatory Notes, UK Ministry of Justice, 2009: 53, section 345.

permitted under the auspices of the statutory formulation of the MPC. Although, prima facie, the legislative amendment of the definition of sexual crimes is not related to the issue of domestic violence, this amendment is crucial to a comprehensive and just legal doctrine of self-defense in circumstances of severe and sustained domestic violence.

The proposed legal arrangement is consistent with the proposals of previous scholars for modifying the doctrine of self-defense in circumstances where battered women have killed their assailant partners.[89] The proposal focuses on the concrete legal structure of the doctrine of self-defense in the MPC and on its particular inadequacies with regard to its application in circumstances of domestic violence: the duty to retreat from one's dwelling and the requirement to respond to an attack in a proportional manner. The proposed arrangement

89 I agree with previous proposals made by researchers in the field. However, these previous proposals have not yet evolved into detailed relevant legislative drafts to regulate the issue in the MPC. I refer particularly to the proposals to abolish the duty to retreat in the context of battered women (see Mackinnon 2001: 745; La Fond, 1982: 762), and in states that have not abolished the duty to retreat in relation to co-dwellers, (Gillespie 1989: xii; Browne 1987: 187–188; Carpenter 2003: 667–700; Downs 1984: 233; Maguigan 1991: 451; Mather 1988: 545, 569). Likewise, I agree with proposals to deal with the requirement of proportionality by expanding the circumstances in which the use of deadly protective force is permitted (Gillespie 1989: 188; La Fond 1982: 284; Schneider 1980: 623, 633; Mather 1988: 545; Ewing 1990: 579–594, 587), and the proposal to create a legal presumption of real danger to life/serious injury in circumstances of domestic violence (Downs 1984: 236). As the language of the MPC allows a relatively broad interpretation of the requirement of immediacy, I do not believe that it is necessary to adopt the proposed amendments to the doctrine in this context, even though I agree with these proposals and believe that they are needed in states which adopted stringent and objective requirements in this context (such as Nebraska, Pennsylvania, Texas, Tennessee, Arizona, Delaware, Georgia, Hawaii and New Jersey). With regard to these states it is desirable, in general, to adopt the proposals expanding the flexibility of the requirement of immediacy in the context of battered women (see for this issue Mahoney 1991: 83–93; Schneider 1980: 634; Maguigan 1991: 449; Mackinnon 2001: 758; Gillespie 1989: 186–187; Mather 1988: 567; Fiora-Gormally 1978: 133, 154; Rosen C. 1986: 11, 34; Talbot 1988: 1527, 1545), and in particular the proposals to include within the wording of the requirement the possibility of an impending assault that may occur at any moment (Downs 1984: 232, 247), inevitable assault (for such a proposal see Leverick 2006: 102–108), an act of defense which is "necessary," even if not immediately (for this proposal, see Rosen R. 1993: 393–394), or an act needed to effectively resolve an ongoing situation of assault (for such a proposal, see La Fond 1982: 280). Likewise, I agree with researchers' suggestions that in states where there is an "objective" reasonableness approach, it is necessary to soften it into a subjective approach relating to the reasonableness of the actions taken by the defendant, in circumstances of domestic violence (Gillespie 1989: 189; Downs 1984: 238, 241; Maguigan 1991: 445–448). For the proposal to create a standard of reasonableness specifically for battered women, see Kinports 1988: 393, 416. Furthermore, it is worth considering the regulation of expert testimony and presentation of evidence, in so far as preliminary evidence is available in the context of domestic violence (Gillespie 1989: 190; Downs 1984: 239; Mackinnon 2001: 760; Maguigan 1991: 449, 456–458; Rosen C. 1986: 38–39; Kinports 1988: 451–453), as well as specific instructions to the jury concerning the proper legal interpretation of the requirements of the doctrine in circumstances of domestic violence (Maguigan 1991: 457–460; Downs 1984: 233–235, 237).

leaves intact the existing legal arrangement in the MPC in relation to three of the traditional requirements for the application of the doctrine (immediacy, repelling an unlawful act and conduct that is not unlawful), as the current wording of these requirements corresponds to the patterns of response that appear to be characteristic of women suffering from domestic violence.

Together with the retaining of these three traditional requirements, and in order to achieve a proper legal arrangement in cases of domestic violence, it is necessary to regulate two other traditional requirements of the doctrine of self-defense: the duty to retreat and the requirement of proportionality. The proposed amendment introduces the following four major amendments to these two doctrinal requirements: *First*, it is proposed to adjust the requirement of proportionality in circumstances of domestic violence by adding these circumstances to the MPC category that currently permits the use of deadly protective force[90] (found in Section 3.04(2)(b)). The inclusion of such circumstances in this category would create a legal presumption that a real and concrete danger exists in cases of severe and continuous domestic violence,[91] such that the use of deadly protective force in these cases would meet the doctrine's requirement of proportionality.

Second, I advocate the explicit abolition of the requirement to comply with the demands of the aggressor (either positive demands to act in certain ways or negative demands to avoid doing something), and/or the particular duty to retreat if and when the aggressor is a co-dweller, in circumstances of severe and prolonged domestic violence. As stated in the proposed amendment, the abolition is explicitly confined to the aggressor's demands "that endanger the personal security, bodily integrity, autonomy or dignity of the victim." This categorical provision should be inserted, in my view, in a separate subsection (Section C), that will follow Section 3.04(2)(b)(ii)(B), which, as currently drafted, refers expressly to the need to comply with these requirements before the use of deadly protective force is permitted.

90 This proposal is consistent with La Fond's proposal (see La Fond 1982: 280). It is also in line with the legal arrangement in the state of Arkansas, which specifically includes circumstances of domestic abuse in the category that permits the use of deadly protective force (see 2010 Arkansas Code, Section 5–2–607).

91 In other words, a real danger to the person's body and/or life and/or autonomy and/or freedom and/or dignity. For the justification of such an expansive approach in the context of the use of deadly protective force, see also La Fond 1982: 238:

> The law of self-defense ought to be grounded primarily in the theory of personal autonomy and, accordingly, that the law should be changed explicitly to permit recourse to deadly force by innocent victims against aggressors whenever necessary to defend effectively against unlawful violence.

See also ibid.: 243–244, 278–282. In this regard, see also the comments supporting the use of deadly protective force in circumstances of rape despite the absence of real danger to life or threat of severe bodily injury, if only because of the brutal interference with the victim's autonomy and humanity. See Leverick 2006: 156–157.

Third, in order to ensure clarity and uniformity in the application of the proposed amendment, it is suggested to insert specific legal definitions of the terms relevant to the circumstances of domestic violence within the section dealing with the general legal definitions relevant to the doctrine of self-defense (Section 3.11). I propose adding the specific legal definitions of "domestic violence" and of a "family member" to the current legal definitions set out in Section 3.11. These legal definitions clarify who will be regarded as a family member for the purpose of domestic violence and, accordingly, what is domestic violence. The proposed definition of domestic violence is in line with current knowledge in this field, and includes a varied repertoire of patterns of violence (physical, mental, verbal, emotional and sexual) employed against a family member.

Fourth, in order to ensure legislative harmony (as well as gender-related justice), it is proposed to introduce an indirect amendment to the definition of sexual crimes set out in the MPC, so that the criminal exemptions applicable today to men committing sex crimes against their female partners will be abolished.[92] Any selective implementation of the three main legislative amendments proposed above, without the implementation of this accompanying indirect amendment to the existing definitions of sexual offenses, may create an absurd legal order that prohibits the commission of physical or mental violence against women in general (including partners), but expressly allows myriad forms of sexual violence in so far as they are directed towards female intimate partners. Such an implicit criminal permission and the distorted legal harmony must be categorically and statutorily abolished.

The wording of the proposed amendments to the MPC in the context of a claim of self-defense made in circumstances of severe and sustained violence in the family is as follows:

Proposed direct amendments to Sections 3.04 and 3.11 of the Model Penal Code

§3.04. Use of Force in Self-Protection

(2) Limitations on Justifying Necessity for Use of Force

(a) ...

(b) The use of deadly force is not justifiable under this Section unless the actor believes that such force is necessary to protect himself against death, serious bodily injury, kidnapping, sexual intercourse compelled by force or threat, *or circumstances of a severe and prolonged pattern of domestic violence;* nor is it justifiable if:

92 For a similar argument criticizing the legal marital immunity from rape as stated in the Model Penal Code's wording, see Denno 2003: 213.

(i) the actor … provoked the use of force against himself in the same encounter; or …

(ii) the actor knows that he can avoid the necessity of using such force with complete safety by retreating or by surrendering possession of a thing … except that:

(A) the actor is not obliged to retreat from his dwelling or place of work, unless he was the initial aggressor or is assailed in his place of work by another person whose place of work the actor knows it to be;

(B) a public officer is justified in using force …

(C) *in circumstances of a severe and prolonged pattern of domestic violence the actor is not obliged to retreat from his dwelling even if the perpetrator is a co-dweller, nor is he obliged to comply with a demand to perform or abstain from performing any action that endangers either his personal security, bodily integrity, autonomy or dignity.*

§3.11. Definitions

In this Article, unless a different meaning plainly is required:

(1) "unlawful force" …

(2) "deadly force" …

(3) "dwelling" …

(4) *"Domestic violence" means – the occurrence of any of the following acts by a person, which is not an act of self-defense:*

(i) *Causing or attempting to cause physical or mental harm to a family or household member.*

(ii) *Placing a family or household member in fear of physical or mental harm.*

(iii) *Causing or attempting to cause a family or household member to engage in involuntary sexual activity by force, threat of force or duress.*

(iv) *Engaging in activity toward a family or household member that would cause a reasonable person to feel terrorized, frightened, intimidated, threatened, harassed or molested.*

(v) *Causing or allowing a child to see or hear violence directed against a person by a family or household member: or putting the child, or allowing the child to be put, at real risk of seeing or hearing that violence occurring.*

(5) *"Family or household member" includes any of the following:*

(i) *A spouse or former spouse.*

(ii) *An individual with whom the person resides or has resided, has or has had a dating relationship, is or has engaged in a sexual relationship, is related or was formerly related by marriage, has a child in common.*

(iii) *The minor child of an individual described in subparagraphs (i) and (ii).*

Proposed indirect amendments to Sections 213.1–213.5 of the Model Penal Code

§213.1 Rape and Related Offenses
Rape. A *person* ~~*male*~~ who has sexual intercourse with *another* ~~*a female not his wife*~~ is guilty of rape …
Gross Sexual Imposition. A *person* ~~*male*~~ who has sexual intercourse with *another* ~~*a female not his wife*~~ commits a felony …

§213.3 Corruption of Minors and Seduction
Offense Defined. A *person* ~~*male*~~ who has sexual intercourse with *another* ~~*a female not his wife*~~ …

§213.4 Sexual Assault
A person who has contact with another ~~*not his spouse*~~ …

§213.5 Indecent Exposure
A person commits a misdemeanor if, for the purpose of arousing or gratifying sexual desire of himself or of any person ~~*other than his spouse*~~ …

Explanations accompanying the proposed statutory amendments to Sections 3.04, 3.11, 213.1–213.5 of the Model Penal Code

The wording of the proposed legal arrangement adds the circumstance of a "severe and prolonged pattern of domestic violence" to the present category that regulates the use of deadly protective force in Section 3.04 (2) (b) of the MPC. The expansion of this category is consistent, in particular, with the legal arrangement in the state of Arkansas that explicitly permits the use of deadly force against aggressors in circumstances of "domestic abuse."[93] This expansion is also consistent with many U.S. state criminal legal systems that allow the use of deadly protective force not only in life-threatening situations but also in other

93 2010 Arkansas Code, Title 5 – Criminal Offenses, Subtitle 1 – General Provisions, Chapter 2, Principles of Criminal Liability, Subchapter 6 – Justification, 5–2–607:

> Use of deadly physical force in defense of a person: (a) A person is justified in using deadly physical force upon another person if the person reasonably believes that the other person is: (1) Committing or about to commit a felony involving force or violence; (2) Using or about to use unlawful deadly physical force; or (3) Imminently endangering the person's life or imminently about to victimize the person as described in 9–15–103 from the continuation of a pattern of domestic abuse.

circumstances where a crime is being committed.[94] The inclusion of circumstances of domestic violence in the legal category that permits the use of deadly force creates, *de jure*, a legal presumption concerning the existence of a real and concrete danger in cases of domestic violence. In doing so, the proposed legal arrangement adjusts the traditional doctrinal requirement of proportionality to the particular circumstances of a severe and prolonged pattern of domestic violence.[95]

In addition, the proposed amendment explicitly abolishes the two existing requirements in the MPC in the context of the use of deadly protective force (the requirement of retreat when the aggressor is a co-dweller, and the requirement of compliance with the demands of the aggressor). The explicit abolition of these two requirements in the context of domestic violence is regulated in a separate section: Section 3.04(2)(b)(ii)(C) of the MPC. The proposal takes note of the indirect amendments with regard to sexual violence against intimate female partners, needed for legal harmony within the regulation of domestic violence. In this respect, the proposed amendment suggests amending the current gender-related criminal exemptions explicitly set forth in Sections 213.1 to 213.5 of the MPC. In effect, the amendment abolishes the existing legal immunity and exception from criminal liability of men for sexual offenses committed against their female partners by substituting neutral, non-gendered terminology for the gendered wording of the definitions. These indirect amendments are consistent with the legislative reforms made in many jurisdictions (in the United States and the world) that criminalize sexual offenses[96] without granting any criminal immunity in this context to one of the partners. Likewise, and further to the gender-neutral terminology adopted in this proposal, it is proposed to adopt neutral language in relation to the gender identity of the victim and the assailant in sexual offenses (the current language is not gender-neutral in view of the use of the terms "male"/"female"/"spouse"/ "wife," instead of the gender-neutral term "person").

Apart from these proposed amendments, the proposal contains an addition to Section 3.11 of the MPC (the section relating to the general legal definitions relevant to the doctrine of self-defense in the MPC) that provides a statutory definition of the particular terms required for the application of the proposed amended legal arrangement. The proposed definitions adopt gender-neutral and egalitarian legislative terminology and relate to domestic violence in general

94 About half the states in the U.S. allow the application of deadly protective force during a felony: Arkansas, California, Florida, Georgia, Idaho, Illinois, Indiana, Kentucky, Louisiana, Minnesota, Mississippi, Missouri, Montana, Nevada, New Hampshire, North Dakota, Oklahoma, Oregon, South Dakota and Utah.

95 The legal arrangement as currently worded exposes battered women who have been prosecuted to the danger of inconsistent and/or mistaken judicial interpretations in this context. See Maguigan 1991: 440.

96 For a comprehensive review of the issue of "marital rape" and the legislative arrangements applied in this regard in the various U.S. states, see Weintraub 1995: 351–378. See also Anderson 2003: 1465–1557; Hasday 2000: 1373–1505.

(not just violence against women), so as to include potential male victims. The addition of subsection 3.11(4) to the MPC is designed to provide a legal clarification of the term "domestic violence," and the addition of subsection 3.11(5) is designed to provide a legal definition of the term "family member." The legal definitions advocated in these subsections are based on several current U.S. state legislative arrangements,[97] and are consistent with the legal definitions of domestic violence in the federal criminal law of the United States.[98]

The legal definition proposed for the term "domestic violence" is broad in three ways: *first*, it not only criminalizes acts that harm the physical integrity of a person but also acts that are harmful to the mental and emotional integrity of the person (in accordance with the language proposed in Sections 3.11(4)(i)–3.11(4)(iv)).[99] *Second*, and in line with the broad definition of domestic violence, the proposed legal definition criminalizes the mere exposure of a minor in the family to any violence directed against a family member (in accordance with the language proposed in Section 3.11(4)(v)).[100] *Third*, and in line with current social trends of maintaining common households, the proposed legal definition affords protection not only to family members but also to household members

97 For example, in Georgia, Wyoming, Arizona, Colorado, Florida, Kentucky and Michigan. Our proposal is based primarily on the legal definition in Michigan and Wyoming; see Wyoming Statutes, Title 35, Public Health and Safety, Chapter 21 – Domestic Violence Protection, Section 35–21–102. Definitions; Michigan Compiled Laws – Domestic Violence (excerpt) Act 389 of 1978 400.1501 Section 1.

98 18 USC Section 2266 Definitions:

> (7) (A)(i) (I) a spouse or former spouse of the abuser, a person who shares a child in common with the abuser, and a person who cohabits or has cohabited as a spouse with the abuser; or (II) a person who is or has been in a social relationship of a romantic or intimate nature with the abuser, as determined by the length of the relationship, the type of relationship and the frequency of interaction between the persons involved in the relationship.

99 It also explicitly refers to non-physical injury as well as violence of all types. Likewise, the legal arrangement in the definition of the states of Michigan and Wyoming refers to both non-physical and physical violence and thereby expands the limiting tendency to define violence as severe only when it entails bodily injury. For the approach regarding the gravity of mental injury and the need to adapt the criminal law so as to include it within the criminal doctrine, see Ewing 1990: 579–594, 587; Cohen 1996: 757–808, 790–791; Kadish 1976: 871, 886–888. This definition is also consistent with Section 2261(a) of the federal criminal law of the United States (interstate domestic violence) that criminalizes stalking, harassment or intimidation of spouses when these acts are committed in an interstate context within the territory of the United States (and/or upon entry or exit from states in the United States):

> 18 USC Section 2261 Interstate Domestic Violence: (a)(1) A person who … harasses or intimidates a spouse, intimate partner, or dating partner … (a)(2) A person who causes a spouse, intimate partner, or dating partner to travel in interstate or foreign commerce or to enter or leave Indian country by force, coercion, duress, or fraud … 18 USC Section 2266 Definitions: (7) (A)(ii): (I) a spouse or former spouse of the target of the stalking.…

100 In accordance with the language adopted in 2005 in Australia: Crimes (Homicide) Act 2005, 9AH:

who live together and may be exposed to violence, without the need for an intimate or blood relationship. This broad definition is set out in the language proposed in Sections 3.11(4)(i)–3.11(4)(iv)).[101]

Along with the broad scope accorded to the definition of "domestic violence," the proposed amendment is restrictive in relation to two main legal principles. *First*, the criminal exemption in this defense is exclusively limited to the criminal liability of the defendant. This restricted arrangement is consistent with the text of the current provision of the MPC that confines the application of the criminal exception relating to the use of deadly protective force to the "actor" (in Section 3.04(2)(b)),[102] and thereby prevents excessive expansion of the proposed criminal defense by applying it to everyone. *Second*, the proposed text in Section 3.04(2)(b) restricts the application of the criminal defense by introducing two cumulative preconditions in circumstances of domestic violence, namely, that the pattern of domestic violence is both severe and prolonged.[103] By adding these two circumscribed yet cumulative requirements, I hope to create a balanced legal arrangement that on the one hand is comprehensive in its consideration of the elements and characteristics of domestic violence, yet on the other hand does not unduly expand the scope of applicability of the exemption from criminal liability.

> (v) in relation
> to a child – (A) causing or allowing the child to see or hear the physical abuse, sexual or psychological abuse of a person by a family member: or (B) putting the child, or allowing the child to be put, at real risk of seeing or hearing that abuse occurring.

With regard to the exposure of children to domestic violence and the traumatic impact of this exposure, see Holt et al. 2008: 797–810.

101 This proposal to include household members follows the broad definition set out in the current criminal statutes in Michigan and Wyoming (see Wyoming Statutes, Title 35, Public Health and Safety, Chapter 21 – Domestic Violence Protection, Section 35-21-102. Definitions; Michigan Compiled Laws – Domestic Violence (excerpt) Act 389 of 1978 400.1501 Section 1).

102 In this way our proposal is consistent with the legal arrangement in the MPC that provide a special defense to third parties (in Section 3.05).

103 This proposal is similar to the definition adopted in the Israeli Penal Law in the context of mitigating the punishment of women accused of killing their partners against a background of domestic violence. See Section 300A(c) of the Israeli Penal Law: 300A. Reduced Sentence (Amendment: 1995):

> Notwithstanding the provisions of Section 300, a more lenient sentence than that stated therein may be imposed, if the offense was committed: ... (c). While the defendant was in a state of severe emotional distress due to severe and prolonged abuse of him or a family member, by the person whose death the defendant caused.

See also La Fond's proposal to expand the doctrine of self-defense and allow the use of deadly protective force in circumstances going beyond a real and concrete threat to life, along with a clear and circumscribed definition of the violence in respect of which deadly protective force may be applied (La Fond 1982: 283).

Conclusion

This chapter proposed legislative amendments tailored to address the unique socio-legal problems that derive from the current legislative structure and wording of the criminal doctrines used in the Model Penal Code and in most U.S. jurisdictions, in circumstances of femicide. The main three doctrines examined in this book relate to the doctrine of provocation, the felony-murder rule and the doctrine of self-defense. These three doctrines, which are practiced in common law countries in general and in jurisdictions in the United States that adopted the MPC in particular, were analyzed and critiqued with regard to their applicability to circumstances of femicide and violence against women.

With regard to Uxoricide, Chapter 2 showed that the current extended doctrine of provocation in the MPC accords legal significance to loss of control by reason of intense emotion and enables the mitigation of the criminal liability of men accused of murdering their female partners. A categorical amendment was thus proposed in this chapter to abolish application of the doctrine to these types of murders by introducing categorical and statutory exceptions to the application of the doctrine of provocation and the EMED in the Model Penal Code, based on circumstances and motives common to the murder of intimate partners (the female desire to end the intimate relationship).

With regard to assaultive-femicide, Chapter 3 demonstrated that the current sub-doctrine of the felony-murder rule that is applied by almost all U.S. jurisdictions and the MPC, the principle of merger, has created a criminal socio-legal anomaly. Blameworthy murderers of women are exonerated and technically exempted from conviction of murder committed by assaultive-homicide on the grounds of the preclusion of assaultive-femicide from felony-murder. This chapter therefore proposed a legislative approach that explicitly includes assault within the predicate felonies in order to prevent the exoneration of assaultive-femicide perpetrators from the heinous murder that they committed.

With regard to the doctrine of self-defense, Chapter 4 showed that the American legal system has yet to offer a comprehensive solution to the problems faced by battered woman, and that American legislators seem to be unwilling to modify the legal approach in order to contend with this disturbing situation. This chapter presented the formulation of particular amendments to the doctrine of self-defense so that the application of the existing self-defense doctrine will accord fair consideration to battered women who use protective force in circumstances of domestic violence against them.

The book posed the challenge of amending the legislative structure of criminal law in order to reflect America's founding principles of justice and the sanctity of human life, irrespective of gender. The choice to delve into the proper treatment of femicide within the particular legal field of criminal law derived from my belief in the central role of the penal law in society. In this respect, it is worth quoting the argument put forth by Wechsler, in his capacity as the chief reporter of the reportorial staff for the U.S. Model Penal Code, regarding the need to re-examine the American penal law:

> Whatever views one holds about the penal law, no one will question its importance in society. This is the law on which men place their ultimate reliance for protection against all the deepest injuries that human conduct can inflict on individuals and institutions. By the same token, penal law governs the strongest force that we permit official agencies to bring to bear on individuals. Its promise as an instrument of safety is matched only by its power to destroy. If penal law is weak or ineffective, basic human interests are in jeopardy. If it is harsh or arbitrary in its impact, it works a gross injustice on those caught within its toils. The law that carries such responsibilities should surely be as rational and just as law can be. Nowhere in the entire legal field is more at stake for the community or for the individual.[104]

In an effort to offer amendments that will rectify current legal flaws affecting the treatment of females killed by their intimate partners, a comprehensive socio-legal look at the phenomenon of femicide has been taken. This socio-legal examination required an inquiry into the type of behavior that should be defined as criminal, and the results of such criminal behavior that should be classified and treated as murder. The specific proposed variations and adjustments to the criminal law relating to femicide presented in this book are the product of a comprehensive examination of typical sociological and criminological behaviors, modi operandi, circumstances and characteristics of both victims and perpetrators of femicide. I hope that the proposed amendments to the U.S. Model Penal Code will constitute a prototype for future legislative state reforms, and establish a suitable criminal doctrinal framework for treating female victims of domestic violence and their perpetrators.

104 Wechsler 1952: 1098.

Bibliography

Alderstein Anne C. 1975. Felony Murder in the New Criminal Codes. *American Journal of Criminal Law* 4 3: 252.

Anderson Michelle J. 2003. Marital Immunity, Intimate Relationships, and Improper Inferences: A New Law on Sexual Offenses by Intimates. *Hastings Law Journal* 54: 1465.

Anderson Ronald Aberdeen. 1957. *Wharton's Criminal Law and Procedure*. Lawyers Co-operative Publishing Company.

Ashworth Andrew J. 1976. The Doctrine of Provocation. *Cambridge Law Journal* 35: 307.

Ashworth Andrew J. 1981. The Elasticity of Mens Rea. In *Crime, Proof and Punishment: Essays. In. Memory of Sir Rupert Cross*. Tapper Colin ed. London: Butterworths.

Barton Russell R. 1990. Application of the Merger Doctrine to the Felony Murder Rule in Texas: The Merger Muddle. *Baylor Law Review* 42: 536.

Beeghley Leonard. 2003. *Homicide – A Sociological Explanation*. Lanham MD: Rowman and Littlefield.

Bendetowies Barry. 1990. Felony Murder and Child Abuse: A Proposal for the New York Legislature. *Fordham Urban Law Journal* 18 1: 399.

Ben Ze'ev Aaron. 2000. *The Subtlety of Emotions*. Cambridge MA: MIT Press.

Ben Ze'ev Aaron and Goussinsky Ruhama. 2008. *In the Name of Love: Romantic Ideology and its Victims*. Oxford: Oxford University Press.

Bergman Bo and Brismar Bo. 1991. Suicide Attempts by Battered Wives. *Acta Psychiatrica Scandinavia* 83: 380.

Berman Mitchell N. and Farrell Ian P. 2011. Provocation Manslaughter as Partial Justification and Partial Excuse. *William & Mary Law Review* 52 4: 1027.

Binder Guyora. 2004. The Origins of American Felony Murder Rules. *Stanford Law Review* 57: 59.

Binder Guyora. 2011. Making the Best of Felony Murder. *Boston University Law Review* 91: 403.

Birdsong Leonard. 2006. Felony Murder: A Historical Perspective by which to Understand Today's modern Felony Murder Rule Statutes. *Thurgood Marshall Law Review* 32 1: 1.

Blackstone William. 1765–1769. *Commentaries on the Laws of England* (4). Oxford: Clarendon Press.

Brown Helen. 1999. Provocation as a Defence to Murder. *Australian Feminist Law Journal* 12: 137.

Browne Angela. 1987. *When Battered Women Kill*. New York: Free Press.

Browne Angela, Williams Kirk R. and Dutton Donald G. 1999. Homicide Between Intimate Partners: A 20-Year Review. In *Homicide: A Sourcebook of Social Research*. Smith Dwayne M. and Zahn Margaret A. eds. Thousand Oaks CA: Sage.

Burke Alafair S. 2002. Rational Actors, Self-Defence, and Duress: Making Sense (Not Syndromes), Out of the Battered Woman. *North Carolina Law Review* 81: 211.

Byrd Sharon. 1991. Till Death Do Us Part: A Comparative Law Approach to Justifying Lethal Self Defense by Battered Women. *Duke Journal of Comparative and International Law* 1: 169.

Campbell Jacquelyn C., Webster Daniel, Koziol-Mclain Jane, Block Carolyn, Campbell Doris, Curry Mary Ann, Gary Faye, Glass Nancy, McFarlane Judith, Sachs Carolyn, Sharps Phyllis, Ulrich Yvonne, Wilt Susan A., Manganello Jennifer, Xu Xiao, Schollenberger Janet, Frye Victoria, Laughon Kathryn. 2003. Risk Factors for Femicide in Abusive Relationships: Results from a Multisite Case Control Study. *American Public Health* 93 7: 1089.

Campbell Jacquelyn C., Glass Nancy, Sharps Phyllis, Laughon Kathryn and Bloom Tina. 2007. Intimate Partner Homicide: Review and Implications of Research and Policy. *Trauma, Violence & Abuse* 8 3: 246.

Canada Senate Debates, June 12, 2012, 41st Parliament.

Carpenter Catherine L. 2003. Of the Enemy Within, The Castle Doctrine and Self Defense. *Marquette Law Review* 86: 653.

Cohen Jane Maslow. 1996. Regimes of Private Tyranny: What Do They Mean to Morality and for the Criminal Law? *University of Pittsburgh Law Review* 57: 757.

Coroners and Justice Act 2009, Explanatory Notes, UK Ministry of Justice.

Corradi Consuelo, Marcuello-Servos Chaime, Boira Santiago, Weil Shalva. 2016. Theories of Femicide and their Significance for Social Research. *Current Sociology* 64 7: 975.

Coss Graeme. 2006. The Defence of Provocation: An Acrimonious Divorce from Reality. *Current Issues in Criminal Justice* 18 1: 51.

Coughlin Anne M. 1994. Excusing Women. *California Law Review* 82: 1.

Crocker Phillis L. 1985. The Meaning of Equality for Battered Women who Kill in Self Defense. *Harvard Women's Law Journal* 8: 121.

Crump David. 2009. Reconsidering the Felony Murder Rule in Light of Modern Criticisms: Doesn't the Conclusion Depend Upon the Particular Rule at Issue? *Harvard Journal of Law and Public Policy* 32 3: 1155.

Crump David and Crump Susan Waite. 1985. Defense of the Felony Murder Doctrine. *Harvard Journal of Law and Public Policy* 8: 359.

Dawson Myrna and Gartner Rosemary. 1998. Differences in the Characteristics of Intimate Femicides. *Homicide Studies* 2: 378.

Della Giustina Jo-Ann. 2010. *Why Women are Beaten and Killed: Sociological Predictors of Femicide*. Lewiston NY: Edwin Mellen Press.

Dobash Emerson R. and Dobash Russell P. 1978. Wives: The Appropriate Victims of Marital Violence. *Victimology* 2: 426.

Dobash Emerson R., Dobash Russell P., Cavanagh Kate and Lewis Ruth. 2004. Not an Ordinary Killer – Just an Ordinary Guy, When Men Murder an Intimate Woman Partner. *Violence Against Women* 10 6: 577.

Dobash Russell P., Dobash Emerson R., Wilson Margo and Daly Martin. 1992. The Myth of Sexual Symmetry in Marital Violence. *Social Problems*, 39 1:71.

Dobash Russell P. and Dobash Emerson R. 2012. Who died? The murder of collaterals related to intimate partner violence. *Violence against Women* 18 6: 662.

Domestic Violence Resource Centre Victoria Discussion Paper No. 10. 2016. *Out of Character? Legal Responses to Intimate Partner Homicides by Men in Victoria 2005–2014.*

Denno Deborah W. 2003. Why the Model Penal Code's Sexual Offense Provisions Should Be Pulled and Replaced. *Ohio State Journal of Criminal Law* 1: 207.

Downs Donald Alexander. 1996. *More than Victims: Battered Women, The Syndrome Society, and the Law*. Chicago: University of Chicago Press.

Dressler Joshua. 1982. Rethinking Heat of Passion: A Defense in Search of a Rationale. *Journal of Criminal Law and Criminology* 73: 421.

Dubber Markus Dirk and Robinson Paul H. 1999. An Introduction to the Model Penal Code of the American Law Institute. *University of Pennsylvania* www.law.upenn.edu/fac/phrobins/intromodpencode.pdf.

Dubin Danielle R. 1995. A Woman's Cry for Help: Why the United States Should Apply Germany's Model of Self Defense for the Battered Woman. *ILSA Journal of International and Comparative Law* 2: 235.

Dugan Laura, Nagin Laura and Rosenfeld Richard. 1999. Explaining the Decline in Intimate Partner Homicide: The Effect of Changing Domesticity, Women's Status, and Domestic Violence Resources. *Homicide Studies* 3 3:187.

Edelstein Arnon. 2011. *Intimate Partner Homicide in Israel: Theoretical and Empirical Aspects*. Ben Gurion University Press.

Erlinder Peter. 1981. Mens Rea, Due Process and the Supreme Court: Toward a Constitutional Doctrine of Substantive Criminal Law. *American Journal of Criminal Law* 9: 163.

Ewing Charles Patrick. 1990. Psychological Self-Defense: A Proposed Justification for Battered Women Who Kill. *Law and Human Behavior* 14 6: 579.

Farr Kathryn A. 2002. Battered Women Who Were "Being Killed and Survived It": Straight Talk from Survivors. *Violence and Victims* 17: 268.

Ferrara Pietro, Caporale Olga, Cutrona Costanza, Sbordone Annamaria, Amato Maria, Spina Giulia, Ianniello Francesca, Fabrizio Giovanna Carmela, Guadagno Chiara, Basile Maria Cristina, Miconi Francesco, Perrone Giacomo, Riccardi Riccardo, Verrotti Alberto, Pettoello-Mantovani Massimo, Villani Alberto and Corsello Giovanni. 2015. Femicide and Murdered Women's Children: Which Future for these Children Orphans of a Living Parent? *Italian Journal of Pediatrics* 41: 68.

Finkelstein Claire. 2005. Merger and Felony Murder. In *Defining Crimes: Essays on the Special Part of the Criminal Law*. Duff Anthony R. and Stuart Green P. eds. Oxford: Oxford University Press.

Fiora-Gormally Nancy. 1978. Case/Comment, Battered Wives Who Kill: Double Standard out of Court, Single Standard In? *Law and Human Behavior* 2 2: 133.

Fletcher George P. 1978. *Rethinking Criminal Law*. Boston: Little, Brown and Co.

Fletcher George P. 1981. Reflections on Felony-Murder. *South Western University Law Review* 12 3: 413.

Fletcher George P. 1990. *A Crime of Self-Defense: Bernhard Goetz and the Law on Trial.* Chicago: University of Chicago.

Fontaine Felix G. 2012. *The Trial of the Honorary Daniel E. Sickles for Shooting Philip Barton Key, Esq., U.S. District Attorney, of Washington, D.C. February 27th 1859.* New York: R. M. De Witt.

Fournier Pascale, McDougall Pascal and Dekker Anna R. 2012. Dishonour, Provocation and Culture: Through the Beholder's Eye? *Canadian Criminal Law Review* 16 2: 161.

Fox James Alan and Zawitz Marianne W. 2007. *Homicide Trends in the United States.* Bureau of Justice Statistics www.bjs.gov/index.cfm?ty=pbdetail&iid=966.

Ganz Daniel. 2012. *The American Felony Murder Rule: Purpose and Effect.* UC Berkeley. Legal Studies Honors Thesis, Supervised by Professor Richard Perry.

Gauthier DeaAnn K. and Bankston William B. 2004. "Who Kills Whom" Revisited: A Sociological Study of Variation in the Sex Ratio of Spouse Killings. *Homicide Studies* 8 2: 96.

Gelles Richard and Straus Murray. 1989. Violence in the American Family. In *Crime and the Family.* Lincoln Alan Jay and Straus Murray. eds. Springfield IL: Charles C. Thomas Publishers.

Gillespie Cynthia K. 1989. *Justifiable Homicide: Battered Women, Self-Defense and the Law.* Ohio State University Press.

Government of Canada, Department of Justice, Bill C-26 (S.C. 2012 c. 9), Reforms to Self-Defence and Defence of Property: Technical Guide for Practitioners. www.justice.gc.ca/eng/rp-pr/other-autre/rsddp-rlddp/p5.html.

Hackney Sheldon. 1969. Southern Violence. *American Historical Review* 74: 906.

Hannawa Annegret F., Hannawa Brian H., Sptizberg Liesbeth Wiering and Christy Teranishi. 2006. "If I Can't Have You, No One Can": Development of a Relational Entitlement and Proprietariness Scale. *Violence and Victims* 21 5: 539.

Hasday Jill Elaine. 2000. Contest and Consent: A Legal History of Marital Rape. *California Law Review* 88: 1373.

Heise Lori and Moreno Garcia Claudia. 2002. Violence by Intimate Partners. In *World Report on Violence and Health.* Krug Etienne G., Dahlberg Linda L.,. Mercy James A, Zwi Anthony B. and Lozano Rafael. eds. Geneva, World Health Organization.

Henton June, Rodney Cate, Koval James, Lloyd Sally and Scott Christopher. 1983. Romance and Violence in Dating Relationships. *Journal of Family Issues* 4: 467.

Herberling Peter D. W. 1975. Justification: The Impact of the Model Penal Code on Statutory Reform. *Columbia Law Review* 75: 914.

Holt Stephanie, Buckley Helen and Whelan Sadhbh. 2008. The Impact of Exposure to Domestic Violence on Children and Young People: A Review of the Literature. *Child Abuse and Neglect* 32 8: 797.

Horder Jeremy. 1992. *Provocation and Responsibility.* Oxford: Clarendon Press.

Horder Jeremy. 2007. The Changing Face of the Law of Homicide. In *Homicide Law in Comparative Perspective.* Horder Jeremy ed. Oxford: Hart Publishing.

Howe Adrian. 1999. Reforming Provocation (More or Less). *Australian Feminist Law Journal* 12: 127.

Howe Adrian. 2002. Provoking Polemic: Provoked Killings and the Ethical Paradoxes of the Postmodern Feminist Condition. *Feminist Legal Studies* 10 1: 39.

Howe Adrian. 2004. Provocation in Crisis – Law's Passion at the Crossroads? New Directions for Feminist Strategists. *The Australian Feminist Law Journal* 21: 53.

Johnson Holly and Hotton Tina. 2003. Losing Control: Homicide Risk in Estranged and Intact Intimate Relationships. *Homicide Studies* 7: 58.

Kadish Sandford H. 1976. Respect for Life and Regard for Rights in the Criminal Law. *California Law Review* 64: 871.

Keetley Dawn. 2008. From Anger to Jealousy: Explaining Domestic Homicide in Antebellum America. *Journal of Social History* 42 2: 269.

Kelly Liz and Radford Jill. 1996. "Nothing Really Happened": The Invalidation of Women's Experiences of Sexual Violence. In *Women, Violence and Male Power.* Hester M., Kelly L. and Radford J. eds. Buckingham: Open University Press.

Kinports Kit. 1988. Defending Battered Women's Self Defense Claims. *Oregon Law Review* 67: 393.

Koss Mary P., Goodman Lisa A, Brown Angela, Fitzgerald Louise F., Keita Gwendolyn P. and Russo Nancy F. 1994. *No Safe Haven: Male Violence Against Women at Home, at Work and in the Community.* Washington DC: American Psychological Association.

La Fond John Q. 1983. The Case of Liberalizing the Use of Deadly Force in Self Defence. *University of Puget Sound Law Review* 6: 237.

Landau Simha and Hattis-Rolef Susan. 1998. Intimate Femicide in Israel: Temporal, Social and Motivational Patterns. *European Journal on Criminal Policy and Research* 6: 75.

LaFave Wayne R. and Wakeman Austin Scott. 1972. *Handbook on Criminal Law.* St Paul MN: West Publishing Company.

Laurent Claire, Michael Platzer and Maria Idomir. 2013. eds. *Femicide: A Global Issue That Demands Action.* Vienna: Academic Council on the United Nations System.

Law Commission for England and Wales, Murder, Manslaughter and Infanticide. 2006. London, Law Com. No. 304.

Lee Cynthia. 2003. *Murder and the Reasonable Man: Passion and Fear in the Criminal Courtroom.* New York: New York University Press.

Legislative Summary of Bill S-7: An Act to amend the Immigration and Refugee Protection Act, the Civil Marriage Act and the Criminal Code and to make consequential amendments to other Acts, Parliament of Canada, library of parliament publications, Publication Number 41–2-S7–E.

Leong Gregory B., Silva J. A. and Garza-Trevino E. S., Ferrari M. M., Komanduri R. V. and Caldwell J. C. 1994. The Dangerousness of Persons with the Othello Syndrome. *Journal of Forensic Science* 39 6: 1445.

Leonning Henry F. 1961. Assault with Intent to Murder – Necessity for Actual Intent to Cause Death – *Wimbush* v. *State. Maryland Law Review* 21: 254.

Leverick Fiona. 2006. *Killing in Self Defence.* Oxford: Oxford University Press.

Levin Mark S. 1983. *People* v. *Watson*: Drunk Driving Homicide – Murder or Enhanced Manslaughter. *California Law Review* 71: 1298.

Levit Nancy and Verchick Robert M. 2006. *Feminist Legal Theory.* New York: New York University Press.

Mackinnon Catherine A. 2001. *Sex Equality.* New York: Foundation Press.

Maguigan Holly. 1991. Battered Women and Self-Defense: Myths and Misconceptions in Current Reform Proposals. *University of Pennsylvania Law Review* 140: 379.

Mahoney Martha R. 1991. Legal Images of Battered Women: Redefining the Issue of Separation. *Michigan Law Review* 90: 1.

Mather Victoria M. 1988. The Skeleton in the Closet: The Battered Women Syndrome, Self Defense, and Expert Testimony. *Mercer Law Review* 39: 545.

McColgan Aileen. 1993. In Defense of Battered Women Who Kill. *Oxford Journal of Legal Studies* 13: 508.

Mendez Miguel A. 2010. The California Supreme Court and the Felony Murder Rule: A Sisyphean Challenge? *California Legal History* 5: 241.

Model Penal Code. 1962. Philadelphia: American Law Institute.

Model Penal Code and Commentaries (Official Draft and Revised Comments). 1980. Philadelphia: American Law Institute.

Model Penal Code and Commentaries (Official Draft and Revised Comments). 1985. Philadelphia: American Law Institute.

Nelson Roth E. and Scott Sundby E. 1985. The Felony-Murder Rule: A Doctrine at Constitutional Crossroads. *Cornell Law Review* 70: 446.

Nicolson Donald and Sanghui Rohit. 1995. More Justice for the Battered Woman. *New Law Journal* 146: 1122.

Noyes Henry S. 1994. Felony Murder Doctrine Through the Federal Looking Glass. *Indiana Law Journal* 69 2: 533.

Pei-Lin Chen Christina. 2000. Provocation's Privileged Desire: The Provocation Doctrine, "Homosexual Panic," and Non-Violent Unwanted Sexual Advance Defense. *Cornell Journal of Law and Public Policy* 10 1: 195.

Perkins Rollin M. 1957. *Perkins on Criminal Law*. Brooklyn New York: Foundation Press.

Pridemore William Alex and Freilich Joshua D. 2005. Gender Equity, Traditional Masculine Culture, and Female Homicide Victimization. *Journal of Criminal Justice* 33: 213.

Puente Sylvia and Cohen Dov. 2003. Jealousy and the Meaning (or Nonmeaning) of Violence. *Personality and Social Psychology Bulletin* 29 4: 449.

Queensland Law Reform Commission (QLRC): A Review of the Excuse of Accident and the Defence of Provocation. 2008. Report No. 64.

Radford Jill and Russell Diana E. H. eds. 1992. *The Politics of Woman Killing*. New York: Twayne.

Ramsey Carolyn B. 2010. Provoking Change: Comparative Insights on Feminist Homicide Law Reform. *Journal of Criminal Law and Criminology* 100 1: 33.

Rapaport Elizabeth. 1996. Capital Murder and the Domestic Discount: A Study of Capital Murder in the Post Furman Era. *SMU Law Review* 49: 1507.

Reece Laura E. 1991. Women's Defenses to Criminal Homicide and the Right to Effective Assistance of Counsel: The Need for Relocation of Difference. *U.C.L.A. Women's Law Journal* 1: 53.

Riley Mitch. 2008. Provocation: Getting Away with Murder? *Queensland Law Students Review* 1 1: 55.

Rosen Catherine J. 1986. The Excuse of Self Defense: Correcting a Historical Accident on Behalf of Battered Woman Who Kill. *American University Law Review* 36: 11.

Rosen Richard A. 1993. On Self-Defense, Imminence, and Women Who Kill Their Batterers. *North Carolina Law Review* 71: 371.

Roth Nelson E. and Sundby Scott E. 1985. The Felony-Murder Rule: A Doctrine at Constitutional Crossroads. *Cornell Law Review* 70: 446.

Rumney Philip N. S. 1999. When Rape Isn't Rape: Court of Appeal Sentencing Practice in Case of Marital and Relationship Rape. *Oxford Journal of Legal Studies* 19 2: 243.

Russell Diana E. H. 1990. Femicide. In *Crimes Against Women: Proceedings of the International Tribunal*. Russell Diana and Van de Ven Nicole. eds. San Francisco.

Russell Diana E. H. 2011. *The Origin and the Importance of the Term Femicide*. www.dianaRussell.com/origin_of_femicide.html.

Russell Diana E. H. and Harmes Roberta A. eds. 2001. *Femicide in Global Perspective*. New York: Teachers College Press.

Sangero Boaz. 2006. *Self Defence in Criminal Law*. Oxford: Hart Publishing.

Saunders Daniel G. and Browne Angela. 2000. Intimate Partner Homicide. In *Case Studies in Family Violence*. Ammerman Robert T. and Hersen Michel. eds. New York: Kluwer Academic.

Scales Ann. 2006. *Legal Feminism: Activism, Lawyering and Legal Theory*. New York University Press.

Schneider Elizabeth. 1980. Equal Rights to Trial for Women: Sex Bias in the Law of Self Defense. *Harvard Civil Rights-Civil Liberties Law Review* 15: 623.

Schneider Elizabeth. 2000. *Battered Woman and Feminist Lawmaking*. London: Yale University Press.

Schopp R. F., Sturgis B. J. and Sullivan M. 1994. Battered Woman Syndrome, Expert Testimony, and the Distinction between Justification and Excuse. *University of Illinois Law Review* 14: 45.

Serran G. and Firestone P. 2004. Intimate Partner Homicide: Review of the Male Proprietariness and the Self-Defense Theories. *Aggression and Violent Behavior* 9: 1.

Siegel Reva B. 1996. "The Rule of Love": Wife Beating as Prerogative and Privacy. *Yale Law School Legal Scholarship Repository.* http://digitalcommons.law.yale.edu/cgi/viewcontent.cgi?article=2092&context=fss_papers.

Smart Carol. 1989. *Feminism and the Power of Law.* London: Routledge.

Smart Carol. 1995. *Law, Crime and Sexuality: Essays in Feminism.* Sage: London.

Smith M. D. and Zahn M. A. 1998. *Homicide: A Sourcebook of Social Research.* Thousand Oaks CA: SAGE.

Smith P. H., Moracco K. E. and Butts J. 1998. Partner Homicide in Context: A Population Based Perspective. *Homicide Studies* 2: 200.

Stephen Fitzjames James. 1883. *A History of the Criminal Law of England.* London: Macmillan.

Stark E., Flitcraft A. and Frasier W. 1979. Medicine and Patriarchal Violence: The Social Construction of a "Private Event." *International Journal of Health Services* 9: 461.

Stout Karen. 1992. Intimate Femicide: An Ecological Analysis. *Journal of Sociology and Social Welfare* 29: 29.

Spatz Melissa A. 1991. "Lesser" Crime: A Comparative Study of Legal Defenses for Men Who Kill Their Wives. *Columbia Journal of Law and Social Problems* 24: 597.

Talbot Jill S. 1988. Note, is "Psychological Self-Defense" a Solution to the Problem of Defending Battered Woman Who Kill? *Washington and Lee Law Review* 45: 1527.

Taylor Rae and Jasinski Jana L. 2011. Femicide and the Feminist Perspective. *Homicide Studies* 15 4: 341.

The Victorian Law Reform Commission. *Defences to Homicide, Final Report.* 2005.

Thomas David L. 1989. The Case of Intent: Should the Elements of Murder Be Expanded in Virginia? *Colonial Lawyer* 18 1: 100.

Tjaden Patricia and Thoennes Nancy. 2000. *Full Report of the Prevalence, Incidence, and Consequences of Violence Against Women.* U.S. Department of Justice, Office of Justice Programs, National Institute of Justice.

U.S. Department of Justice, Bureau of Justice Statistics. 2013. *Homicide in the U.S. Known to Law Enforcement 2011* www.bjs.gov/content/pub/pdf/hus11.pdf.

Vandiver Frank E. 1964. The Southerner as Extremist. In *The Idea of the South.* Vandiver Frank E. ed. Chicago: University of Chicago Press.

Van Zanten Douglas. 2008. Felony Murder, the Merger Limitation, and Legislative Intent in *State* v. *Heemstra*: Deciphering the Proper Role of the Iowa Supreme Court in Interpreting Iowa's Felony Murder Statute. *Iowa Law Review* 93: 1565.

Victorian Law Reform Commission. Defences to Homicide: Final Report. 2004. www.lawreform.vic.gov.au/sites/default/files/VLRC_Defences_to_Homicide_Final_Report.pdf.

Walker Lenore E. 1979. *The Battered Woman.* New York: Harper and Row.

Wallace Alison. 1986. *Homicide: The Social Reality.* New South Wales Bureau of Crimes Statistics and Research, Attorney General's Department.

Warner Tara D. 2010. Violent Acts and Injurious Consequences: An Examination of Competing Hypotheses about Intimate Partner Violence Using Agency-Based Data. *Journal of Family Violence* 25 2: 183.

Warren Oscar L. 1938. *Warren on Homicide Permanent Edition.* William S. Hein Incorporated.

Websdale Neil. 1999. Understanding Domestic Violence. Boston MA: Northeastern University Press.

Wechsler Herbert. 1952. The Challenge of the Model Penal Code. *Harvard Law Review* 65: 1097.

Wechsler Herbert. 1968. Codification of Criminal Law in the United States: The Model Penal Code. *Columbia Law Review* 68: 1425.

Wechsler Herbert. 1982–1983. Revision and Codification of the Penal Law in the United States. *The Dalhousie Law Journal* 7: 219.

Weil Shalva. 2015. Combating Femicide in Multiple Ways: the Cost Actions IS1206 on "Femicide Across Europe." In *Femicide, Targeting of Women in Conflict: A Global Issue that Demands Action*. ACUNS 3: 139.

Weil Shalva. 2016. Failed Femicides Among Migrant Survivors. *Qualitative Sociology Review* 12 4: 6.

Wells William and DeLeon-Granados William. 2004. The Intimate Partner Homicide Decline: Disaggregated Trends, Theoretical Explanations, and Policy Implications. *Criminal Justice Policy Review* 15 2: 229.

Weintraub Siegel Lalenya. 1995. The Marital Rape Exemption: Evolution to Extinction. *Cleveland State Law Review* 43: 351.

Williams Glanville. 1983. Convictions and Fair Labeling. *Cambridge Law Journal* 42 1: 93.

Willoughby M. J. 1989. Comment, Rendering Each Woman Her Due: Can a Battered Woman Claim Defense When She Kills her Sleeping Batterer? *Kansas Law Review* 38: 196.

Wilson Margo and Daly Martin. 1998. Sexual Rivalry and Sexual Conflict: Recurring Themes in Fatal Conflicts. *Theoretical Criminology* 2 3: 291.

Wilson Margo and Daly Martin. 1993. Spousal Homicide Risk and Estrangement. *Violence and Victims* 8 1: 3.

Index

For Product Safety Concerns and Information please contact our EU
representative GPSR@taylorandfrancis.com
Taylor & Francis Verlag GmbH, Kaufingerstraße 24, 80331 München, Germany

www.ingramcontent.com/pod-product-compliance
Ingram Content Group UK Ltd.
Pitfield, Milton Keynes, MK11 3LW, UK
UKHW011018180926
475701UK00004B/809

* 9 7 8 0 3 6 7 5 8 9 9 8 1 *